SEC
YANTR
AND
TANTRA

Unveiled in this book are the secrets of these occult sciences to help the reader achieve worldly success and spiritual enlightenment. Detailed instructions are given for the preparation and application of Yantras for specific purposes: to win favours, defeat enemies and cure diseases, among others. The methods of selecting and using Mantras to attain miraculous powers, and fulfilment of one's desires, are explained fully. In the Tantra section of the book are given methods of treatment of diseases by herbs. Information is provided about Tantric articles and where to obtain them.

Dr. L.R. Chawdhri has an experience of 39 years in the fields of Astrology, Palmistry and Numerology. He has specialised in remedial measures developed by these sciences. He is author of 17 widely acclaimed books on occult subjects.

By the same author:

Secrets of Astrology: Based on Hindu Astrology

Secrets of Occult Science: How to read Omens, Moles, Dreams and Handwriting

Published by
Sterling Publishers Private Limited

SECRETS OF YANTRA, MANTRA AND TANTRA

Dr. L.R. Chawdhri

STERLING PAPERBACKS
An imprint of
Sterling Publishers (P) Ltd.
L-10, Green Park Extension, New Delhi-110016
Tel : 6191023, 6191784/85; Fax : 91-11-6190028
E-mail: ghai@nde.vsnl.net.in
Website : www.sterlingpublishers.com

Secrets of Yantra, Mantra and Tantra

ISBN 81 207 1365 6
Reprint 1993, 1995, 1996, 1997, 1998, 1999

Published by Sterling Publishers Pvt. Ltd., New Delhi-110016.
Printed at Ram Printograph (India), New Delhi-110051.
Cover design by Seema Srivastava

PREFACE

Yantra, Mantra and Tantra is part of Indian occult science, with each term having its own importance in the lives of people. Earlier, two separate books entitled, *Practicals of Yantras* and *Practicals of Mantra and Tantra* respectively, had been published. However, many readers had requested that all three aspects be combined in one comprehensive volume for their convenience. Keeping this in mind, I am publishing this work on Yantra, Mantra and Tantra.

However, I would like to insert a warning at the very outset that neither the author nor the publishers are in any way responsible if any reader uses the information provided in this book for any harmful or injurious activity. The success of the Yantra, Mantra and Tantra provided in this volume are entirely dependant on the "Sadhaka". Hence I would like to reiterate that these should be employed only for the service and benefit of humanity and not for any nefarious activity, for which the author, publisher and printer accept no responsibility.

I am confident that this complete handbook would be of immense interest to all those who want to gain a meaningful insight into Indian occult science.

Dr. L.R.Chawdhri

Jyotish Tantra Kendra,
110, Pratap Chambers,
Gurudwara Road, Karol Bagh,
New Delhi-110005

CONTENTS

Part I

YANTRAS

I

YANTRAS

Yantra is not magic, but a path or technique which has been frequently mistaken with "Jadoo Toona" and superstition. In technical terms, Yantra means an instrument, an apparatus, a talisman or mystical diagrams. By following certain techniques and instructions, one can attain "siddhi" and fulfil one's desires and ambitions speedily.

Our ancient "rishis" and seers practiced Yantra and attained perfect peace of mind so essential in modern life. The "Shastras" or ancient texts have held the power of Yantra in high esteem as an effective tool in the path towards realising God.

The Aims and Objects of Yantras

A man expresses himself through signs, speech or writing. While Yantras include signs and writings, Mantras and Tantras are inter-linked since they are expressed through the medium of Yantra. Different Yantras are connected with different deities and are combined with different Mantras. The five basic elements of Earth, Water, Fire, Air and the Sky are related to Yantras, and by performing Special "Pujas" or prayers one can control nature for one's own advantage. According to our Shastras, Yantra is a science which can be used through the five elements of Nature and by the recitation of certain Mantras. Deities are worshipped in different forms and each form is linked to a Yantra. Each planet is said to have a beneficial or harmful effect. Yantra is believed to remove their malefic effects and increase their beneficial aspect. A "Bindu" or a zero is the basic primary sign through which a triangle is developed, indicating various desires, methods or knowledge. The "bindu" is a focal point of increasing one's powers of concentration. It is often expanded to form various types of triangles and other round, long or broad figures which are called "Yantras".

While anybody can draw the yantra, it does not yield the desired results unless it is energised by a "Sidh Mantra". This task can be performed only by a competent "tentrik". Yantras are generally prescribed by astrologers and tantriks to ward off the evil effects of the planets, spirits or one's adversaries.

In general, a Yantra is a particular design drawn on bronze, lead, copper, silver, stainless steel, or gold. A durable material is used so that when a "Puja" is performed, the wearer will be protected from all those forces which are inimical. Yantra thus becomes the medium through which the invisible forces of energy act on an individual. The medium is sanctified and the person who wears it should recite certain "mantras" so that the effectiveness of the yantra is increased. In order to enhance the benefits of the yantra, the utmost skill and sincerity is required of the person who energises it.

The yantras sadhana is verifiable at every stage as it is a rational science based on a set of doctrines, which may be tested by any individual at any level. In order to otain "Siddhi", the sadhana must be done selflessly and with all faith and humility. It must be admitted that despite the best of intentions, the desired results are not always achieved. People become disheartened and are often known to label both yantra and its "Sadhakas" as hoaxes. However, just as scientists do not always succeed in their endeavours, so to the yantras and those who practice its prescribed rituals may register failures on some occasions.

The preparation of yantras is a difficult process as there are many prescribed steps and rituals that have to be followed exactly. The great tantrik yantra diagrams represent time and space, especially the "Shri Yantra" which is the most sacred and effective yantra in Hinduism.

Since tantriks are dealing with inner experiences, the descriptions given in different texts vary from each other. Hindu and Buddhist tantras agree in principle on the major aspects, with some minor differences on certain matters which are less important. During the last few centuries one notices a harmonious blending of Hindu and Buddhist traditions in Nepal. Tantriks have traditionally taken a keen interest in astronomy and astrology and study various time charts that depict the significant events in life. Many works of tantrik art are related to this essential phase of ceremonials. In the next phase the tantrik identifies the inner central column of his spine or "sushumna". The axis or centre is at "Meru" so that he visualises himself as the centre around which the whole circuit of his world revolves.

The aim of a Hindu tantrik is that his "Kundalini" (Sleeping serpent) shall ascend the 'sushumna' as often as possible and ultimately remain there permanently. This is considered the highest step in the tantrik sadhana. A series of lotuses is present vertically up the central 'sushumna' as seen in Figure 1.1. There are six chakras or lotuses, with a seventh at the critical root of all existence, at the top of the skull.

The Kundalini

Sushumna is the yogic nerve through which the kundalini passes. The tantrik has to do intense sadhana to arouse the "Kundalini" and achieve success. A few pointers to Kundalini Yoga are provided below in alphabetical order for the guidance of tantriks and sadhakas.

1. ANAHATA chakra is the lotus of the heart with twelve petals.
2. BRAHMARANDHRA is the role of brahman at the crown of the head.
3. CHAKRAS are focal points of power in the astral body.
4. DIET those who are sadhakas or yogis should have a moderate and nutritious diet.
5. EKAGRATA or the single-minded concentration of the mind is obtained through the practice of kundalini yoga.
6. GURU the teacher or guru's help are essential.
7. HATHA YOGA prepares the sadhakas for the practice of kundalini yoga.
8. INA NADI (Chandra Nadi) flows through the left nostril.
9. KUNDALINI is the coiled up strength or "shakti" that lies dormant in Muladhara.
10. LALANA CHAKRA is placed at the space above Ajna and below Sahasara.
11. MULADHARA is the Chakra that is located at the base of the spinal column.
12. PADMASANA is very good for practicing kundalini yoga.
13. PURAKA MANI Chakra is situated near the naval. It has ten petals and has the colour of a storm cloud (Nimbus).
14. SVA DHISH THANA is the chakra with six petals located at the root of the reproductive organ.
15. VISUDDHA CHAKRA, with sixteen petals, is located in the Sushumna Nadi at the base of the throat.

The Six Chakras or Lotuses

The six chakras, which constitute the centres of consciousness are described below. One's vision should be directed inwards to Sushumna, the path of air between Ida and Pingala and situated in the spinal column spreads from Muldhara (Anus) to Brahmara Dhara (crown of the head), and shines brightly like the sun. In its centre is the fine lotus fibre-like capillaries, from where the kundalini shakti shines as in a streak of lightning.

The Sushumna has six centres known as Chakras or kamals, each of which has a different appearance and powers.

1. *The Mooladhara Chakra*: is situated at the base of the spine between the anus and the genitals. The lotus is blood red in colour and has four petals on which are four letters Vam, Sam Sham and Sam (वं, श, ष, स) in golden hues. In the centre is a yellow coloured square representing the earth. On this is the elephant Iravatham, which bears the letter "Lam" (लं). In the centre of the bindu is the four-faced or four armed Lord Ganesha (some say Brahma), who is the presiding deity. In the centre of the lotus is Dhakini Shakti. There is also a triangle at the centre which bears the Kama Bija (क्लीं) or Kleem. Over that is a black sivayam bhulinga and above it a thrice coiled kundalini. Those who have awakened this lotus are said to have been absolved of all their sins. In fact, the objective of Raj Yoga is to rouse this lotus.

2. *Swadhistana Chakra*: lies at the root of the reproductive organ. It has a deep vermillion colour like that of 'sindhur'. It has six letters with bija letters Bam, Mam, Yam, Ram and Lam (बं,भं,मं,य,रं,लं,). In the middle is the white varuna mandala or the region of water, which is half-moon shaped. Gliding on the water is makra (alligator) with the bija vam(वं), on whom rides Lord Vishnu with all his ornaments. In the centre is the fearful-looking Rakini Shakti , which has four arms and three eyes. The Subhumna passes the centre of this lotus.

3. *Manipuraka Chakra*: is the lotus that is situated at the navel and is violet in colour. It has ten petals with bija letter which symbolises the region of the Agni Mandal (fire). In the middle is the bija ram (डं,ठं, णं,नं,थं,दं,धं,नं,पं,फं) on a goat, and on the bija is Rudra riding a bull. The three-eyed, three-faced, four-armed Lakini Shakti is in the centre.

4. *Anahata Chakra*: is situated in the region of the heart which is also the seat of the Jiv-Atma or the individual soul. There is a central core which is red in colour, which is surrounded by twelve petals which are

golden pink in hue. The bija letters is the vayu mandala which has a hexagonal shape and a smokey colour. In the middle is an extraordinarily bright inverted triangle. On this is the Vayu Bija (यं) riding on a black deer. There is also the presiding deity Ishwara, with two arms and three eyes. Over the centre on a red flower with yellow clothes is a deity called Kakini, who promises freedom from fear. In the triangle there is a bana linga, below which there is an eight-petalled lotus on which the Jiv-Atma moves around.

When an individual medidates and concentrates on this lotus, ten kinds of sounds are heard. These sounds produce different physical effects on individuals.

Note: The Jiv-Atma is commonly known as "Atma Ram". After death, when the bones are taken from the ashes of the funeral pyre, we sometimes find "Atma Ram". Sometimes it is in perfect condition, sometimes it is found that the Atma Ram of a saintly person is found in perfect condition.

5. *Visudha Chakra*: is the lotus located at the base of the throat, with sixteen petals which are grey in colour . There are red letters on the petals (अं, आं, इं, ईं, उ, ॐ, ऋं, ॠं, लं, ॡं,) At the centre there is a white circular space which represents the sky (Akash Mandala). In the middle is a triangle, on which there is the Chandra Mandala or the region of the Moon. On it, riding on a white elephant, is the Akasa Bija. In the bindu sitting on a bull is Sada Siva, with five faces, three eyes and ten arms, holding various weapons and wearing a tiger skin. In the centre of the Chandra Mandala is the deity Sakini, who has five faces three eyes and four hands.

The person who has a vision of this lotus does not suffer from any disease.

6. *Ajna Chakra* lies between the two eyebrows and is called "Trikuti". It consists of two white petals bearing the 'bijas' (हं, क्षं) and in the circular core resides a deity known as Hakini Shakti, whose face is white in colour, with three eyes and arms. It has six faces. There is a triangle with the bija, (ओं)and the Rudra Granthi. The triangle also contains the white 'hita longa' which gives off sparks similar to those occurring during lightning. The sparks go as far as the brahmarandhra, which is the centre of the dynamic mind which radiates the inner will. Beyond this lies the Sahasrara Kamal, or the thousand petalled lotus. Herein lies the third eye. The person who is able to concentrate on this point destroys all his past "karmas" and becomes a "jiva mukta" or one who

has become all-knowledgeable and is liberated from the life cycle.

7. *Sahasra Dala Kamala:* lies beyond the Ajna Chakra and at the base of the sushumna. The thousand petals contain the fifty letters repeated twenty times. When the kundalini shakti, after piercing the six chakras enters the Sahasrars, the person enters a superconscious state and enters 'samadhi', which is the state of union between individual consciousness and infinite consciousness. Some consider this to be the union between Shakti and Shiva.

This shad chakra is both Vedic and Tantric. According to Gandharva Malika Tantra, it is in the Sahasra that one finds Kalpa Vriksha, the divine tree which fulfils all desires. Man is freed from old age and death merely by seeing it.

The Division of Yantras

Since yantras are mainly used for pujas, our shastras have classified the pooja of yantras into five types, such as:

1. *Bhoo Prishth Yantras:* These yantras are made from materials and the very name indicates the use of earth etc, which may be sub-divided into the following.

(i) These are raised yantras and include vern mantras and beej mantras.

(ii) the others are carved.

2. *Meru Prishth Yantras*: These yantras are shaped like mountains as they are broad at the base, slender in the middle and peaked at the top. These are raised yantras.

3. *Patel Yantras* : These are shaped like an inverted mountain and hence are the opposite of the Meru structure. They are carved

4. *Meru Parastar Yantras*: These are cut yantras.

5. *Ruram Prishth Yantras*: has the shape of a rectangle at the base and a tortoise back on top.

Each yantra mentioned above serves a different purpose. The objective of an individual is gained through a particular yantra. While some yantras are worn around the neck, shaped in triangles or rectangles, others are tied to the arms or kept as close to the body as possible. In many parts of the country yantras are placed in temples and worshipped after due ceremony. In Gujrat for example, the Gayatri Yantra is worshipped at the Bahu Chari Mata Mandir and the Beesi Yantra in the Amba Maata temple. The beesi Yantra is found written on the top of grave of Mehboob Mian in Baghbad Shariff and at the Jama Masjid in Agra.

The Hindus are guided by the shastras which decree that the yantras are divided into seven categories, depending on their uses.

1. *Sharir Yantras*: The kundalini in the body is awakened through six chakras in the body. There are specific yantras for each chakra which is worn or used in the body. Each yantra carries separate mantras which, if recited, indicate or result in different gains to the individual.These are known as sharir yantras.

2. *Dharan Yantras*: These are worn on various parts of the body, depending on the requirements. Certain results are bestowed on the wearer if used with certain rituals.

3. *Aasan Yantras*: These are kept under the aasan at the time of sadhana and are thought to bear fruits earlier than others. They are frequently placed under the foundations of houses and temples, as well as under deities so that there are good results within a short span of time.

4. *Mandal Yantras*: In this there are nine participants who are made to sit in the formation of the yantra itself. While one person sits in the centre, four persons sit in four main directions viz. North, South, East and West and another four sit in the sub-directions such as north-east, south-west etc. The person in the centre performs the puja, of the Ishat mantra, while the others recite other specified mantras.

5. *Puja Yantras*: They are those which are installed in houses and temples while puja is performed. These yantras are of different kinds and for different purposes. They may be of various deities or of the planets. These yantras are installed in various ways:-

i) prior to performing puja, the yantras are installed as idols or devas. The yantras are written in digits and accordingly, while performing the puja, the names of respective devas are recited through the mantras. The Muslims write 786 which indicate the word "Bisham Allah".

ii) in yantras, the name of the deva is written in the centre and puja is performed thereafter.

iii) Some yantras are prepared while writing the mantras. In some cases the full mantra is written, while in some other cases either the first word or the beej mantra is written.

iv) The photograph, painting or etching of the deva and deities are pasted on before performing the puja.

v) In such yantras, colours are used in the pictures of the devas, and deities.

6. *Chhatar Yantras*: are kept under one's cap or turban or in one's pocket.

7. *Darshan Yantras*: They are those which, if seen by the Sadhaka in the morning, are beneficial to the subject, giving him success. There are several places in the country where purified yantras have been installed, such as at the temple of Lord Jagannath in Puri and the Sri Nath Devar temple, where these yantras are performed to alleviate the troubles of people.

How to Write Yantras

A certain methodical, system must be followed while writing yantras. There is a prescribed pattern which must be adhered to. The sadhaka must face a certain direction and use different materials for different purposes. In this way, the yantras used and recited are powerful and bestow the desired results.

In writing and drawing lines of yantras, lines are drawn from east to west when used for a good purpose. Yantras for uchattan, death, and one's enemies are written from west to east. Lines for progress are made from up and then proceed downwards.

The correct and auspicious time or mahurat is very important. It has generally been laid down that yantras relating to good causes be written early in the morning. Yantras for peace or 'shanti' at midnight, for videshan at noon, for death in the evening, for Uchattan in the afternoon and for Mohan, Vashikaran, Aakarshan etc., in the forenoon.

Specific Horas (horas mean hours) are used to write certain yantras as for example the hora of Jupiter is auspicious for writing yantras for good causes.

HORA OF PLANET	PURPOSE
Jupiter	All yantras for good causes' love, affection and the cure of diseases.
Venus and Mercury	For yantras related to love affairs, Mohan,Vashi Karan, Aakarshan, Business and Sale, and control of one's speech.
Sun	For love, disease, affection, power authority favours and meetings with superiors/dignitaries.

Saturn	Maran, Uchattan
Mars	Litigation, enemies, videshan, maran and for creating differences between people.
Moon	Love, affection and attraction between the sexes.

The sadhaka should write the yantras at an auspicious and appropriate hora, failing which the work started will not yield success.

Material for Writing Yantras

Hindus believe that there are many articles prescribed for writing of the yantras, one of the most commonly used being the "Ashat Gandh".

(a) Ashat Gandh includes eight items consisting of agar, tagar, gorochan, kasturi, white chandan sandoor, lal chandan and kesar.

(b) Camphor, Kasturi, Kesar, Gorochan, Chandan, Tagar, Agar, and Wheat.

(c) Kesar, Kasturi, Camphor, Hengul, White Chandan, Red Chandan, Agar and Tagar.

(d) Camphor, Chandan, Agar, Tagar, Turmeric, Kumkum, Gorochan, Shilajeet.

The powder of the articles mentioned in any group is called "Ashat Gandh". The powder is mixed with holy water to form the medium for writing the yantras. Rose water or scent may also be used.

Pen(Quill)

Pens are required for writing yantras. Usually pens made of jasmine or pomergranate wood are prescribed, or else those made of different metals such as iron, gold or copper are used for various purposes. Pens made of bird feathers and the branches of trees and bushes may also be used for writing yantras must be followed exactly. Ball pens must not be used. The ink should be prepared at home and all materials used should be purified with holy water.

Materials used by Muslims

Materials used by Muslims in writing yantras are given below. Yantras are prepared on a particular day and a particular Hora of the planet, depending on the purpose of the yantra.

1) For Jupiter–camphor, barley, red sandal, sugar and musk
2) For Venus–amber, musk, aud, white sandal, camphor and aspand

3. For Mercury –aud, camphor, red sandal, Karankal and salt.
4. For Sun –aud, mushak, and cinnamon.
5. For Moon –honey, camphor and aud.
6. For Saturn –aud, looban, real and Karankal.
7. For Mars –looban, aud and real.

For souls –gugal, asafoetida and mustard seed.

Method of Yantra Puja

In order to reap the benefit of yantras, it is essential that the puja be performed according to specified rituals.

1. Since every yantra is associated with a particular deva or deity, the sadhaka must keep in mind the particular ishat. One should take flowers in both hands and offer them to the yantra while reciting the Beej Mantra.
2. Panch armit or Ganges water should be offered to the yantra.
3. Sandal wood paste or chandan must be offered to the yantra.
4. Unbroken rice, flowers and garlands must be offered.
5. Incense sticks and 'diyas' or lamps must be lit with the chanting of appropriate mantras.
6. Fruits, betel nuts and betel leaves are to be offered.
7. 'Aarti' and "pradakshina" in which the yantra is propitiated is necessary.
8. At the end flowers and prayers with folded hands must be offered.

In case a sadhaka cannot comply with all the rituals prescribed above, he is advised to light incense sticks, the oil lamp, apply sandal wood paste, vermillion and scent or Ashat Ghand while reciting Beej Mantras. The puja should be performed by the sadhaka himself at his own convenience rather than allowing some person who is not well-versed in the required rituals and ceremonies.

Practical uses of Yantras

When prepared according to prescribed directions yantras are used as follows:

1. *Vashi Karan:* Brings any person, animal, deity or soul under one's control, including one's adversaries.
2. *Shanti Karan:* These yantras deal with the cure of diseases and aids in warding off the malefic influence of soul and planets.

3. *Stambhan* : Means to stop or to prevent. These yantras are used to thwart the efforts of one's enemies or opponents who may be plotting for one's downfall.
4. *Videshan* : Means creating differences between people.
5. *Uchattan* : These yantras deal with the distraction of one's enemies so that they remain away from their homes, country, business, families etc.
6. *Maran* : These are death-inflicting yantras through which anybody's death can be plotted.

Note: The above divisions apply equally to mantras and tantras.

2

YANTRAS IN PRACTICE

Yantras should be written and used with due reverence and faith. Yantras must be prepared according to prescribed rituals and instructions, and the 'puja' should be performed by a competent person. Yantras may be worn around the neck, on the finger or on one's person as detailed below.

Shri Yantra

Hindu 'shastras' designate this yantra as the most important one as it has a powerful effect on the attainment of power, authority and financial success. It also bestows popularity on those as who are in power such as kings, political leaders and officers.(Refer figure 2.1)

Beej Mantra

The Beej mantra used during puja is as follows:

"ॐ श्रीं ह्रीं कलीं ह्रीं श्री महालक्ष्मैय नमः"

"Om Shareeng, Hareeng, Kaleeng, Hareeng, Shri Mahalakshmaiya Namah".

This Yantra is worshipped in almost all temples and houses in South India, where it is called "Shri Chakra".

The author has done extensive research on this Yantra and has evolved the method of wearing it on the body, either as a ring or a necklace. It has been highly effective, irrespective of whether it has been worn by a Chief Minister, a business man or an ordinary man or woman. The author has found that when the Sun is afflicted in any horoscope by the debilitating effect of Saturn, Rahu or Ketu, the use of the Shri Yantra is highly beneficial to the wearer. Depending on the position of the planets in the horoscope, the yantra is used on gold, copper or silver. The'puja' of the yantra takes one week, and is to be worn on a Monday morning. The performance of 'Surya Namaskar' by the wearer is necessary in order to obtain the desired results speedily.

Bagala Mukhi Yantra

This is a highly effective yantra prepared at a particular time when the maximum power is generated from the planet Mars. It is useful for Stamban, mohan, Vashi Karan and Uchattan aspects of Tantrik Vidya. It is effective as a means of achieving success in competitive examinations and to attain victory over one's adversaries, especially during law suits. This yantra also offers protection for cuts, scars, operations and accidents. A diagram of the yantra is given in Figure 2.2.

This yantra should be written on bronze or engraved on silver, copper or gold. The Beej mantra for 'Japa' must be recited 1500 times daily for 45 days. According to Meru and Tantra Druma, the 'puja' is to be performed with yellow beads, yellow dress, yellow flowers and while seated on a yellow 'asan' or carpet. The goddess Bagla Mukhi is the presiding deity.

Beej Mantra

"ॐ ह्रीं बगलामुखयै नमः"

"Om Hareeng Bagla Mukhai Namaha"

Any person using this yantra, either worn around the neck or arm, or carried in one's pocket or in any other way as prescribed, should avoid meat, fish and co-habitation on Tuesday in order to get immediate results.The yantra is to be drawn with turmeric, datura flower's juice or yellow orpiment on a piece of stone or carved in copper metal and then worshipped.

The following points must be observed during puja:

a) the dress should be as specified above;
b) the 'japa' or beej mantra' should be in the mind;
c) the incence sticks and 'diya' should remain lit and in front of the person performing the 'puja';
d) while performing these rituals, the person performing the puja should have wholesome vegetarian food, sleep on the ground and avoid sex;
e) if something happens during 'sadhana', no one should be told about it;

f) the sadhana should not be started when the Moon is positioned in the 4th, 8th or 12th house according to the person's birth sign.

Kali Yantra

Kali yantra or Dakhina Kalika Maha Yantra bestows on the sadhaka the fulfilment of desires, wealth and the comforts of life. This yantra is required to take care of the harmful effects of Saturn, which is usually responsible for misfortunes, sufferings and sorrows in human life. This yantra is prepared and used at a time when Saturn has the most beneficial effect on Earth. When worn, this yantra is the surest remedy against chronic diseases like blood pressure, paralysis and nervous disorders. It has the occult power of protecting the wearer from evil forces such as Bhuta, Preta, Pisacha, Kala Purusha and Brahma Rakshyasas.

Any person wearing this yantra is protected against planetary malevolence, as well as from accidents, misfortunes and dangers. Since Saturn is the planet for longevity it has the additional benefit of bestowing long life on the person who keeps this yantra on his body. (Refer Figure 2.3 for Kali Yantra.)

Ther Kali Yantra is very powerful and should be written on bronze embossed on gold, silver or copper plates before offering prayers. While performing the puja, the person should concentrate on the image of Kali.

Japa Beej Mantra

"ॐ क्री कालिकाये नमः ॐ कापालिन्यै नमः"

"Om Karing Kalikaya Namah, Om Kapalinyai Namah".

After performing Pranayam, Rishi Nyas, Karanga Nyas etc., the devotee should invoke Kali Devi . According to Swanan Tantra, Kali Tantra and Bhairon Tantra, Japa should be performed for one lakh mantras by taking rice and ghee together. A sadhaka practising "Birachar" should worship with clarified butter. This yantra is also known as Sasaan Kali, Mahakali and Bhadra Kali yantra, to be performed under the guidance of one's Guru.

Shri Bhairon Yantra

This yantra should be written according to prescribed directions and one thousand mantras should be chanted for forty-one days. The mantras of Bhairon are contained in "Kavich Path". The Sadhaka is bestowed with good luck and the fulfilment of all his desires. It is effective for Vashi Karan, Maran and for the removal of poverty. This sadhana is particularly useful during the present Kaliyug. (Refer Fig.2.4)

Beej Mantra

"ॐ ह्रीं बुटकाये अपदुद्धारणाय कुरू कुरू बुटकाय ह्रीं ॐ स्वाहा"

"Om Hareeng, Butkaya Aapaduddharanay Kuru Kuru Butkaya Hareeng, Om Swaha".

It is important for the Sadhaka to remember the following points:

a. Bhairon sadhana is to be performed at night only;
b. it should be performed only for a specific purpose;
c. Bhaironji has to be offered a spiritual liquor or wine;
d. Offerings during Bhairon puja have to be changed from day to day-
 –on Sunday –rice cooked in milk;
 –on Monday –a sweet shaped in the form of a ball;
 –on Tuesday –ghee and gur, or articles prepared with ghee;
 –on Wednesday –curd and sugar;
 –on Thursday –basen ladoos;
 –on Friday –roasted gram;
 –on Saturday –pakoras made of urad dal are offered.

In addition to the items mentioned above, jalebis, roasted papad, apples and gram are offered.

Bhairon yantra is very useful also for self-protection. Maran, Vashi Karan and the removal of poverty.

1. *For Vashi Karan*

At sunrise on Thursday mornings, the Bhairon mantra should be recited ten thousand times on the banks of a river or in a jungle. This ritual gives immense power to the Sadhaka to bring his opponents under his influence.

2. *For Protection*

In order to give protection, the mantra reads thus:

"ॐ ह्रीं भैरव भैरव थयक्रहर मां रक्ष रक्ष हुं फुट स्वाहा"

"Om Hareeng Bhairve Bhairve thekarhar maang raksha raksha hoong phut swaha"

3. *For Maran*

At midnight on a Tuesday, recite the above mantra ten thousand times, while sitting at a crossroad. Perform a 'hom' with ghee, kheer, wood and lal chandan and utter the enemy's name. This will lead to his death.

4. *To Remove Poverty*

At night, one should face the West, light a lamp of mustard oil and recite the mantra ten thousand times. This will remove poverty.

Saraswati Yantra

Maha Neela Saraswati Devi is the presiding deity of the planet Jupiter, as shown in Figure 2.5 Saraswati bestows intellect, intelligence and is the patron goddess of learning and music. For those who are dull-witted and have suffered breaks in their education, and for those who are suffering from the bad effects of a malefic Jupiter, this occult yantra sharpens the intellect, and ensures success in studies and high achievement in competitive examinations.

Saraswati Devi is also revered by married ladies to ensure a happy conjugal life. Unmarried girls also seek her blessings in order to have a good husband and a peaceful married life.

This yantra is a sure remedy for all mental disorders, weak intellectual growth and lunacy. Those wearing this yantra must avoid meat, fish and sexual relations on Thursdays.

Beej Mantra

Ganges water should be sprinkled on the yantra, a tilak of kesar should be applied, a ghee lamp lit, and fruits and flowers offered. A jug of water must be kept alongside, and the following mantra must be recited 1.25 lakh times in forty days–

"ॐ विद्या दायनी सरस्वतिये नम:"

"Om Shri Vidya Dayeni, Saraswatiya Namaha".

On the 41st day, a homa should be performed for 20,000 mantras, after which sweets should be distributed to virgin girls.

Shri Ganesh Yantra

Before undertaking any new venture, it is necessary to perform a Ganesh Puja in order to ensure the successful completion of one's objectives. The 'upasana' and puja of Ganapati is essential and may be performed through the worship of an image , a photo or a yantra. The swastik is the sign of Lord Ganesh. The Yantra can be made on Booj Patra, gold, silver or copper. Figure 2.6 shows the Shri Ganesh Yantra.

The Shri Ganesh yantra should be writen according to prescribed canons at an auspicious time. With the chanting of mantras, the yantra is purified. The yantra is composed of six triangles which are closed on all sides, with a central triangle and 'bindu' inside. The Beej word can also be recited for purifying the yantra.

After attaining 'siddhi' of the yantra, the sadhaka will be blessed with the fulfilment of his desires, and the achievement of his goals of securing wealth, power and authority. The yantra must be worshipped for a period of thirty days and the chanting of one thousand mantras a day. Flowers, honey, milk and coconuts should be placed as offerings.

Japa Mantras

Three Jaap Mantras are given below for purifying the yantra.

"ॐ ह्रीं श्रीं ग्लौ गं गणपतये वर वरद सर्वजनं मे वशमानय स्वाहा"

a) "Om Hareeng Shareeng Galo Gang Ganpatya Var Vard Sarvjanam Me Vashmanaye Swaha"

"ॐ ह्रीं श्रीं ग्लौ गं गणपतये वर वरद सर्वजनं मे वशमानय ठः ठः"

b) The mantra is the same, except that the word" tha tha" is used instead of "Swaha".

"ॐ गं गणपतये नमः"

c) "Om Gang Ganpataya Namah".

Mrit Sanjivani Yantra

This yantra offers protection from all diseases and like the Maha Mritanje yantra it bestows the 'sadhaka' with wealth, good fortune, fame and happiness.

Figure 2.7 shows the yantra which should be carved or embossed on copper or silver plate. It may also be written on Bhooj Patra in an auspicious time. The yantra can be purified with one thousand mantras daily for 45 days. Coconuts, fruits, flowers and incense must be offered. The yantra can be kept in the temple for puja or can be worn on the body. In the end homa should be performed with 10,000 mantras, along with fruits, til, cooked rice with milk and sugar, mustard, milk, curd, durba grass samadha of banyan tree, palasa tree and the catech plant.

Mantras

"ॐ जूँ सः मां पालय पालय"

a) "om Joom Sah Ma Palay, Palay".

"ॐ हौ जूँ सः (अमुकं) जीवय-जीवय पालय पालय सः जूं हौ"

b) "Om Hon Jung Sah (amuk) Jivae–Jivae palay palay Sah Joom Hon Om"

In the above mantras, replace the name of the diseased person or sadhaka where the words "Ma" "मा" and "Amuk" "अमुकं" appear.

Mangal Yantra

The Mangal Yantra is in the shape of a triangle and is embossed or engraved on copper plate. It is composed of 21 sub-triangles enclosed by a big triangle. In each triangle, the different names of the lord Mangal are inscribed, as shown in Figure 2.8.

After installing the yantra in the place where puja is conducted in the house, the yantra is worshipped with red flowers, and sweets made from gur or rice.

This yantra is very powerful and gives quick results. It frees the sadhaka from debts and cures blood pressure and rash temper. It also offers protection from accidents, cuts and wounds and enables the sadhaka to recover speedily from operations. In the case of severe diseases, the yantra should be worshipped on a daily basis starting from a Tuesday.

Mantras

"ॐ क्रां क्रीं क्रौं सः भौमाय नमः"

a) "Om Karang Kareeng Karoong sah Bhoomaya Namaha"

"ॐ क्रां क्रीं क्रौं सः भौमाय नमः सः क्रौं क्रीं क्रां ॐ"

b) "Om Karang Kareeng Karoong sah Bhomaye Namah sah Karoong, Kareeng, Karang Om".

This yantra is assigned to Lord Hanuman and the Mars planet.

Other Uses

The author has used this yantra in different ways, apart from those prescribed above and has got 95% success with immediate results after applying the rules of astrology.

i) Mars is significator of husband in the case of ladies rather than the planet Jupiter. When the position of Mars is weak in the birth chart or positioned in the 6th, 8th or 12th house, the lady's marriage is invariably delayed.

The author has found that in such cases, the yantra can be prepared and puja is performed by the girl starting from Tuesday for 41 days, a suitable match is found within a short span of time.

ii) In those cases where a lady's marital life becomes strained on account of bickerings leading to a separation between the couple, this yantra has shown remarkable results in patching up relations between the spouses.

iii) In those cases where a man or a woman is of harsh temperament, it has been noticed that by wearing this yantra after puja, troubles arising from the person's behaviour are controlled.

iv) In those instances when a man is lacking in courage and boldness, or is shy and unable to express himself, very good results have been seen merely by keeping the yantra on the person's body.

Any person who is wearing this yantra on his or her body or in the place of puja, should avoid fish, meat and sexual contact on Tuesdays in order to get rapid results.

Nava Graha Yantras

Whenever a particular planet, or planets in a horoscope are positioned in a way that results in harm or retards the individual's health, prosperity and peace of mind, one should put a yantra of the planet (Refer to Figure 2.9).

The procedure for making a yantra is as follows:

Red sandalwood should be mixed with ashat gandh and with a pen of pomegranate wood,write the yantra on Bhooj Patra or Palm leaf. The pen may be of peacock feather. The yantra should be written at an auspicious time when the planet is in Shukal Paksha (bright phase).

The yantra should be placed before Graha Shanti Vidhan with 'homa Jap' and 'puja'. After purification, sadhana and prana pratishta the yantra may be placed either in gold, silver, copper or ashat dhatu talisman and worn around the neck or arm, with an appropriate metal for each planet.

On the day of yantra puja, the wearer should not eat any meat or fish, should not use oil and must have his meal before sunset. The next day, when the yantra puja is completed, the yantra should be placed near a tulsi plant at sunrise. The wearer should have a green coconut and should offer 'Arghya'to the sun thrice before wearing the yantra. The yantra can be embossed or engraved on copper, silver or stainless steel and worn after the puja is completed.

Every planet is associated with a particular metal. This metal is used in making the yantra either by engraving or embossing. Consequently, the talisman of the appropriate metal is worn around the neck or arm of the person. Given below is a table in which the planet, the metal associated with it and the Beej Mantra is listed for the convenience of readers.

	PLANET	METAL	BEEJ MANTRA
1.	Sun	Gold	Oang Rang Raviaya Namha
2.	Moon	Silver	Oang Soong Somaya Namha
3.	Mars	Gold/Copper	Oang Bhaung Bhoumaya Namha
4.	Mercury	Brass	Oang Hrang Hring Bung Budhaya Namha
5.	Jupiter	Gold	Oang Gung Guruaya Namah
6.	Venus	Silver	Oang Sung Sukraya Namaha
7.	Saturn	Iron	Oang Eang Haring Sring Sani Charya Namaha
8.	Rahu	Brass	Oang Rang Rahuaya Namaha
9.	Ketu	Copper	Oang Bhung Ketuaya Namaha

Combined Navgraha Mantra

To counteract the adverse planetary influence, the yantra shown in Fig. 2.9A can be used. The yantra should be inscribed on gold, silver, copper or stainless steel and worn around the neck. Fruits, honey and a variety of spiced rice may be offered as puja. The yantra can be purified by chanting the Navgraha mantra for 45 days, 1000 times a day.

Mantra

"ॐ सूर्य नमः चन्द्रये नमः बुध्ये नमः ब्रहस्पतिये नमः मंगलये नमः शुक्रये नमः शिये नमः राहुये नम केतुये नमः नवग्रहये नमः"

"Om Suryee Namaha, Chanderye Namaha, Budhae Namaha, Brahaspatiae Namaha, Mangala Namaha, Shukrae Namaha, Shaniae Namaha, Rahuae Namaha, Ketuae Namaha, Nav Grahae Namaha".

Karia Siddhi Yantra

The author has found this to be a highly effective yantra. It may be engraved or embossed on copper plate. The yantra is composed of a circle, which is divided into seven equal segments. Each segment contains a figure and a number. In one segment there is a snake which has number 38 on it. Guitar carries number 91 on it, tree 47, jewels 17, sun 61, arrow 52 and ship 33. The sum total of all the numbers is 339, as shown in Fig.2.10.

The figures shown on the yantra indicate the following:

1. *Snake*: Bestows knowlege, wisdom and a means of healing from disease.
2. *Guitar*: Denotes music, confidence and happiness.
3. *Tree*: Family progress at all times, including in the future.
4. *Jewels:* Offer protection from all troubles and stand for health, wealth, prosperity and a comfortable and happy home.
5. *Sun*: Indicates power, authority and finances of the individual and those dependent on him. It signifies success in politics favours from superiors and the fulfilment of desires.
6. *Arrow*: Denotes protection against the 'evil eye' and other dangers to both the individual and his family.
7. *Ship:* Is a unique mark as it indicates courage for the individual against any odds and ensures his success in all activities.

These yantras ensure the individual's well-being and success in life. After performing yantra puja, the yantra should be hung in the house at a prominent place or in the temple. The sadhaka will thus be blessed with success in all his endeavours.

Vashi Karan Yantras

The yantra shown in Fig. 2.11 is used for winning over the affections of one's lover. The yantra should be carved on gold, silver stainless steel or copper. The yantra must be worshipped by the sadhaka while facing the North. The yantra should be worn around the neck or kept on one's body.

The mantra given below must be recited for 55 days, 1000 times a day. Milk gruel is given as offering during worship.

Mantra

"ॐ दरिद्राणीं चिन्तामणिगुणनिका जन्मजबधौ"
"निमन्गानां दष्ट्रा मुररिपुवराशहस्य भवति"

"Om Daridrani Cinta-mani Gunanika Janmajabadho.
Nimanganam Dastram Muraripu-varahasya Bhavati".

Fig.2.12 shows a Mohammedan yantra whch may be used during love affairs, particularly to combat the restlessness which affects the individual during such infatuations.

i) The yantra should be written on plain paper in black ink and hung from a pomegranate tree. Whenever the yantra moves due to the breeze, one's lover will increasingly yearn to be with the beloved.
ii) It should be buried in the desert.
iii) The yantra should be made with flour. There should be either 11 or 21 pills made from flour, which should be thrown into a river early in the morning for 21 days.
iv) A wick should be made of the yantra, dipped in mustard oil and burnt, with the wick facing the house of one's beloved. The objective of securing the affections of the person will be attained immediately.

Pandhara Yantra

This yantra should be written on plain paper with black ink or engraved or embossed on stainless steel or copper plate on a Friday in Venus 'hora'. This is a tried and tested yantra, which, if kept on the person of a man or a woman will lead to attraction between the two. Refer Fig. 2.13.

Fig. 2.14 denotes a yantra which can be used to bring about cordial relations between husband and wife when there is discord between them. The yantra should be tied aroud the arm of either husband or wife.

Fig. 2.15 shows a yantra which should be written and then dissolved in water and given to the person who one wants to entice. Prior to writing the yantra, the words, "YA SHAFI" should be recited 11 times. Success in getting one's lover is guaranteed.

Fig. 2.16 shows a yantra which is very effective for Vashi Karan. The yantra should be written on Bhoj Patra with lac water, turmeric and manjith. Replace the word "Sham" given in the yantra with the name of the lady or man who has to be brought within one's control. Yantra puja is to be performed by collecting the dust from under the feet of the concerned person and an idol of dust must be made. The yantra should then be kept in a secret place near the idol. Success is assured in gaining the affections of the concerned man or woman.

Fig. 2.17 shows another yantra in which success is assured in attracting the love of a person of the opposite sex. The yantra should be written on Bhooj patra with camphor, kumkum, gorochan and kasturi. Replace the name of the person concerned with that of the word 'sham' given in the yantra.

When performing yantra puja, Bramhacharya should be observed for three days. On the fourth day, a Brahmin should be given lunch. In the morning put the yantra in a three metal talisman and tie it around the arm or neck. The person concerned will undoubtedly be won over.

Kamakashya Yantra

This is a highly auspicious yantra and is shown in Fig. 2.18. The yantra is used for Vashi Karan of ladies of royal families or those connected with high status.

The yantra is written on Bhooj patra with gorochana, kumkum and camphor, with a pen of chameli wood. Write the name of the concerned lady instead of the word "Devi" as used in the yantra. While writing the yantra, the writer should wear white clothes and should perform the puja with full devotion and confidence with flowers and incense during the night. The figure or image of the concerned lady should be kept in mind while performing the puja. The puja should be performed for seven days and after that lunch should be served to Brahmin ladies. The words "कामाक्षी प्रियताम" "Kamakshee Priyatam"should be recited and enclosed in the three metal talisman to be worn on the right arm. It is a very powerful yantra which has been used to win over ladies of royal families.

Subhagya Vijay Yantra

This is a highly auspicious yantra for the Vashi karan of ladies in order to win over members of the opposite sex. Fig. 2.19.

Gorochan should be mixed with water and the yantra be written on Bhooj patra. Flowers, 'Diyas' and incense should be used in performing the puja.The yantra can be carved on stainless steel, copper, silver or gold. It should be wrapped in a golden talisman and worn on the right arm by men and around the neck by women. This is a tried and tested yantra which brings good luck to the wearer.

Fig. 2.20 shows a yantra which should be written on a paper with saffron, kesar or kasturi in order to bring anyone under one's control. The Yantra marked 'A' should be kept by the person on his or her body. The yantra marked 'B' should be dissolved in water and the water drunk by the concerned person. Infatuation between the two parties is assured.

Shanti Karan Yantra

Shanti Karan Yantras include the cures of diseases and warding off the evil influences of planets, the evil eye and spirits. These are also known as 'Pacification Yantras', a few of which are given below.

Fig. 2.21 (i and ii) show yantras for the cure of rheumatism and stomach problems as also for epilepsy. The following yantra must be written with Ashat Gaund on Bhooj Patra and worn around the neck or kept on one's person. The yantras can be worn either embossed or engraved on copper or stainless steel plate. The patient is cured by the constant use of the yantra.

Cure for Old Fever

It is shown in Fig. 2.21 (iii). When a fever persists for any length of time, the yantra should be written in black ink on Bhooj Patra and worn around the neck. This ensures a quick recovery.

Cure From Gout

This is a yantra of Mahamritanje mantra carved on copper plate and tied like a bangle around the wrist of the right hand on Thursday morning. Refer to Fig. 2.21(iv). The constant use of this yantra will cure gout. The mantra should be recited 108 times before wearing the yantra.

Cure From Flatulence

Fig. 2.21 (v) indicates the yantra which will cure the problem of flatulence. The yantra should be written with kesar on a Sunday, before sunrise, it should be washed and the water taken by the patient for 41 days. The name of the patient should replace the world "Sham" in the yantra.

For Heart Attacks and Heart Problems

Any of the yantras should be written on Bhooj Patra with Saffron and worn around the neck with a talisman made of copper or silver, as indicated in Fig. 2.21 (vi).

To Cure the Evil Eye

Fig. 2.22 shows a yantra which is highly effective in those cases in which a child has been affected by the "evil eye." "नजर लगाना" The yantra should be written on paper with black ink and be engraved or embossed on copper or stainless steel plate and put around the child's neck.

Another use of this powerful yantra is for the child who weeps too much, remains sick upto the age of 3 or who urinates in the night. The use of this yantra will alleviate the problem.

This yantra is also effective in aiding the child in studies.

When a child weeps too much during the day or night or during sleep, or gets frightened in sleep and sees dreadful dreams either of the yantras can be used around the neck for relief. Refer Fig. 2.23.

To remove the Fear of Souls

i) This yantra (Fig. 2.24) should be written with chandan on the stone which must be washed. The water should be taken by the person concerned . One will be cured.

Stambhan

Stambhan Means immobilisation or to STOP the enemy's speech or back biting. The persons who oppose may be a woman or a man, officers or Ministers etc., wishing for your downfall. They can be stopped from doing evil and bringing harm through the following yantras.

In order to prevent the enemy, officers, or others from harassing unnecessarily, the following yantra can be used as shown in Fig. 2.25, Either of the yantras should be written on a new earthen pot and buried in Fire. The enemy will stop causing trouble. The name of the enemy should be written below the yantra.

This is a Tested yantra from Saundria Lahri to win over the enemy. Write this yantra with the name of the enemy on a Gold plate as shown in Fig. 2.26. Puja should be done and Jaggery and gruel offered for the Puja. The author has used this yantra, worn around the neck or kept on the body extensively. It should be carved on copper or stainless steel plate, after Pooja. It was found to be very effective in combatting the enemy.

Shatru Mukh Stambhan Yantra

When a person has created trouble resulting in losses to an individual then use the yantra in Fig 2. 27 to stop him doing further mischief. Write this yantra on the wall of your house with the name of the enemy with "Kharia Mitti". Puja of the yantra should be performed by offering white flowers, fruits, incense and by wearing white clothes. Offer lunch to a Brahmin and recite the word 'Shri Shiv' 41 times. The enemy will stop talking against you. This is a tested Yantra by the author.

Engrave or emboss this yantra shown in Fig 2.28 on a silver ring. As and when you will approach any officer or anybody else for any work. Wear this ring. The person will favour you.

Write this yantra with Kesar or Saffron on a piece of paper. Keep it under your tongue and approach the enemy, who will not be able to talk against you. Refer Fig 2.29 for this yantra.

For A Missing Person

When a person is missing or has left the house without intimation and their whereabouts are not known, the following yantras can be used to trace him or her

i) Write the yantra in Fig. 2.30A on a piece of paper with black ink. Put this yantra in a small bucket and lower into a well. If you hear a sound of laughing, the missing person is alive. If you hear weeping, the person is dead. If nothing happens, mystery shrouds the missing person but, the man is certainly alive.

ii) Write the yantra in Fig 2.30B on a paper with black ink. Mount it on a spinning wheel. A virgin girl should revolve the spinning wheel seven times and after that the spinning wheel should be placed erect facing the sky. The missing person will come back.

For victory over the enemy, write the yantra in Fig 2.31 on a paper or emboss or engrave it on a copper plate and keep it on your body.

As and when you will approach the enemy, the enemy will surrender and will not oppose you. He will work as per your wish and desire.

Videshan Yantra

Videshan means creating differences between two or more persons. This is used when persons are harming you and do not come around in spite of all efforts, or they are beyond control.

Through yantras, you can create misunderstandings and quarrels between two or more persons. Our shastras allow us to create differences between husband and wife, two friends or brothers only in self-defence.

To create videshan between persons write the yantra in Fig 2.32 with the blood of a crow and owl and monthly blood of a widowed lady on Bhooj Patra with a pen made of the wings of a crow.

After writing the yantra, perform Puja with flowers, bury or place the yantra in the house of the person.

As long as this yantra remains in the house, there will be constant quarrels and bickerings. Write the name or names of the persons concerned are written in the centre.

To Create Enmity Ref Fig 2.33

i) Write this yantra on a paper with black ink. It should be buried or thrown at the place of residence. They will fight between themselves.

ii) Write this yantra on paper with excreta of an ASS, and throw it in the house of persons concerned. Write the names of the persons below the yantra.

Write this yantra, Fig. 2.34 on Sunday with black ink on a paper. Perform pooja, and put it on the fire. The relations will break between persons whose names are written.

ii) Write this yantra with coal on paper and perform pooja. Show the yantra to the persons or throw it in their house. Relations will become strained.

Uchchattan

Enemy Uchattan Yantra: - Fig 2.35

i) Write this yantra on a copper plate and with a steel pen. The yantra should be kept with you.

ii) Write this yantra on a Silky cloth piece with black ink. Make a talisman of it. The person whose Uchattan is required must be asked some way or the other to wear it on his neck or on his arm. He will be subject to Uchattan

iii) Write this yantra on Bhooj Patra with Red Chandan. Light a fire in a broken piece of earthen pot and put the yantra over it. As and when, smoke emerges from the fire, the enemy will be subjected to Uchattan.

This yantra is best suited for Uchattan of a person. Ref Fig 2.36. Write this yantra on Bhooj Patra with blood of Anamika (Jupiter) finger. Pooja of the Yantra should be performed by wearing red clothes and rosary of red flowers. The Sadhaka should paint his body with red colour. Pooja be performed during Krishna Paksha night with red flowers and Red scented articles. Invite Brahmin for lunch after Puja.

The most important point for this yantra is to perform Ganesh Puja before writing the yantra and doing pooja of Yantra.

After 21 days Puja of the yantra, cut the yantra into pieces and mix it in left over eaten lunch (जूठे भात) and on the last day throw to the crows.

The enemy will face Uchattan. Change the name of enemy in the yantra in place of word 'Ram'.

Maran Yantras

Maran yantras are death inflicting yantra. This being a nefarious action has not been detailed here in this book.

Note : These yantras are supplied by the author for the welfare of mankind.

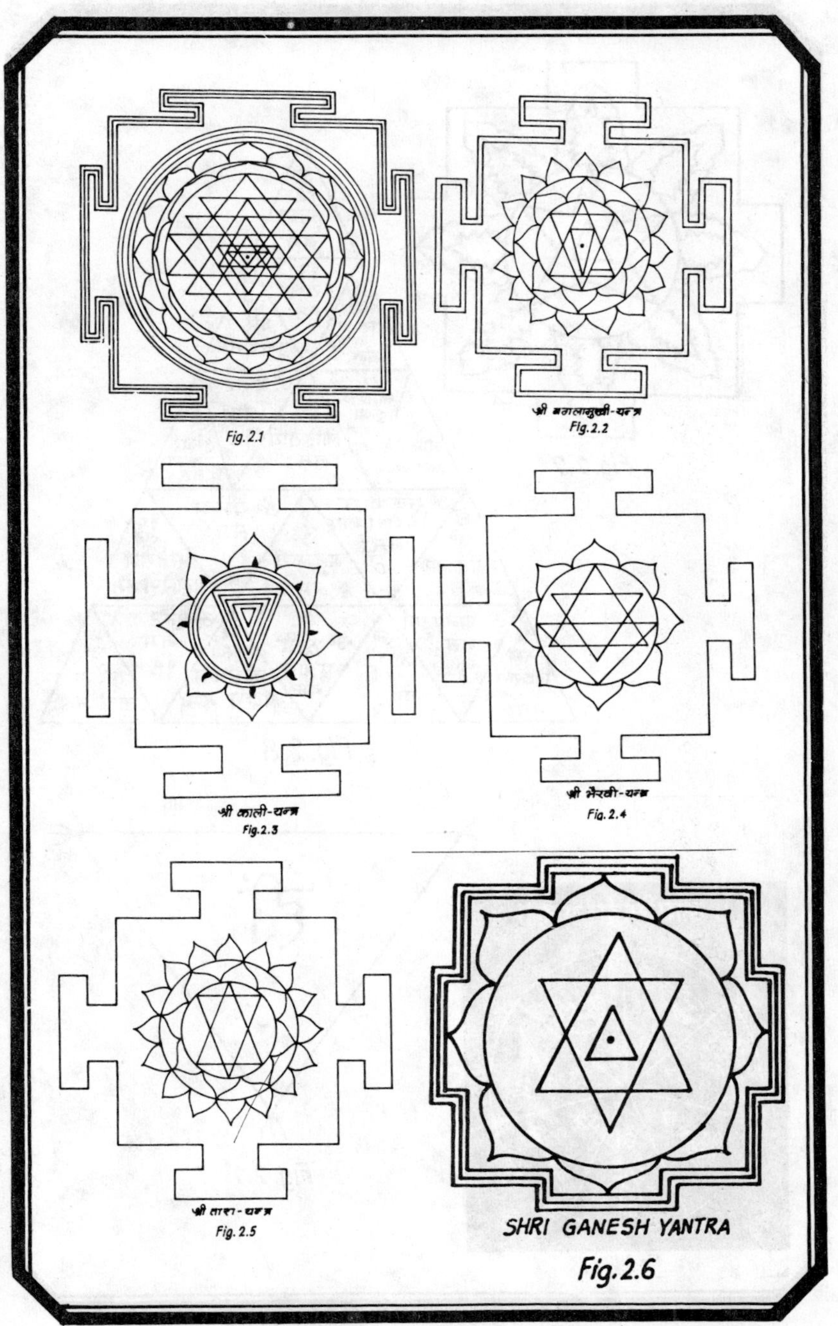

Fig. 2.1

श्री बगलामुखी-यन्त्र
Fig. 2.2

श्री काली-यन्त्र
Fig. 2.3

श्री भैरवी-यन्त्र
Fig. 2.4

श्री तारा-यन्त्र
Fig. 2.5

SHRI GANESH YANTRA
Fig. 2.6

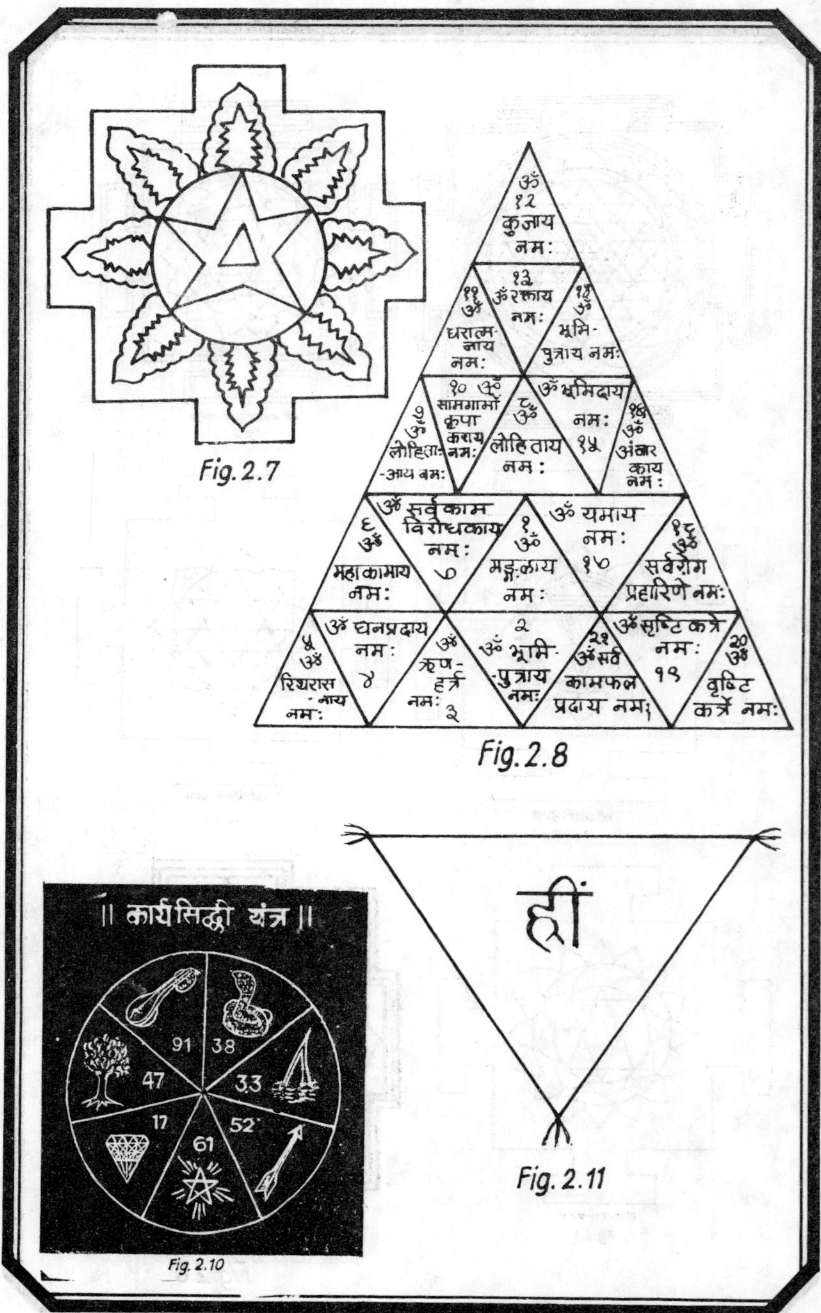

Fig. 2.7

Fig. 2.8

Fig. 2.10

Fig. 2.11

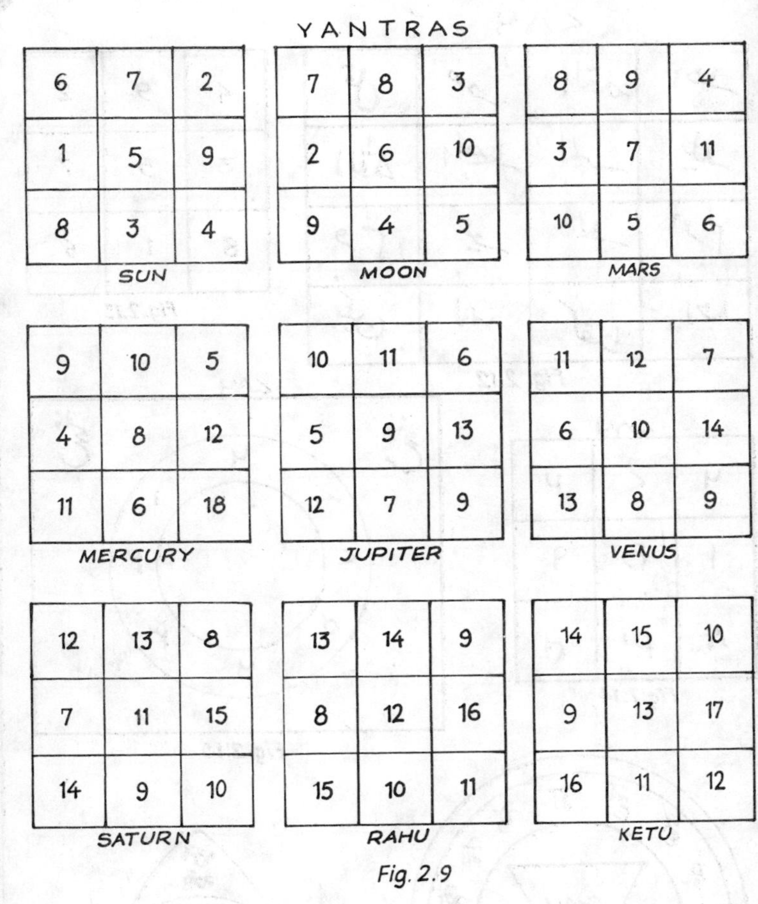

YANTRAS

SUN

6	7	2
1	5	9
8	3	4

MOON

7	8	3
2	6	10
9	4	5

MARS

8	9	4
3	7	11
10	5	6

MERCURY

9	10	5
4	8	12
11	6	18

JUPITER

10	11	6
5	9	13
12	7	9

VENUS

11	12	7
6	10	14
13	8	9

SATURN

12	13	8
7	11	15
14	9	10

RAHU

13	14	9
8	12	16
15	10	11

KETU

14	15	10
9	13	17
16	11	12

Fig. 2.9

बु	शु	च
गु	रा	के
मं	शं	सु

Fig. 2.9A

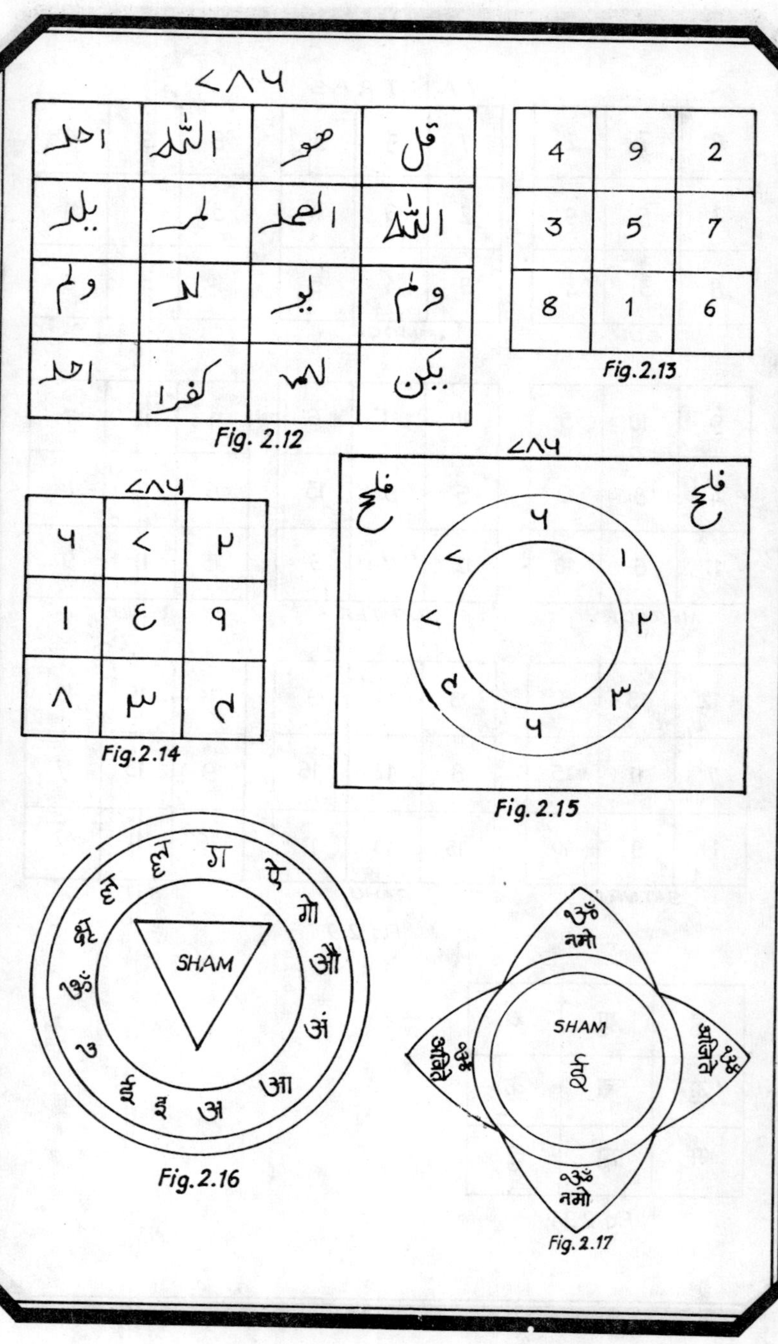

Fig. 2.12

Fig. 2.13

Fig. 2.14

Fig. 2.15

Fig. 2.16

Fig. 2.17

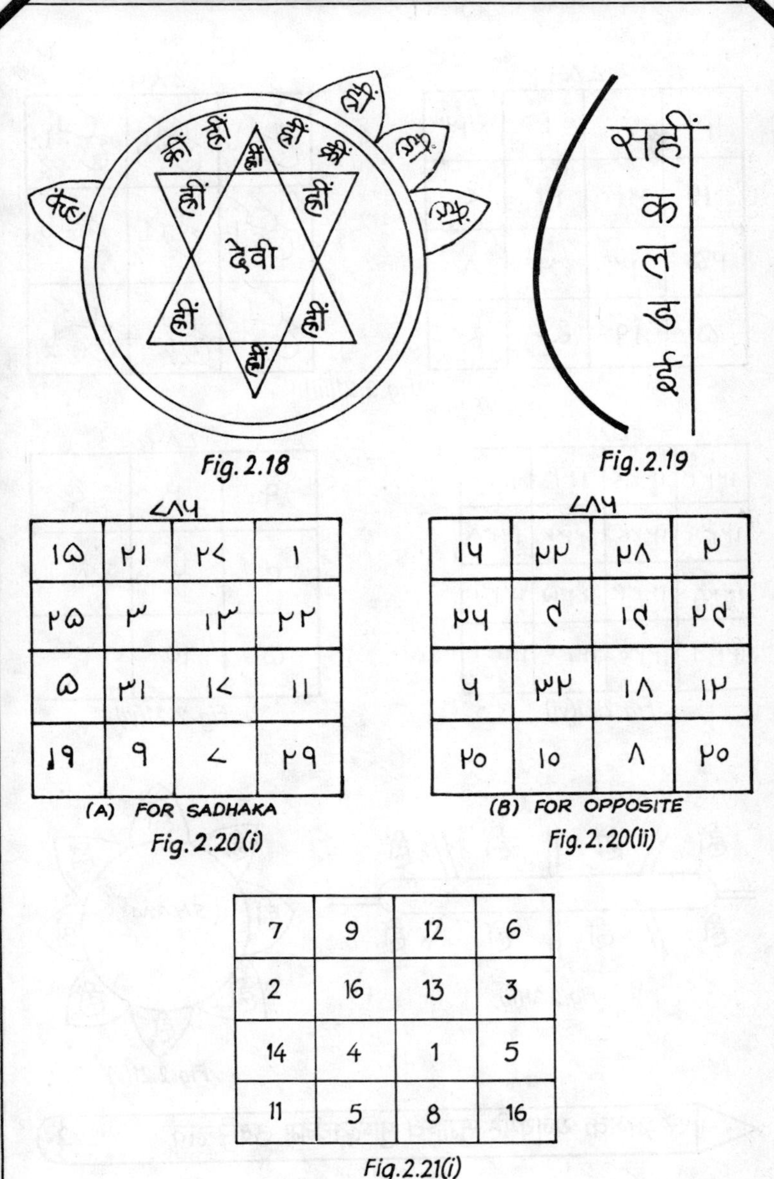

Fig. 2.18

Fig. 2.19

٧٨۶

١۵	٢١	٢٧	١
٢۵	٣	١٣	٢٢
۵	٣١	١٧	١١
١٩	٩	٧	٢٩

(A) FOR SADHAKA

Fig. 2.20(i)

٧٨۶

١۶	٢٢	٢٨	٢
٢۶	٩	١٩	٢٩
۶	٣٢	١٨	١٢
٢٠	١٠	٨	٢٠

(B) FOR OPPOSITE

Fig. 2.20(ii)

7	9	12	6
2	16	13	3
14	4	1	5
11	5	8	16

Fig. 2.21(i)

۷۸۶

۳	۸	۱	۲۳
۲	۳۲	۲۱	۷
۲۵	۳	۶	۸
۵	۱۹	ع	ع

۷۸۶

یا کبیکج	یا کبیکج	یا کبیکج
یا کبیکج	یا کبیکج	یا کبیکج
یا کبیکج	یا کبیکج	یا کبیکج

Fig. 2.21(iii)

۷۸۶

۱۲۳۲	۱۲۳۷	۱۲۴	۱۲۲۶
۱۲۳۹	۱۲۲۷	۱۲۳۲	۱۲۳۸
۱۲۲۸	۱۲۳۲	۱۲۳۵	۱۲۳۱
۱۲۳۶	۱۲۳۰	۱۲۲۰	۱۲۴۱

Fig. 2.21(vi)

۷۸۶

۹	۲	۷
۴	۶	۸
۵	۱۰	۳

Fig. 2.21(vi)

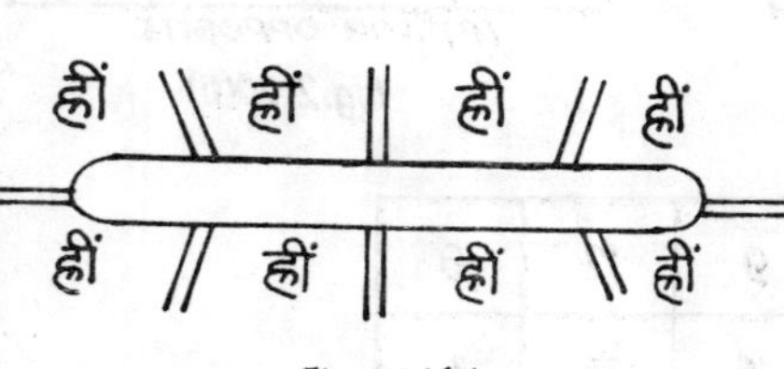

Fig. 2.21(ii)

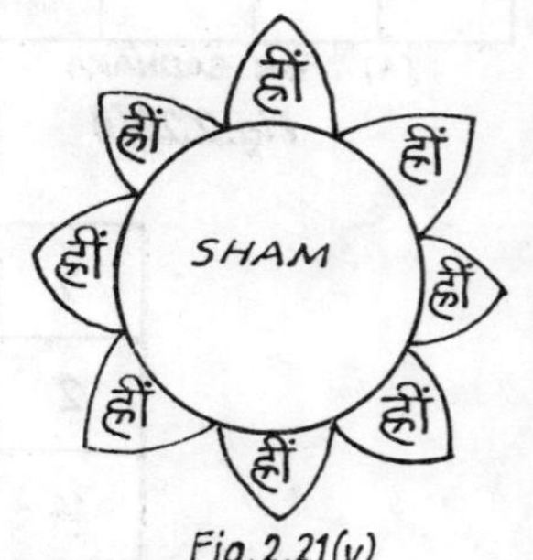

Fig. 2.21(v)

ॐ मभकं यजयमहे सुगन्धिं पुष्ट्विवर्धनम उर्वारुमेव ---

Fig. 2.21(iv)

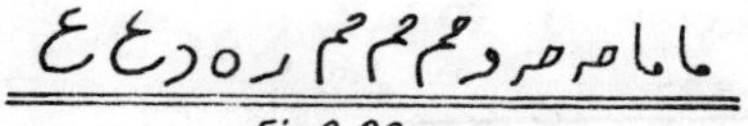

ما ما مر و مم مم ر ه د ح ع ع

Fig.2.22

۷۸۶

د	ت	ب
ج	ح	خ
ح	ل	د

Fig. 2.23(i)

۷۸۶

۸	۱۱	۱۴	۱
۱۳	۲	۷	۱۲
۳	۱۶	۹	۶
۱۰	۵	۲	۱۵

Fig.2.23(ii)

٩١ʃ	ɛɛ	٩	૪
०	ɤ	०	ɛ٩
ς	=	०١	०١०
ɛ	٩	ς	ɤ०

OR

०	०	ɛ	ɔ
ς	૪	ɤ	ɛ
ɤ	١١١	ς	٩٩
ɛ٩	૪	٢١١	١١

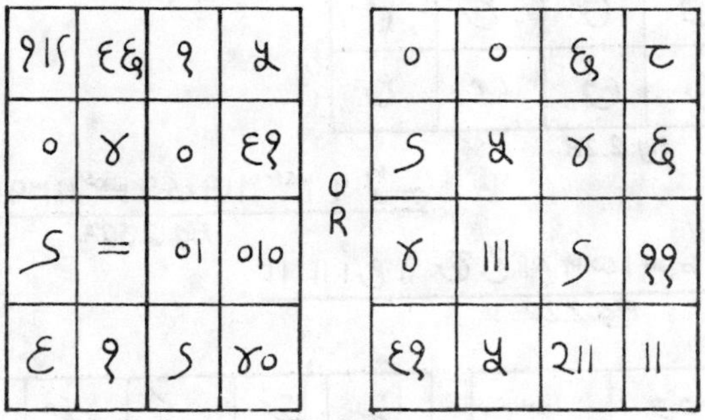

Fig. 2.24

۷۸۶

۴	۹	۲
۳	۵	۷
۸	۱	۶

۷۸۶

۲	۷	۶
۹	۵	۱
۴	۳	۸

Fig. 2.25

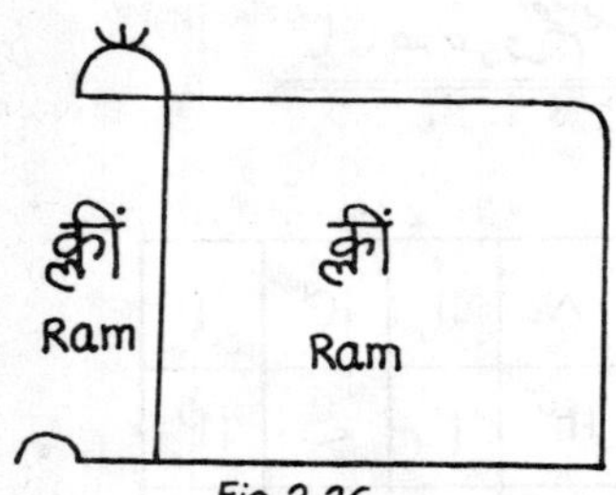

Fig. 2.26

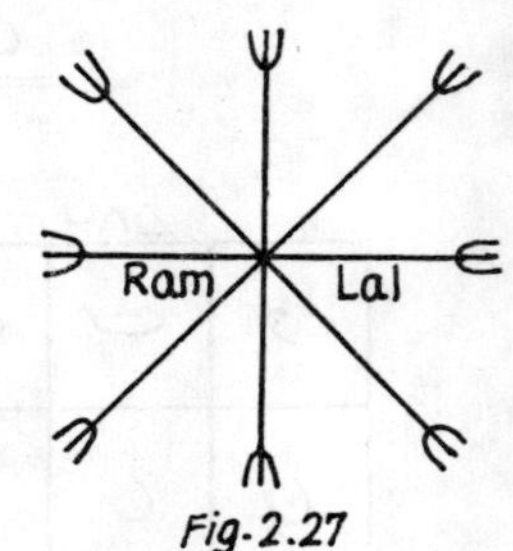

Fig. 2.27

ق	س	ع	م	ح
ع	م	ح	ق	س
ح	ق	س	ع	م
م	ح	ق	س	ع

Fig. 2.28

۱۱۲۹۲۱۱۹۱ عمر ۹ ی ۶۱۹ عمر ۳ ۶ لوٗ–

Fig. 2.30A

۱۱ ۱۱ ۱۱ اُع ۱۱ ج ج ۱۸۹ ۵ ۱ هر ۱ ط ۱۲۱ لح ۸

Fig. 2.29

دا۲	وه	۳
دوا	۵ ع	۱۵ ی
پیرسیدی	باصره	راه

Fig. 2.30B

ببینا	فتحا	لک	فتحنا	انا
ببینا	لک	فتحا	لک	فتحنا
فتحنا	لک	فتحا	لک	ببینا
انا	فتحنا	لک	فتحا	ببینا

Fig. 2.31

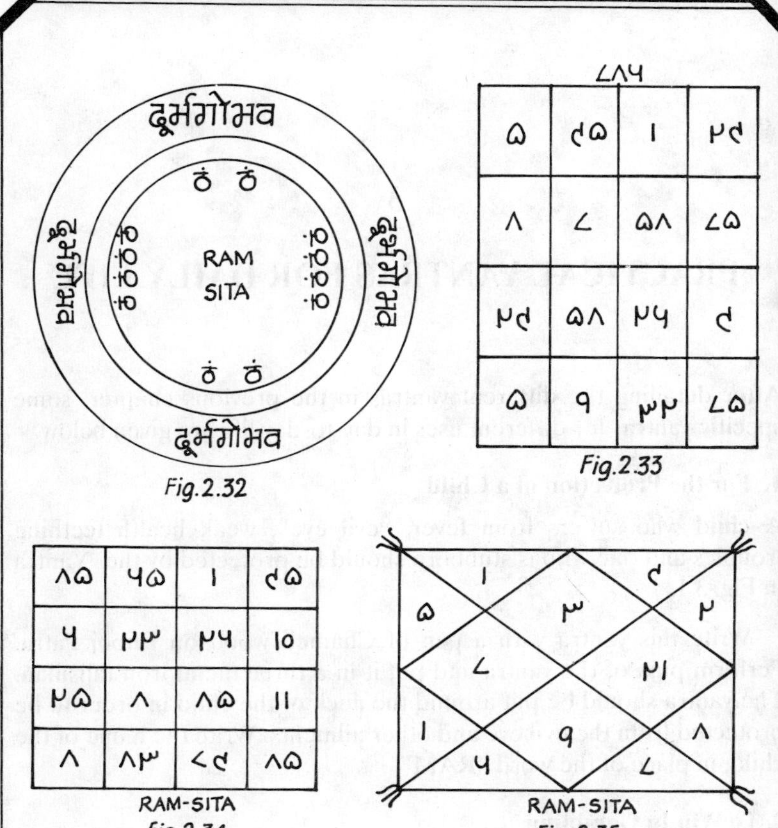

Fig.2.32

Fig.2.33

Fig.2.34

Fig.2.35

ॐ गं गणपति प्राहस्तं

हुं गं RAM

हुं गं घं स्घां म हा

Fig.2.36

3

PRACTICAL YANTRAS FOR DAILY LIFE

After detailing the different yantras in the previous chapter, some specific yantras for different uses in day-to-day life are given below.

1. For the Protection of a Child

A child who suffers from fever, "evil eye", weak health teething troubles and one who is stubborn should be protected by the Yantra in Fig. 3.1.

Write this yantra with a pen of Chameli wood on Bhooj Patra. Perform puja of the yantra and put it in a three metal iron talisman. The yantra should be put around the neck of the child in order to be protected from the evil eye and other ailments. Write the name of the child, in place of the word "RAM"

2. To Win In Gambling

On Sunday in Pusy nakshastra bring the root of Aapamarg(Chirchitta) plant with Ashat Gand and with a pen of the chameli plant, write the yantra shown in Fig. 3.2 on Bhooj Patra, stainless steel or copper. The Yantra should be wrapped in the root of Aapamarg.

Puja of the yantra, should be performed with Dhoop and Gugal. Take 310 grams of sweet and throw it away so that mice may eat them. The yantra should be tied on the right arm before going to gamble in order to ensure victory.

Note: For gambling Tantric articles like "Hath Jori" and "Billi Ki Jeer" have shown remarkable results whenever they have been given for use by the author.

3. To Win Law Suits

We have already detailed "Bagla Mukhi Yantra" for this purpose. "BEESI YANTRA" given in Figure 3.3 is also useful. When a man is involved in law suits or quarrels or enmity with anybody or in those cases in which the promotion of a person is held up, this yantra should be written on Tuesday with Ashat Gand on Bhooj Patra and worn around the neck. It will yield success. The yantra can be written on stainless steel or Copper sheets also.

4. To Get Relief From Debt

Either of the Yantras shown in Fig. 3.4 may be written in Shukal Pakash on Sunday or Tuesday with Ashat Gand on Bhooj Patra. The yantra should be kept on the person or put around the neck, so that the person becomes able to pay his debts.This yantra can be engraved on copper, silver or stainless steel plate also.

5. Gauri Shankar Yantra

This is the most powerful yantra for success in achieving all desires, comforts and acquiring worldly objects. The yantra must be written on Bhooj Patra with Red Chandan and be used around the neck or kept on one's person. The yantra is shown in Fig. 3.5 and should be written on Monday or Tuesday. This Pandrah Yantra can be engraved on copper or stainless steel plates also.

6. For Birth of Son

This Mohammadan Yantra shown in Fig. 3.6 is very effective and *TESTED* yantra which is very useful for ensuring the birth of a son.

The yantra should be written with Mushak and Saffron on Bhooj Patra or engraved on Copper, Silver or Stainless steel plate. After puja the yantra must be tied around the waist of the woman for 40 days. After conception, it should be removed. Again, when the 9th month starts, the yantra must be tied around the waist. After the birth of the son, the yantra should be put around his neck. The boy will remain safe from troubles and evil eyes.

7. For Barren Ladies

This too is *TESTED* yantra. It is shown in Fig. 3.7. If a barren woman or a lady whose conception has been delayed recites this yantra ten thousand times she will become pregnant. If she ties this yantra around her waist and performs intercourse, she will be blessed with pregnancy and a son. If a man recites this yantra as above, all his desires will be fulfilled. In case a man writes this yantra with the blood of his first finger on his forehead, all will become his friends. This yantra should be carved on copper or stainless steel plate or on a paper with black ink.

8. For Increasing Sale in Business

A very widely *TESTED* Yantra by the author in shops, offices and in factories etc., where the business was not up to the owner's expectations. Refer to Fig. 3.8. This yantra must be carved, engraved or written on gold plates or copper and stainless steel plates. After puja the yantra should be fixed at the place of business or on the shop etc. Sweet Pongal should be offered for puja. The following mantra must be recited for 45 days 1000 times daily in order to boost sales.

Mantra

"ॐ शिवः शक्तिः कामः क्षितरथ रवि शोतकिरणा
स्मरो हंसः शकृस्तदनु च परमारहयः
अमी हल्लेखाभिस्ति ऋभिखसानेषु घटिया
भजन्ते वर्णास्ते तव जननि नामावयवताम्"

"OM Sivah Sakti Kamah Ksitrath ravi Sotakiranah
Smaro Hansah sakristadnu Cha Para -mara-hayah.
Amni Hrallekhabhist Rishibhikh avasanasu Ghatiya
Bhajanta Varnaste Tava Janani Namavayavatam."

9. To Remove Stammering

When a person stammers or a child does not speak on time, the Yantra shown in Fig. 3.9 is very beneficial. Write this yantra on a piece of paper with saffron or engrave it on stainless steel or copper plate. After that the yantra should be put for puja. The yantra should be washed in water 60 times and the water taken by the person, who stammers. Put this yantra around the neck of the person or child in a talisman. Stammering will stop and the child will also start speaking. If somebody keeps this yantra with him he is blessed with wealth and comfort.

10. To Prevent Abortions

When a lady faces continuous abortions and desires the birth of a child, either of the yantras shown in Fig. 3.10 must be used.The yantra should be written on Bhooj Patra with Ashat gand or with musk on plain paper. The Yantra can be embossed or engraved on copper or stainless steel plate and the yantra tied around the waist of a lady after pregnancy. The tendency to have miscarraiges will stop.

11. To Stop the Drinking Habit

When a man is in the habit of drinking and becomes a problem to his family and requires to be controlled, this yantra can be used. Write the yantra on white cloth. Put the talisman around his neck. He will leave the habit of drinking. This yantra is also useful to eradicate poverty. Refer to Fig.3.11.

12. To Find Match For A Girl

When the marriage of a girl is delayed the yantra in Fig. 3.12. must be used. This yantra should be read by the girl 21 times and the yantra wrapped in yellow silken cloth. The talisman should be worn around the girl's neck. Her marriage will be fixed with a good boy and she will have good children.The yantra can be written on paper with black ink or engraved on a Copper Plate.

Some Important Yantras

In YANTRA SHASHTRA our sages have provided Maha Yantras for TEN Maha Vidyas, which are as below:-

1. Shri Yantra
2. Baglamukhi Yantra
3. Kali or Maha Kali Yantra
4. Bhairon Yantra
5. Tara Yantra
6. Bhuvaneshwari Yantra
7. Chinamsta Yantra
8. Dhumavati Yantra
9. Matangi Yantra
10. Mahalakshmi or Kamla Yantra

All Ten Maha Yantras, have been discussed in the previous chapter.Other yantras are now provided for the guidance of readers.

13. Bhuvaneshwari Yantra

This yantra is made as shown in the Figure 3.13. The Yantra bestows wealth and happiness. The sadhaka wins over worries. After all Nayases, Puja of the yantra should be completed after reciting Kavach of Bhuvaneshwari.

The Japa Mantra of Yantra is as :-

1. ॐ ऐं ह्रीं श्रीं

2. ॐ ह्रीं श्रीं

According to Sarada:Thirty-two lakh japas and thirty-two thousand "Homa" are to be performed. After obeisance to the Guru a worshipper is to perform one lakh 'Japa' after which Homa is to be performed with 'Lotuses'. Japa is to be performed by taking boiled rice with ghee and by subduing passions. Homa must be performed with Honey and Kinshuka. According to "JUARANAB" tarpan is to be performed after one lakh Japa and ten thousand Homa.

14. Chhinmasta or Parchand Chandika Yantra

This yantra is very powerful and effective. It blesses the sadhaka with progeny removes troubles and protects him from poverty. This yantra is also known as PARCHAND CHANDIKA YANTRA. In Vishwas Ratan and Rudrayamal its upasana has been given in detail.

Japa Mantra

"ॐ श्रीं कलीं ह्रीं ऐं वज् वैरोचनीये हुं हुं फट् स्वाहा"

"Om Shareeng, Kaleeng, Hareeng., Aeeing Vaj Vyrochaneeye Houng Houng Phut Swaha"

The mantra be recited one lakh times and after that Homa be performed for one-tenth mantras with Bilwa wood and clarified butter. In Homa use red flowers and ghee. Daily after Japa, offer sweetened rice boiled in milk (khir-Pongl), dry fruits etc. The puja be performed in a vacant house, cremation ground or in a temple.

After obtaining Siddhi of the Yantra, wear the yantra on the body for the above purposes. The yantra can be made on Bhooj Patra, or on a metal like gold, silver or copper.

15. Dhumavati Yantra

The upasana of Dhumavati Devi is to be performed during the night. The place for worship is a cemetery where sadhakas should perform, puja bare bodied except for underwear in a lonely place.

The Yantra has been shown in Fig. 3.15 Dhumavati Devi is not commonly known. She has fat body, fierce eyes, wears dirty clothes, and has dry hair. Due to old age she has a bend in her spinal chord.

JAPA MANTRA

"धूँ धूँ धूमावती ठः ठः"

"Dhoong Dhoong Dhumavati Tha Tha".

A sadhaka is to perform one lakh japa on the 4th day of Krishna Paksha (Dark Night) in solitude or in a cremation ground or in the forest by observing fast and remaining silent the whole day and night. Wear wet clothes and a turban. Homa be performed with ghee. Ten thousand mantras are to be performed for Homa. Further details are available in Maharnab Tantra and Meru Tantra.

The Yantra is used for all round success and spiritual uplift and should be written on Bhooj Patra with Ashat Gand or on gold, silver or copper plate.

16. Matangi Yantra

Shri Matangi Devi bestows siddhi of speech, and promotes sangeet or music of the sadhaka.

This yantra as shown in Fig 3.16 is made on Bhooj Patra with Ashat Gand or on gold, silver or Copper plate. After its installation, daily pooja of the Devi is be performed with mantra while sitting in sidhasana.

The mantra is as follows:

"ॐ ह्रीं मातंग्यै नमः"

"Om Hareeng Matangaya Namah"

After doing all Nayas, Kavach path of Devi should be recited and then puja of the yantra performed for one lakh times, followed with "Homa" for ten thousand mantras.

Japa Mantra

"ॐ ह्रीं कलीं हूं मातंग्यै फट् स्वाहा"

"Om Hareeng Kaleeng Houng Matangaya Phut Swaha"

17. Mahalakshami or Kamala Yantra

This yantra is very powerful and effective as the worship of Goddes Lakshami .This Yantra brings good fortune and prosperity. All desires are fulfilled by uttering the Mantra of this goddess. Refer Fig.3.17 for the yantra.The yantra must be written or prepared during an auspicious mahurta and installed, after which pooja of the yantra should be performed.

Lakshami Pooja

Mantra: The one letter Bij, Shreeng (श्रीं) is known as Lakshmi Mantra. For pooja use this Mantra.

"ॐ श्री महालक्ष्मैय नमः"

"Om Shree Mahalakshamiaya Namaha"

Light incense, diya and offer flowers. Do the puja while in a comfortable asana.

After doing all " Nyas " , the sadhaka should meditate on the goddess yantra and offer "panch pushpa" to her. Ten lakh "Japas" of the mantra are to be made with one lakh mantra and "homa".

According to Sarada , three lakh japa and homa for thirty thousand japa is to be performed with clarified butter. Ten thousand Tarpana should be offered with cool and pure water.

According to Prapanchasara, One lakh jap and ten thousand Homa (Sacrificial Fire) with Bilwa fruit and honey should be performed .This is recommended to the sadhaka.

18. Mahamritanje Yantra

The Upasana of Lord Mahamritanje SHIVA is most auspicious and bestows the devotee with health, wealth and happiness, good fortune and fame. This yantra particularly relieves one from all dreadful diseases. The yantra can be carved or embossed on copper or silver plate. It can also be written on Bhoja Patra in an auspicious lagna and Hora. Purify the Yantra with mantras .This Yantra can then be worn as directed for Shri Yantra. The Yantra dispels all sorts of fears, influence of evil planets, fear of ghosts, accidental death, diseases etc.

The Yantra must be purified 108 times with Mahamritanje Mantra with samput. This mantra is given in part I. For the convenience of the sadhaka we again provide the mantra. Homa should be performed with ten thousand mantras, Bilwa fruit, til, rice cooked with milk and sugar, mustard, Milk, curd, durba grass, Samdha of Banyan tree, Palasa tree, and catech plant (10 articles).

Mantra

" ॐ हौं जूं ॐ भूर्भव स्वः
ॐ त्र्यम्कं यजामहे सुगन्धि
पुष्टिवर्धनम् धियो यो नः प्रचोदयात
उर्वारूकमिव बन्धनान्मृत्योंमू माऽमृतात्
स्वः भुवः भूः ॐ सः जूं हौ ॐ

"Om Hoong Joong Om Bhoorbhava swah
Om Tryamakam Yajamaha Saugandhim

Pushtivardhanam diyoyona Parchodyat.

Urvarukmev Bandhananmrityomu mamritamat Swaha

Bhoova Bhooh om Sah joon Houng Om."

Use of camphor, scent, chandan etc., for Pooja and other rituals should be followed as in the case of " Shri Yantra". The Yantra is specially powerful for all chronic, and severe diseases. The person who has to perform pooja keeps good health and is free from ailments.

For the siddhi of the yantra, the matra should be recited for 45 days one thousand times daily. It should be carved or inscribed on copper or silver plate. Coconut, fruits, flowers, incense are particular items of food and offerings.

This is a *TESTED* Yantra used by the author.

19. Winning Over Enemies

This yantra has also been tested by the author. It has a remarkable effect for winning over enemies.

The yantra should be inscribed or engraved on gold, copper or silver plate. It should be written with a special black ink. This can be kept by, or worn as a talisman by the sadhaka. The mantra should be worshipped for 45 days, one thousand times daily. Honey, fruit and Jaggery are used as offerings. Meditate on the Devi along with the mantra for successful results.

Mantra :-

" ॐ ताडिल्लेखातन्वीं तपनाशशिवैधानरमयीं निषण्णमप्युपरि क्मलानाँ तव कलाम्
रहापदमातव्यां मुदित्तमलमायेन मनसा महात्तः पश्यन्तोदधति परमाह् दलहरीम"

"Om Tadil-lekha-tanvim tapana-Sasi-Vaidanara-mayim nisannam
pyupari Kamalanam tava kalam;
Raha padmatavyam mudita-mala-mayen manasa
mahaktah Pasyanto dedhati Paremahda Iaharim."

The above mantra means that great men, who, with their minds bereft of impurity and illusion, look on Thy Kala slender as a streak of lightning of the essence of the Sun, the Moon, and fire, and abiding in the great forest of lotuses, standing far above the lotuses, desire a great flood of infinite bliss.

This yantra is *TESTED* by the author personally, and has been used by him for many years with success.

20. For Infatuations

This yantra is for infatuation of women, men, animals, Devas and demons. The mantra deals with the power bestowed by meditation on the Devi presiding over the kamaraja kuta in the form of Iccha Sakti.

The Yantra should be inscribed, engraved or written on Gold plate, sandal flowers, Saffron or turmeric. The mantra must be recited for 45 days, one thousand times daily. The food for offering is milk gruel and Pansupari.

Mantra:

The mantra is pronounced thus:-

"तनुच्छायाभिस्ते तरुणातरीण श्रीधरणिभिर्दिवं सर्वमुवींमरूणिमनिमग्नं स्भरति यः। भवन्स्यस्य त्रस्यदूनहरिणशलीननयनाः सहोर्वश्या वश्याः कति कति न गीर्वाणागणिकाः"

"Tanucchayabhiste taruna-tareena-Shri-dharanibhirdvim Sarvamuveenmarunima-nimagnam Sabhrati yh. Bhavansyasya trasyadoona harina-Shalina-nayanah Sahorvamshya vashyh Kati Kati Na geervan-gani kah." II

21. Some Mohammadan Yantras

These five yantras have been passed on to the author by a practising tantric. He claims that these are very effective, tested yantras. However, the author has not used any of them and sadhakas are requested to use them and test their authenticity.

1. *To Remove Effects of Evil Eye and of Souls*

This yantra, shown in Fig. 3.21(1),should be written on the paper and used around neck by putting it in a talisman. The effects of the evil eye and souls will be removed and one remains protected from such effects. Write the name of person at bottom.

2. *For Separation*

This yantra has to be used in three ways. Refer Fig. 3.21(2)

A) i. Write this yantra on paper and exorcise it 41 times (फुंक मारना) Write the names of persons to be separated at the bottom of the yantra. The yantra should then be buried in a cemetery or at "shamshanghat." Both will be separated.

ii. Alternatively, place the yantra at a place from where both are likely to pass and put their feet on the yantra.

B) Recite this yantra over a piece of salt for one lakh times in three days and then put it on the fire. Both will face trouble and will be separated.

C) Mix salt in water in new earthen pot. Put the yantra inside also. Both will face troubles and separate as the salt will mix in water. After that, water should be thrown in running water.

3. *To Get the House Vacated*

When a tenant or anybody else does not vacate a house or premises, write the yantra, shown in Fig. 3.21(3) on a piece of paper. Put it in a bottle and bury in the ground. The name of the occupant should be written at the bottom of the yantra. He will vacate the place.

4. *To Create Enmity Between the Two*

This is a very useful Yantra. Write the yantra on paper. Burn it in fire, Separation will take place between the two or else there will be a constant bickering between them.

Write the name at bottom of yantra. Ref Fig. 3.21(4)

5. *To Create Love Between Two*

Write the yantra shown in Fig. 3.21(5) on a piece of paper and dissolve it in water. The water should be taken by both persons. Their differences will be resolved and there will be love between the two.Then bury it underground.

You will achieve your objective.

Note : All yantras duly purified ar supplieed for the benefits of mankind.

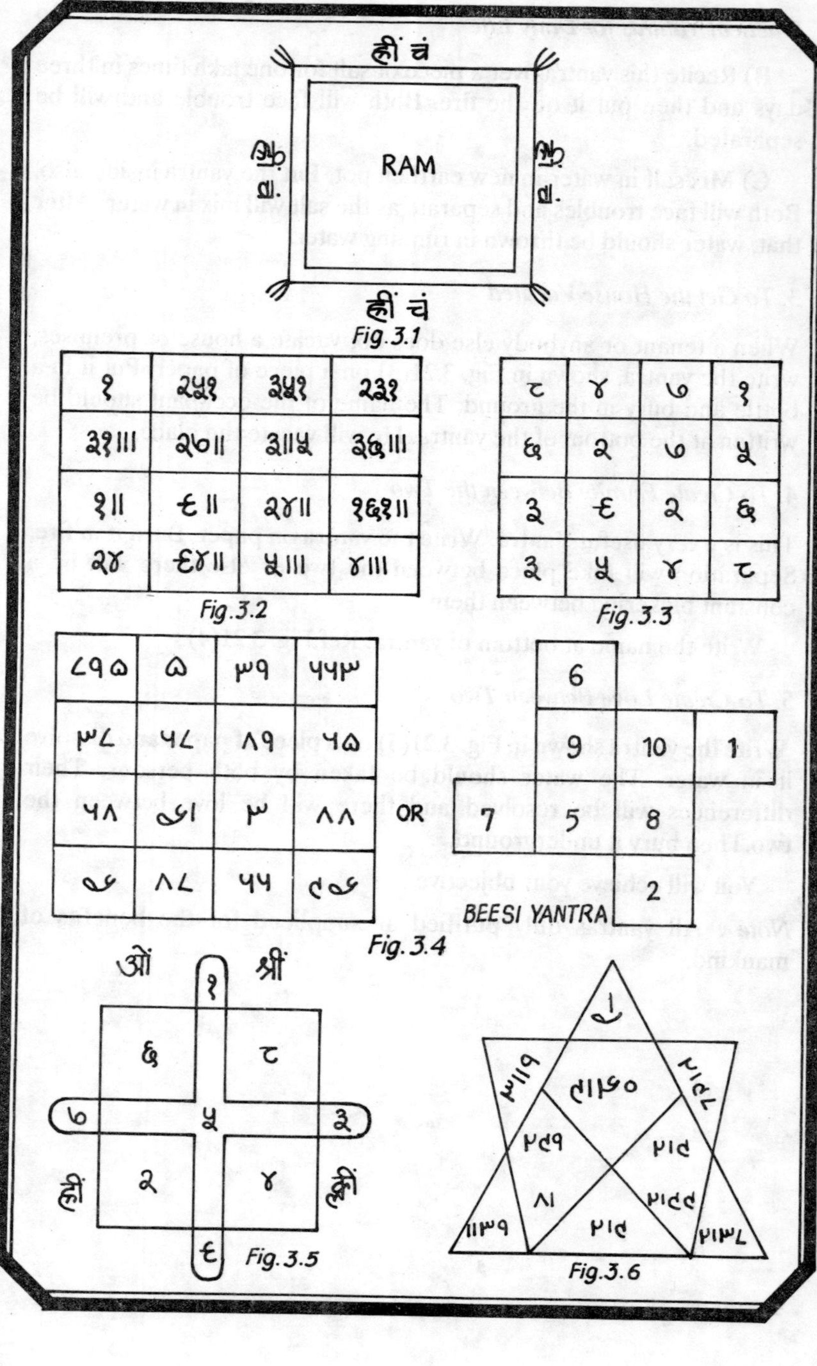

Fig.3.1
Fig.3.2
Fig.3.3
Fig.3.4
Fig.3.5
Fig.3.6

ر	صو	م	ال
۳۹	۳۲	۱۹۹	۹۷
۳۳	۴۲	۹۴	۱۹۸
۹۵	۱۹۷	۳۴	۴۱

Fig.3.7A

ق	ل	ا	خ
۵۹۹	۳۱	۲۹	۱۵۱
۳۸	۹۸	۳۰۲	۳
۲	۶۱	۹۹	۲۷

Fig.3.7B

Fig.3.8

۷۸۶

ب	ب	ب
ب	ب	ب
ب	ب	ب

Fig.3.9

۷۸۶

۳۸	۳۳	۴۰
۳۹	۳۷	۳۵
۳۴	۴۱	۳۶

OR

۷۸۶

۸	۴	۱۴	۴
۱۶	۲	۹	۱۳
۴	۱۷	۱۲	۶
۱۱	۷	۴	۵

OR

۷۸۶

علے الارض	ان تقع	السما	یمسک
۱۳۲	۱۳۷	۱۰۴۱	۲۳۰۲
۱۳۸	۱۳۲۰	۲۲۹	۱۰۴
۲۳۰	۱۰۳۹	۱۳۹	۱۳۳

OR

۷۸۶

۸	۱۱	۴۱۵۱	۱
۴۱۵۰	۲	۷	۱۲
۳	۴۱۵۳	۵	۶
۱۵	۵	۴	۴۱۵۲

Fig.3.10

۷۸۶

۱۱۷۲۳۹	۱۱۷۲۳۴	۱۱۷۲۴۱
۱۱۷۲۴۰	۱۱۷۲۳۸	۱۱۷۲۳۶
۱۱۷۲۳۵	۱۱۳۲۴۲	۱۱۷۲۳۷

Fig.3.11

۷۸۶

۹۹۸۲۰	۹۹۸۲۳	۹۹۸۲۷	۹۹۸۱۳
۹۹۸۲۱	۹۹۸۱۴	۹۹۸۱۹	۹۹۸۲۴
۹۹۸۱۵	۹۹۸۲۹	۹۹۸۲۱	۹۹۸۲۸
۹۹۸۲۳	۹۹۸۱۷	۹۹۸۱۶	۹۹۸۶۸

Fig. 3.12

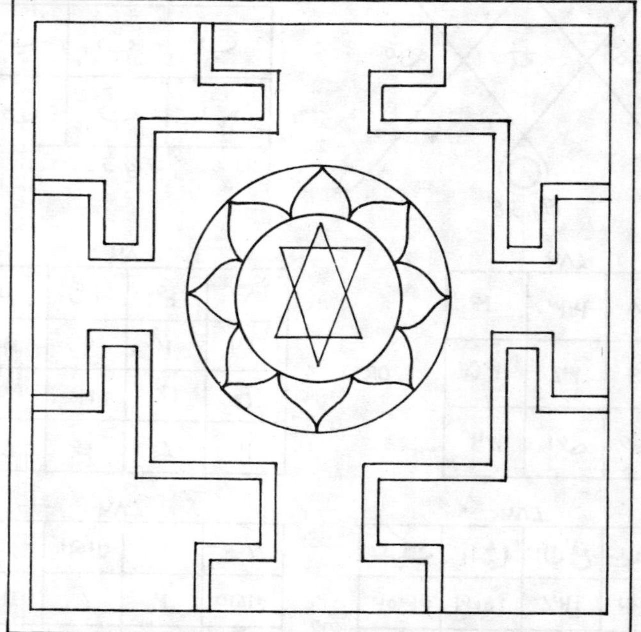

श्री भुवनेश्वरी - यन्त्र

Fig.3.13

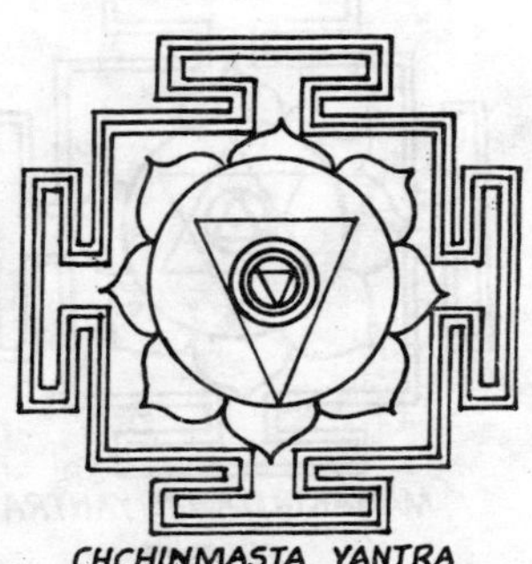

CHCHINMASTA YANTRA

Fig. 3.14

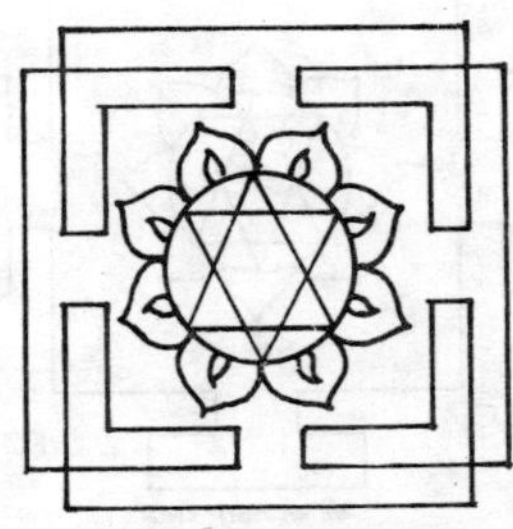

DHUMAVATI YANTRA

Fig. 3.15

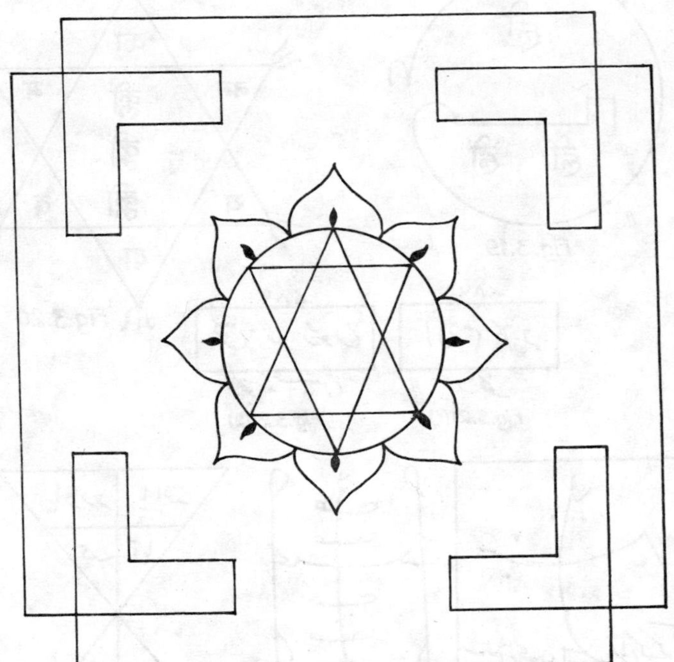

श्री मातंगी-यन्त्र

Fig. 3.16

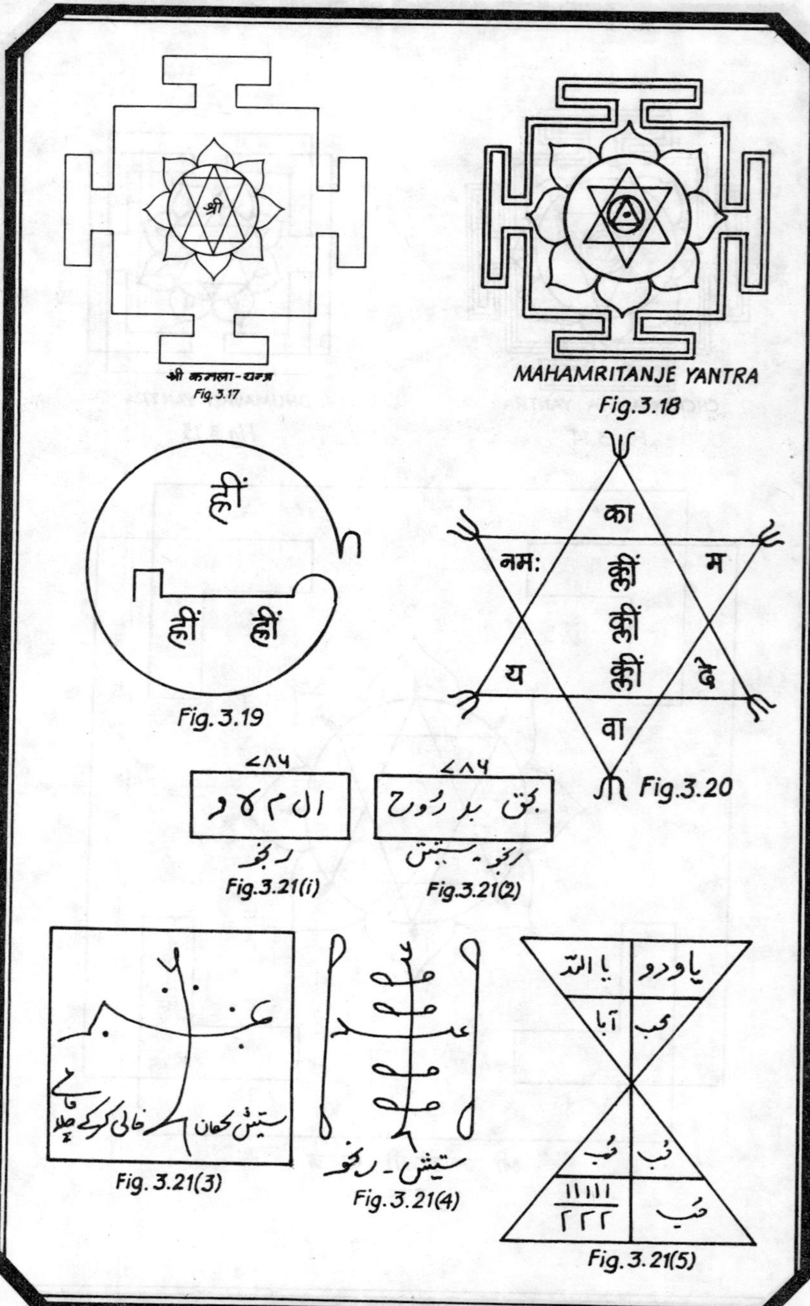

श्री कमला-यन्त्र
Fig. 3.17

MAHAMRITANJE YANTRA
Fig.3.18

Fig. 3.19

Fig.3.20

Fig.3.21(i)

Fig.3.21(2)

Fig. 3.21(3)

Fig. 3.21(4)

Fig. 3.21(5)

4

CHARMS, CRYSTAL GAZING AND MYSTIC EYE

Belief in charms, mascots, amulets and the like have been present since ancient times. As far back as we know, people were found to have written strange words, made peculiar marks, or carried some item on their person to ward off evils or to bring good luck. The belief is widespread even today. Everywhere people carry a lucky sign, or some talisman to bring in good luck. In some quarters certain objects are constructed to ward off evils or to bring good fortune. The signs should be worn after they are purified by a competent Tantrik.

CHARMS

The right charm has been studied by a great many people and such items are available with Indian Gypsies and others. These signs are known as LUCKY SIGNS. These are to be used in copper, bronze, silver, Gold or written on Bhooj Patra etc.

The author has supplied to many to use these lucky signs according to their requirements on a specific metal, after checking the individual horoscope and Palm. The results obtained are marvellous, whenever the signs were used after their purification and puja.

The following signs are treated as Lucky signs and are being used since ancient times. These signs are YANTRAS and a list of a few such symbols is provided below for guidance.

1. Om

This is a lucky sign for prosperity, comforts and all round success. This may be worn around the neck or on a ring. The sign can be of Gold, silver or copper.

2. Swastika

It is the most auspicious and tested replica, attributed to LORD GANESHA son of LORD SHIVA. The sanskrit meaning of the word is "purveyor of good fortune". It bestows luck and prosperity on the wearer. It can be used around the neck, or on the ring in gold, silver or copper.

3. Trishul

This sign is attributed to LORD SHIVA, a perfect sign of good luck. Not only does it save the wearer from opposition and enemies but is also used for spiritual advancement.

4. Cross

This sign is attributed to Jesus Christ. It ensures prosperity, peace of mind, purity in life and finally helps the wearer to realise Christ.

5. Hand

The figure of the hand is a symbol of the good qualities of hospitality, generosity, strength and goodness. Usually the hand is that of FATIMA, the daughter of the prophet MOHAMMED and the wearer of the symbol is supposed to be endowed with those qualities represented by the hand.

6. Sham Rock

It is a national symbol of Ireland. It is a plant with three leaves and a white clover. This is a symbol of good luck and is worn, either in natural state or in the form of a symbol, by many people to bring fortune and prosperity.

7. Sword

It is a sacred symbol among Sikhs. An auspicious sign for prosperity, bravery and courage. It keeps the enemies at bay, and ensures the wearer has victory over enemies.

8. Beads

Beads are worn for prosperity,cures from diseases and for spiritual advancement. Coral beads are used by children to protect them from the evil eye or from disease. The best beads are of Rudraksh, wood, Chandan, Tulsi and Coral.

9. Acorn

It is a nut or fruit of the Oak tree called oak apple. For a long time people have been known to carry a dried Acorn, believing that it would give them youth. Also many believe that it will cause a lover to return and repent for leaving his beloved.

10. Angle

A right angle, like the letter "L" is the harbinger of learning and deep understanding for those who are scholarly.

11. Arrow Head

An Arrow Head offers protection against evil, especially from the "EVIL EYE". It is usually worn around the neck, and one that is found is better than one which the wearer makes himself.

12. Axe

An Axe head, carved from an attractive piece of stone, is believed to be a charm against evil. Usually it is worn around the neck either with a string or chain.

13. Badger Tooth

Since ancient times when playing cards were invented, players have worn a badger tooth in order to have luck at the game. It is especially good for children.

14. Bamboo And Serpent

This is an ancient and complicated symbol. It consists of a circle around which numerous triangles are inscribed. Across the circle lies a Bamboo stick of seven sections crossed by a serpent. This charm is supposed to bring skill in learning and is worn by students.

The circle represents eternity. The triangle having three sides, represents the Trinity. The Bamboo stick has seven knots to represent, the seven stages of wisdom through which the scholar must pass to attain perfect knowledge.

The serpent has always been a symbol of wisdom and knowledge. Each one of them can be used as lucky charm but when added together, all these bring luck and success to the student and the wearer.

15. Bees

In Jewellery, figures of a Bee or Bees in a precious metal, like gold etc are made and embedded with precious stones. This when worn, brings great success in Business. The wearer will be energetic, will persevere and will have success in any enterprise in which buying and selling is involved.

16. Bull

This is a symbol of strength, power and determination. To wear the replica of a Bull, especially its head will bring to the wearer, the above qualities. One will be powerful, strong and determined.

17. Clover

The four leaf clover has long been considered a source of much luck. According to tradition, one leaf of the clover brings fame, another wealth, a third a faithful lover, and the fourth good health. Hence the CLOVER is considered a source of good luck and fortune.

18. Dolphin

This is a fish-like creature. The replica is worn for success in music, literature and painting. Its influence on these arts is said to be great.

19. Fish

The ancient Hebrews along with other people, adopted the fish as a religious symbol and it has come down to the present in various religious rites. Due to its great fertility, it is a sign of wealth and prosperity. Many people wear little carvings of fish as a means of ensuring wealth and good luck.

20. Heart

It is a symbol of love. Lovers give each other a symbol or small replica of a Heart as a pledge of Love and fidelity. To wear it means that the wearer accepts the pledge of Love in all sincerity.

21. Horse Shoe

Universally accepted as a charm of good luck. It is used everywhere and is always used in ways to keep the luck from spilling over.

A black horse shoe or its ring is specially used to ward off the evil effects of the Planet SATURN and that of the evil eye. It also removes the effects of SADESATI and the wearer is benefited with wealth. It stands tested many times by the author with remarkably good results. It is fixed on doors also.

22. Ekk Onkar

This is a universal replica for brotherhood and advancement of spiritual upliftment being used by Sikhs throughout the world. This replica is on the lines of Hindus wearing an Om and Swastika. It brings peace of mind and is worn around the neck and made of gold, silver and other metals.

23. Khanda

Khanda is a religious emblem of the Sikhs which is composed of three parts. The Central sword belongs to Guru Hargobind Sahib. The two swords on the side are attributed to the 10th Guru, Gobind Singh Ji and the central circle used to protect and destroy the enemies. This emblem indicates courage, valour, protection from enemies and the destruction of all evils. Sikhs use this emblem as a lucky Charm made of Gold, silver etc., and worn around the neck to attain all the virtues of Khanda.

24. Key

Three keys are usually worn together. In this charm, the keys stand for love, wealth and health and the wearer is believed to be able to unlock the doors to these.

25. Knots

Knots tie things together. Sacred Knots are used in marriage. It is worn to indicate unbreakable bonds between those who wear them.

26. Owl

The owl is a symbol of deep knowledge and wisdom. The wearer is blessed with both these qualities.

27. Penny

The ordinary Penny is not a source of good luck . The Penny which has lucky powers is one bearing the date of a leap year. If this is carried on a person, it is supposed to bring good fortune.

28. Ring

A ring signifies eternity as it has the perfect circle with no end. If worn, it indicates a vow made and which is to be kept for eternity.The wedding ring as also the gift of a ring to a loved one carries the same idea.

29. Serpent

This is the most auspicious replica which STANDS TESTED for knowledge, wisdom, and healing from disease. It enables one to excell in either the arts of learning or those of healing. It should be worn as small image of a serpent around the neck.The author has used a serpent ring in healing diseases after proper pooja of the ring with a large measure of success.

30. Tau

It consists of two straight lines, one vertical and the other horizontal. People wear this symbol to ward off diseases of skin.

Note: The above charms and lucky signs have been shown in Figures 4.1, 4.2

31. Planetary Signs

When a planet is malefic and is not giving favourable results, use a replica or sign of another planet, as advised to neutralise the evil effects. The wearer will be blessed with fortune.

32. Birthday Sign

You can use the replica of your SUN SIGN (Aries to Pisces) in the prescribed metal for good luck, happines and prosperity.

Many people make and carry their own charms. This is perfectly permissible. If an object seems to be connected with one's success, it is permissible to use this object as a charm and a source of good luck.

Often an heirloom, which has brought good fortune to the family, will be passed on to the child and heirs in the family, so as to retain good luck.

Use of Rudrakshas

Holy rudrakshas are of 38 types and normally available upto sixteen faces. The bead or Rosary is very auspicious and is believed to draw man close to the Almighty. All religions have advised the use of this Bead. In the Hindu religion the wearer of Rudrakshas is blessed by LORD SHIVA. It has miraculous effects on our body, mind and soul and is used for the propitiation of planetary afflictions and the cure of diseases. These rudrakshas are worn around the neck individually as talisman or as Lucky charms and are available with the Author. The main points are as below:-

ONE faced rudraksha when found is very rare and is ascribed to Lord SHIVA. It blesses the wearer with power, authority, wealth and all comforts of life and cures one from Heart attacks. It may be placed where pooja is performed, and wealth remains in abundance, all troubles vanish and people of that house lead a comfortable life. One gets Bhakti, Mukti and peace of mind. This is the most auspicious and sacred Rudraksha. It is often found that people wear it by enclosing it in Gold, which is not correct, and must be avoided.

TWO faced rudraksha when used as Lucky charm increases spiritual strength. It is beneficial to end Tamsic habits for concentration of minds. Pregnant ladies should wear it round their waist or on the arm for the successful birth of a child. It is also used to avoid abortions and for Vashi Karan.

THREE faced rudraksha bestows good luck, and is used for wealth and education. The fever which starts after three days is cured by its use.

FOUR faced rudraksha is auspicious for health, wealth and advancement of spiritual achievements. It also increases the intellect and power of speech.

FIVE faced rudraksha is commonly used by people as it is easily available. It blesses the wearer with fulfilment of all his desires and helps in the recovery of diseases.

SIX faced rudraksha is used on the right arm or around the neck. One is blessed with all comforts of life and success in work and in business etc. Students should use it. It is also useful for hysteria, fainting fits and other diseases of ladies.

SEVEN faced rudraksha blesses the wearer with respect, wealth and spiritual power.

EIGHT faced rudraksha blesses the wearer with all comforts of life.

NINE faced rudraksha blesses the wearer with wealth, family comforts, children's welfare and the fulfilment of hopes and desires.

TEN faced rudraksha gives protection from the malefic effects of planets and evil effects of souls. One remains safe from all TANTRIK attacks and the effects of the evil eye.

ELEVEN faced rudraksha is especially beneficial to ladies. Her husband will be blessed with prosperity and longevity. She will have sons and all comforts.

TWELVE faced rudraksha bestows comforts, employment and the blessings of all deities.

THIRTEEN faced rudraksha too is very auspicious. The wearer gains moksha, victory over enemies , attainment of ambitions and is endowed with good health and the comforts of life. One can also attract anybody one wishes to.

FOURTEEN faced rudraksha cures diseases. It bestows all comforts of life on the wearer.

Note:- For more details, readers should refer to the author's books, "Complete Astro Palmistry" and "Practicals of Mantra and Tantr"

Crystal Gazing – History Of Crystal Ball

Crystal Gazing in some form has been practised for at least 3000 years in almost every part of the world. It has been found among the civilizations of Assyria, Persia, Egypt, Ancient and modern Greece, Rome, China, India, Japan, North American Indians, and the Fez, Zulus and Maoris. It is also practiced by the Incas, by Australian, Aboriginals Polynesians, the Shamanas, in Eastern Russia and in Madagascar.

The art of crystal gazing, which was attributed in early times to divine power, came to be regarded in the middle ages by the Christian church as the work of evil spirits. This was looked upon as heresy and was treated accordingly.

However it continued to flourish and Crystal Gazing lingered on until it received new impetus and reached its highest development in the hands of Dr. John Dee (1527-1608) Dr John was the Astrologer to Queen Elizabeth-I and his divinations helped to make history. His famous "SHOW STONE" is now kept in the British Museum.The Crystal Ball itself is the product of Skilful craftmanship and obviously was not available to primitive seers. Crystal vision has been induced by vessels containing liquid poured into the palm of the hand, and by various reflecting gems, but the most successsful and enduring method has been the use of a clear, polished ball. Crystal balls have always been made of material other than "CRYSTAL". Genuine rock crystal is a freak of nature. Glass made by nature through volcanic actions are rare and the few existing specimens are museum pieces. The houseware industry uses the term "Rock Crystal;" to identify household glass-ware of extra clear quality.The ball should be as clear as possible. In some cases, balls of optically perfect quality are available Modern techniques have produced perfect balls in both optical, acrylic, plastic and optical glass.

Can you Really See Anything in A Crystal Ball?

Crystal vision occurs to greater or less extent with many persons of saintly nature.

Perhaps one man or woman in twenty viz 5% of these will be able to, by practice, develop the faculty to a point where it will sometimes convey information not attained by ordinary means.

Is Crystal Gazing Dangerous?

Crystal Gazing appears to be absolutely harmless and the author knows of no kind of injury resulting from it, since most experiments are made with scientific care.

Crystal Gazing

The author has procured 4" diameter Crystal Ball of optical glass from the USA and is practicing through it with much success. Crystal Gazing is an ancient Hindu art. Through its use, crimes have been solved, lost articles are found, hidden facts or lives have been discovered and unrealised aspects of one relationship with others have been revealed. It also indicates the future and gives replies to one's questions. Though crystal Gazing has been used with remarkable success in piecing together the facts of the past, looking to the future and discovering what is about to happen has to be done cautiously.

The basic conception of crystal Gazing is "CONCENTRATION". The persons endowed with natural ability to concentrate are aided in their use of the sphere. To what extent this power exists in the would be experimenter can be told by a first class Phrenologist.

A famous Hindu Crystal-Gazer in old times has said that there are streams from the human eyes and a flow of Magnetism, projected from its reservoir in the cerebellum, when the gaze is concentrated upon a given point.

The ancients also taught the importance of strict purity in relation to the amatory nature, when either Crystal Gazing, clairvoyance or other occult efforts are to be put forth, and the use of boys and virgins in crystal divination.

Purity of blood is important to the purity of power. Food, digestion, sleep, drinks, all must receive a proper degree of attention. Sound physical organs are not absolutely essential, but nevertheless it is best to enjoy a healthy brain, heart, liver, kidney, stomach, lungs and pelvic organs if one desires to attain a high degree of lucidity, or clarity of mental vision, all of which largely depends upon the condition of the blood. Clairvoyance depends as much on air, light, diet, sleep., labour, music, and health, as upon mechanically induced magnetism.

Phenomena of Crystal Gazing

The phenomena of Crystal Gazing may be classified as follows:-

FIRST: Images of something unconsciously observed. New reproductions, voluntary or spontaneous, and bringing no fresh knowledge to the mind.

SECOND: The images of ideas unconsciously acquired from others, by telepathy or otherwise. Some memory or Imaginative effect, which does not come from the Gazer's ordinary self. Revivals of memory, illustration of thoughts.

THIRD: Images, clairvoyant or Prophetic, Pictures bringing information as to something past, present or future which to interpret the gazer has.

Method of Crystal Gazing

1. The Crystal Ball must be clean, without any blemishes or bubbles.
2. For successful gazing, the person should be highly sensitive and receptive.
3. Ability to concentrate is the key to success. Everything around you should be completely "shut out" from your thinking.
4. Use frequent ablutions(washing) and prayers three or four days before consulting the crystal.
5. The MOON must be in SHUKAL PAKSH (on the rising side to FULL.) It should not be neglected, as it is of great importance to your success.
6. When the SUN is in its greatest Northern declination it is the best time for crystal gazing.
7. Light incense, "Dhoop" and "Deep" before beginning Crystal Gazing.
8. The person for whom you are going to give a reading may hold it in their hands for a few minutes prior to its use, but no one else, except yourself and the gazer should touch it.
9. The gazer should seek to put everything out of his mind except the problem. There should be no noise in the room otherwise it will distract and reduce concentration.

10. Gaze steadily at the Crystal without batting an eye or moving the muscles of the body.
11. It requires constant practice. You will not succeed initially but constant practice will make you perfect thus controlling your body, eyes and other factors.
12. The crystal or Magic Mirror should frequently be magnetised by passes made with right hand, for about five minutes at a time. This gives it strength and power. Similar passes with the Left hand add to the sensitiveness of the crystal.
13. The back of the crystal ball should be held towards the light, but never its face.
14. Very often, all that you can do is to describe what you see and allow the person whose life you are reading to make his own interpretation. The place you see may have a meaning for him but none for you. The face you see may be that of somebody he knows closely.
15. Sometimes, the scenes in the crystal will change as you gaze and you should tell what you see and what is happening before your eyes. Do not add to it. Be honest in revealing what you have seen.
16. Do not use the crystal ball as entertainment.

Pictures you May See in the Crystal Ball

Few phenomenon strike one as more fantastic and incredible than crystal vision. The visions appear without any set pattern and it seems to depend on mere chance whether one sees a skeleton, a scene of one's childhood, a string of letters or a picture of what a friend is doing at a distance. The vision often begins with a milky clouding of the ball. The cloudiness obscures any extraneous reflected image and out of the cloudiness is formed the clear images of the crystal vision.

The author cannot explain this clouding as it occurs too often and too independently to be the mere effect of suggestion, as it does not seem to depend on any optical condition.

The cloudiness may persist for some time , and usually comes at the beginning of one series of pictures and the next.

The pictures seen in the ball will sometimes be clearly defined in the ball and will be limited to it. Sometimes all perception of the ball disappears and the seer is introduced to a group of lifesize figures.

As a general rule, the crystal vision is a thing which changes and develops somewhat as a dream does, following some trivial chain of associations but not maintaining any continuous pattern.

The Scientific Explanation of Crystal Vision

How is it that the seer sees everything in the crystal ball? Common experiments supply obvious answers, but they cannot be stretched to cover a quarter, perhaps not even a tenth, of the phenomena that occur.

On the whole it seems safest to attempt no further explanation of crystal gazing than to say that it is an important method of inducing visions, of externalizing pictures which are associated with changes to the sensory portions of the brain, due partly to internal stimuli, and partly to stimuli which may come from minds external to the seer's own.

The crystal vision is what we must call a random reflection caught at some odd angle from the universe as it shines through the medium of that special soul.

Normal and supernormal knowledge and imagining are blended in strongly mingled rays, memory, dreams, telepathy, precognition. All these are present alongwith indications of a spiritual communication.

Instructions for Crystal Gazing

The ancient method of Crystal Gazing for the purposes of "Divination" involved somewhat elaborate rituals, including the use of swords, pentacles, candles, incense lighting and many accompaniments usually associated with the performance of magical rites. The object in view was not, as at present, the cultivation of mere "Personal Clarivoyance" in the gazer but rather to compel the actual presence in the crystal of certain genie or spirits to reveal themselves and to obtain answers to questions put forward by the gazer.

However the crystal gazer of today has no desire to compel the presence of a spiritual being in the crystal. It is quite unnecessary for him or her to draw magic circles, or to go to the trouble and expense of acquiring and using special or costly apparatus with the exception of the crystal itself.

What is desired is that through regular crystal gazing one should cultivate a personal clairvoyant power so that visions of things or events, past, present and future, may appear clearly to the interior vision or eye of the soul.

In the pursuit of this effort only, the crystal becomes at once both a valuable, interesting and useful channel of development and instruction, shorn of its former dangers and one which is conducive to spiritual development.

In order to attain these goals attention should be paid to the following practical directions, which, if carefully followed, will lead to success.

Practical Directions

1. Select a quiet room where you will be entirely undisturbed, taking care that it is as far as possible free from mirrors, pictures, glaring colours, and the like, which may cause distraction. Avoid any light rays from being reflected or in any manner directly reaching the crystal.

The room should not be dark, but rather shadowed, or charged with dull light, such as that prevailing on a cloudy or wet day.

2. The crystal should be placed on its stand on a table, or it may rest on a black velvet cushion, but in either case it should be partially surrounded by the black silk or any similar wrap or screen, so adjusted to cut off any undesirable reflection.

Before beginning to experiment, remember that most frequently nothing will be seen on the first occasion and possibly not for several sittings. However some persons, if strongly gifted with clairvoyance or psychic power in a state of unconsciousness, and sometimes conscious degree, may be fortunate enough to obtain good results at the first trial especially if a small amount of temple incense is burned just before using the crystal. If nothing is perceived during the first attempt, do not be disheartened or impatient or imagine that you will never see anything. Be calm and have patience and perseverance.

3. Commence by sitting comfortably with eyes fixed upon the crystal, not a fierce stare but with a steady and calm gaze for thirty minutes only on the first occasion. After that carefully pack up the crystal.

At the second sitting at the same place, same position and at the same time, you may increase the time to forty minutes, and continue for this period during the next five or six sittings after which, the time may be gradually increased, but should in no case be more than two hours.

4. Any person or persons admitted to the room should keep absolute silence and remain seated at a distance from you. When you have developed Occult powers, questions should be put by the person present in a gentle low and slow tone of voice, never suddenly or in a forceful manner.

5. When you find, the crystal begins to look dull or cloudy with small pin points of light glittering therein, one can say the stage of "Crystalline Vision" begins. This cloudiness alternately appears or

disappears as in a mist. Quite suddenly, you may find a blindness but a blue or bluish ocean of space as a background will be clearly apparent.

6. The crystal should not be used soon after taking a meal. Contentment and love of simplicity in living will lead to more success. Mental worry or ill health will not bear fruit. Attention to correct breathing is important.

7. The crystal gazer will see visions appearing in the extreme background which indicate a time more remote, either past or future, than those perceived near at hand, while those appearing in the front, or close to the gazer, denote the present, or immediate future.

8. Two principal classes of visions will present themselves to the gazer:

a) Symbolic, indicated by the appearance of symbol such as flag, boat, knife, gold etc.

b) Actual scenes and personage, in action or otherwise. Persons who are active, exciteable, and decisive, normally see symbolic visions. Passive persons will find direct or little revelation. Be truthful, unselfish, grateful and have confidence in yourself to gaze and concentrate the mind.

Astral Appearance in the Crystal

In the end, we tabulate the results of Astral appearance in the Crystal.

CLOUDS	RESULTS
1. White cloud	Good, the affirmative, favour
2. Black cloud	Bad, inauspicious
3. Violet, Green, Blue	Coming joy, excellent
4. Red, Crimson, Orange or Yellow	Danger, trouble, sickness, beware, deception, grief, betrayal, slander, loss, surprises of a disagreeable nature.
5. Ascending clouds	Affirmative replies to questions asked. If the query is a silent one it makes no difference.
6. Descending clouds	The negation of all questions. No.
7. Clouds or shadow	Moving towards the left hand mean 'The real' or a pictureof an actual thing. Whatever appears on the RIGHT hand side is symbolical.

	Presence of spiritual beings, and their interest.
8. Moonlight	Benefits the Magic Mirror or Gazing crystal
9. Sunlight	The chemical and active rays or influence of the direct sunlight are injurious, and will ruin the magnetic susceptibility of the crystal
10. Extreme of Heat or cold	Injurious

Warning

A sure and certain low exists, Viz–that if the seer's purpose is evil when he or she uses the crystal or Magic mirror, it will react upon the seer sooner or later with terrible effect. All are strictly cautioned to be good and do good only.

THE MYSTIC EYE

This is modern yantra which the auther finds marvellous. It is being used successfully and is shown in the photograph in Fig 4.4 The yantra has been procured from the USA.

The basic use of the Mystic Eye is that it SEES ALL, KNOWS ALL, TELLS ALL.

The yantra can give your unknown date of birth. A brief note and method of use is explained below:-

Do you Believe?

There are things in the universe that surpass anything the normal man can envisage. There are wonders and mysterious phenomena that defy explanation and challenge credibility. There is matter, form and vision, faith, fear and folly, magnetism and mind. There is the good, the static and the evil: There is the known, the unknown and the mysterious. Do not scoff at what you are about to read and discover. Don't ridicule what you are about to learn and experience, for the MYSTIC EYE is in truth a phenomenon of physical reaction to your conscious subconscious and super conscious mind. Remember, less than a century ago, the most brilliant man in the world of that era did not dare envisage anything as wondrous as radio (sound without wire) or Television (Pictures through Air).

Instructions For the Use of Mystic Eye

The mystic eye consists of Psycho-activated Pendulum and answers YES and NO. You can see it in the photo.

FIRST: Relax–Hold the string of the Pendulum between the thumb and forefinger as shown in the photo. Rest your elbow on the table, so that the Pendulum is suspended about 1/4 inch above the "EYE".

SECOND: Think of a question or ask a question in a fairly loud tone. Remove all skepticism from your mind and CONCENTRATE Your attention on the Eye. The Pendulum will then swing in the direction of the answer. Do not move your hand or attempt to control the motion of the Pendulum. You will discover that your subconscious thoughts are as powerful as a giant motor.

Type of Question you May Ask

You may ask a question about any subject relevant to yourself or your surrounding, your past, present or future, about love, health, business, money or success. The MYSTIC EYE may also be used as a LIE DETECTOR OR SELF ANALYSER.

How the Mystic Eye Responds

When you ask or are asked a question, the pendulum will start moving or swinging in the direction of the answer. It is not necessary to stop the motion of the pendulum when asking a new question. If the pendulum is answering "YES" to a question and the next question calls for a "NO" answer, the Pendulum will automatically slow down with a circular motion and then swing to "NO" answer.

If there is slight delay in motion of the Pendulum it indicates lack of concentration. This can be corrected by starting with a more jotting question.

How to Determine Birth Date

If you wish to determine the birth date of your client, guest or that of your friend etc., handle the pendulum and proceed as follows:-

1. Ask what is the month of your birth. The pendulum will swing in the direction of one of the months.
2. Next ask, what is the first number of your birth date? The pendulum will swing in thedirection of one number; If the pendulum should swing to "2" you would know that birth date is either 2nd or in the twenties.
3. Ask "Is 2nd the entire date?" If the pendulum swings to "NO"

then ask, "what is the second number? If the pendulum swings to "7" the birthdate would be 27th, Verify the birthdate by asking, "Is March 27th the correct date"?

Conclusion

You are about to experience one of the thrills of your life in working with the MYSTIC EYE. It can be used by one person or a group of people. Understand that this is also one of the psychological wonders of the world. Here is a phenomenon of physical reaction that challenges the imagination.

Typical Questions

1. Are you in Love?
2. Is your husband true to you?
3. Are you going to inherit some money soon?
4. Are you happy in your work?
5. Will you be drafted?
6. Will you recover your lost ring?
7. Will you get a raise in pay soon?
8. Will you travel soon?
9. Are you going to get a new car?
10. Will I get place of my choice on transfer? etc. etc.

The use of "MYSTIC EYE" can be extended to interested persons only by appointment. So far it has stood up to the tests of the author. The MYSTIC EYE can be supplied for the use of others and for the welfare of the public at large.

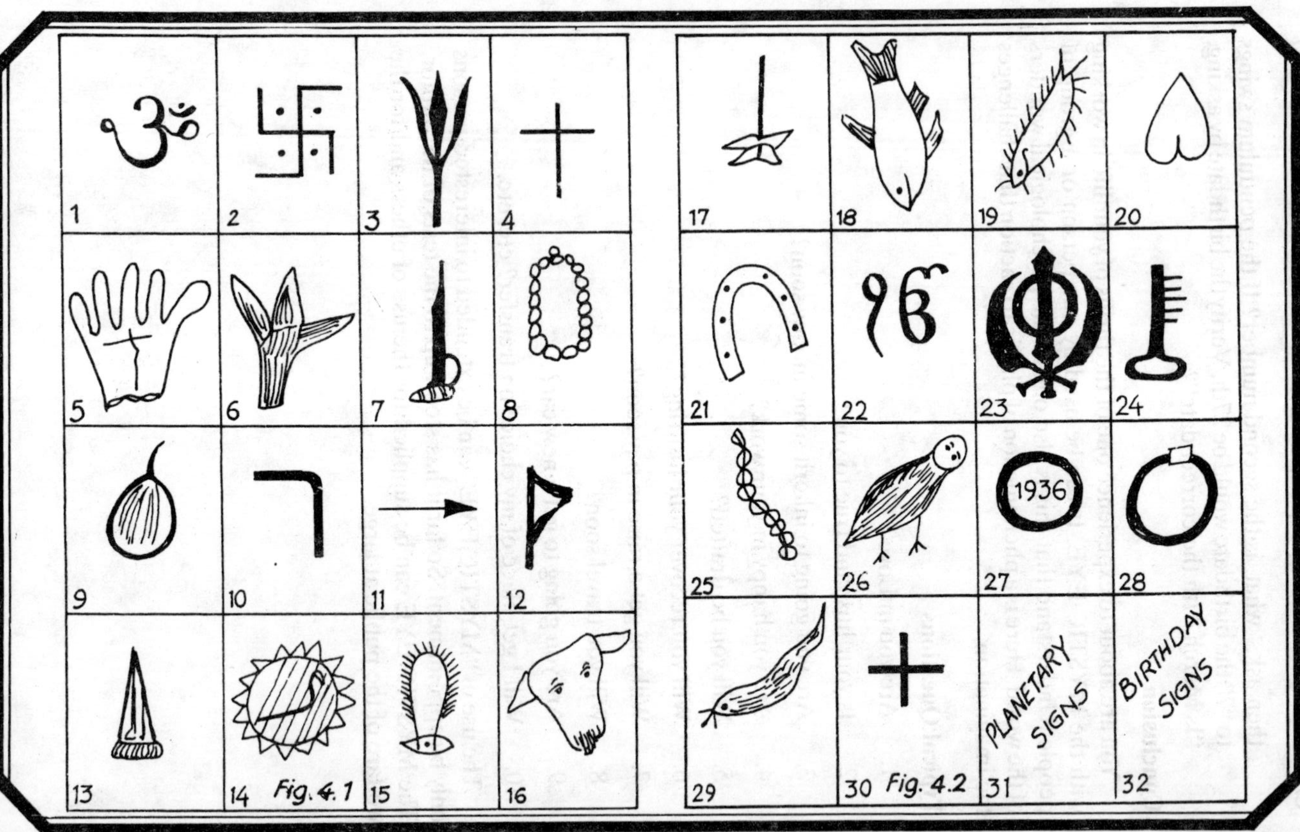
1
2
3
4
5
6
7
8
9
10
11
12
13
14
15
16
17
18
19
20
21
22
23
24
25
26
27
1936
28
29
30
31
PLANETARY SIGNS
32
BIRTHDAY SIGNS
Fig. 4.1

Fig. 4.2

Part II

MANTRAS

5

HOW TO WORSHIP MANTRAS

Definition

Mantra is a complete set of words from the Vedas attributed to the deities or Devas. Mantras have come down to us from our Maharishis, saints, Sadhus and yogis who after recitation of Mantras for several thousand years guided us to follow them. Mantras are single or strung together syllables.

Mantras are used in Tantrik sadhanas or rituals, whispered or chanted in different combinations and contexts, setting up patterns of vibrations. One must learn to pronounce them properly as well as to understand their meaning. Hindus believe that god, good health, good fortune and victory over one's enemies can be attained by chanting the right mantra. According to the Puranas, Shastras and Maharishis, Mantra is the only way to attain one's desires, provided one recites them with complete faith and the prescribed methods and rules. The recitation of words of mantras should be pure and correct in order to create the right vibrations.

Mantra sadhana is very difficult. If during practice some drawbacks remain, it can inflict losses. Without faith and belief, such practice should be avoided. Guidance of a competent Guru or preceptor is quite necessary to attain success.

Guidelines for Sadhaka

A sadhaka is the person who recites the Mantras, meditates and performs all the rites to attain sidhi through Mantras.

The sadhaka should observe some rules and regulations very strictly while practicing Mantra Shakti.

The following guidelines are provided for the Sadhaka:-

1. Complete faith unflinching loyalty backed by a clear heart towards the deity is required for Sadhana.
2. Do not start Mantra Shakti under any pressure.
3. Trust in God, Cosmic love, kindness and patience should be the virtues of a Sadhaka.
4. Avoid harsh speech, lust, anger, restless thoughts, evil company and egoism
5. Do not get emotional. On the other hand to be devout is good
6. Mantras on hearsay should be avoided as they must be authentic
7. Sadhana without any specific aim bears fruits early.
8. In case you see any miracle, do not fear. Keep your WILL POWER strong and continue your Sadhana. All troubles will vanish.
9. Brahmacharya or celibacy should be observed during sadhana.
10. In case of failure, do not lose heart. Try it again and again and you will be crowned with success.

How Mantras are Useful

All our problems are self-created. Usually they are the outcome of our Karmas and the reasons can be checked from the individual Horoscope. One's subconcious mind can help to find the solution through meditation and recitation of Mantras.

Life is a complex combination of incidents and accidents. Can we use MANTRAS AND TANTRAS in the right way to derive benefits out of them so as to solve or eliminate the incidents and accidents ? Yes, these can be avoided or solved by the right use of the right Mantras.

Purity of thoughts, words and deeds, sincerity and deep seated belief in repeating mantras systematically and without any stress or strain on the brain or body, are the key-notes for the efficacy of Mantras.

Concentrate and meditate without having any of your problems and desires in mind. The Mantra should be recited softly so as to be audible only to the person concerned and not to others. Mantras should be recited in a pleasing musical tone which will help in concentration.

Continuous sadhana will enable the sadhaka to find solutions to the problems, attaining peace of mind and reducing mental strain. The Mantras must be recited as they are. Any addition or alteration in the Mantra must be avoided. If distorted or recited incorrectly, the power of the mantra is lost and it ceases to have the desired beneficial effect.

FOOD: The sadhaka should have a light meal, hot and well cooked and in small quantity, as overeating leads to the excitement of the sensory organs which aggravate passions. Onion, garlic and meat have a stimulating effect on the sensory organs and do more harm to the body than good. Intoxicants and smoking of any kind should be avoided. Lack of control in the diet is a great obstacle to progress. Small quantities of wholesome food purifies the mind and a pure mind retains the memory of God.

Asanas During Meditations

KRIYA YOGA is the posture or Asana arousing Mantra Shakti.

1. *Siddh Asana*

This Asana is very useful to acquire Sidhi. Even fat persons can practice it. Place one heel at the anus and keep the other heel at the root of generative system. The feet or legs should be so arranged that the ankle joints should touch each other. Hands should be placed straight on the knee joints. Sit for 15 minutes with closed eyes concentrating on God. This ASANA is useful in curing rheumatism and keeps the mind and body in order.

The eyes must be focussed if not closed, on the space between eye-brows (TRIKUTI)

2. *Padma Asana*

Place the right foot on the left thigh and then carefully bring the left foot on the right thigh. This is the physical position for the spiritual process. One must press the tongue against the teeth and chin against Heart. The sight should be focussed on the tip of the nose. Breathing should be slow. It destroys diseases.

3. *Pranayam*

Pranayam removes all diseases, purifies the Nadis, steadies the mind in concentration, i.nproves digestion and increases the appetite. It helps awaken the Kundalini.

Sit in Padma or Sidh Asana. Close the right nostril with the thumb. Draw in the air very slowly through the left nostril. Then do it likewise with the right nostril. Retain the air as long as you can comfortably . Then exhale very very slowly, through the nostril after removing thumb or finger. Do twenty rounds in the morning and twenty in the evening. Increase it gradually.

4. *Trataka*

This involves steady gazing at a particular point or object without blinking to increase concentration. It is a very effective method to control the mind and improve the eyesight and develop will-power. It can be done by concentrating one's attention on a black or white dot on the wall, a picture or on OM etc.

5. *Pooja*

Deva or Deity should be kept in one's mind while reciting the mantra. Each mantra has a tremendous force and draws maximum benefits. This can be performed in three ways:-

1. Vaikhari (Verbal) by speaking loudly.
2. Upamsu (Whispering).
3. Mansik (Mental).

6. *Agni Hotra*

Homa is performed with fire in accordance with prescribed rituals.

Mandala Vidya and Bhuchari

Mandala yaga has been mentioned in Mandala Brahman- Upanishad. It is stated that various kinds of lights manifest themselves during meditation. If one concentrates below the tip of the nose at a distance of four, six, eight , ten and twelve inches, one will see Blue, ash or grey, red, white and yellow colours slightly mixed. If the sadhaka concentrates at a distance of four inches the red Agni mandala i.e. fire is seen. Again at 10 inches is seen the white Jala Mandala or water. At twelve inches one sees the Prithvi mandala or the earth. One who can see the five mandalas is known as a Yogi. If twelve inches above the Head, one sees effulgence, one is a liberated soul or has attained salvation.

Concentration on Sky or on AKASA Mandala leads to peace of mind. With vayu mandala, the body remains still without any movement. In Jala Mandala one feels, cool, while in Agni hot. In such case, the body will be in an eminently fit condition.

Practice

For practice of Mandala vidya, one can sit in a dark room and first concentrate at a distance of four inches below the tip of nose, then one will see a blue spot. Increase the distance gradually as stated above. One must spend at least two sittings for each mandala. This vidya enables one to concentrate and consequently achieve progress in all spheres of activity. While concentrating on the tip of the nose, and if the light is allowed to flow towards the earth, we see a red effulgence. This is called BHUCHARI. The body is enveloped by this light. This acts as a shield for the practitioner against evil spirits. Instead of seeing below, if one sees twelve inches above the head, according to Mandala Bramham-Upnishad and sees a bunch of light beams, as it were, his vision gives Amrita Tatva or Moksha.

Bright Jyoti

While observing light at Trikuti, one can gradually see the light enlarge as it extends gradually in all directions without seeing any particular object. This is called BRIGHT JYOTI which literary means a big and powerful light. During practice, one feels a sort of peace of mind and stillness which cannot be described but has to be experienced.

Lights in Meditation

Various kinds of lights as detailed above are manifested during meditation. In the beginning a bright white light, the size of pin point will appear in the forehead in the TRIKUTI, which is called AJNA CHAKRA. You will notice, when the eyes are closed, different coloured lights, white, yellow, red, smokey, blue, green, mixed lights, flashes as in lightning, fire as in burning charcoal, fire flies, Moon, Sun and Stars. These lights appear in the mental space, and are Tantric lights, having its specific colour.

Yellow and white lights are generally seen. Red and Blue lights are rarely seen. Frequently there is a combination of white and yellow lights.

Initially small balls of white light float about before the mind's eye. When you first observe this, be assured that the mind is becoming more steady and you are progressing in concentration. After some months you will see bigger lights, bigger than the Sun. At first these will not be steady causing peculiar sensation of extreme joy and happiness. A desire to see the lights intensifies. After continuous practise, these lights become steady. It gives encouragement, and creates faith in the physical elements. The appearance of these lights denote that you are transcending the physical consciousness. You are in a semi-conscious state when the lights appear. You must NOT shake the body when you experience such lights. You must be perfectly steady in Asana or the state in which these lights manifest themselves. You must breathe very slowly.

Sometimes in meditation, you will see a brilliant dazzling light.You will find it difficult to gaze on this light.You will be compelled to withdraw your mental vision from this light. This dazzling light is the light from the Sushumna in the heart.

Dazzling Lights

Sometimes during meditation you will see very powerful dazzling lights, bigger than the Sun. They are white and become steady slowly. The light is so powerful and dazzling sometimes that you have to withdraw yourself from looking at it and break the meditation. By constant practice, the mind is engaged in concentration and will be used to it, and fear will vanish. Concentration on Trikuti rather than the top of head as it is easy. Be steady, do not make changes. Sometimes you will feel invisible help, possibly from your Ishta Devata or Lord when you are in trouble. The invisible power assists you.You will have to mark these changes carefully.

Advance Stage of Lights

Sometimes during meditation, you will see much advanced lights and objects than those described above. You will see an infinite blue sky and ethereal spaces. You will see yourself in the blue light sometimes. After that you will notice highly vibratory, rotating particles in the light or else you will see physical forms, human forms, children, women, adult, males, rishie's with beards etc. Those forms are of two types:-

1. Lustrous forms of Devatas
2. Physical forms

You will see Ishta Devata or tutelary deity (guiding Devata) or your lord in handsome dress and with valuable ornaments, flowers, garlands, with four or many hands and weapons, Sadhus and Rishis etc, appear to encourage you. You will find a huge collection of Devatas and celestial ladies with various musical instruments in their hands etc. You will see beautiful flower gardens, fine palatial buildings, rivers, mountains, golden temples, picturesque sceneries etc.

Warning

Swami SIVA Nanda has stated that one should not waste one's time in looking at these visions.This is only a curiosity. These all are encouragements to convince you of the existence of super physical, metaphysical realities and the solid existence of God. Drive these pictures away and focus your attention on the goal.

Personal Experience

The AUTHOR has experienced the former type of lights of various colours, during meditation,while sitting in office or sometimes in any state particularly in a passive mood. The author has felt these lights to be soothing, with the mind becoming joyful and at peace.

These appear in a dot, expand and form the shape of a Jyoti of a deepak (Light emanating from a burning Jyoti) in yellow colour followed by change of colour to red and Blue. This Jyoti remains for a good period, till the eyes are opened.

Once, when the author was engrossed in deep meditation in the house at night and was alone, there came such a dazzling light in the dark room that everything was enveloped in celestial light, which was frightening in the initial moments. However on controlling the mind he enjoyed the situation peacefully.

So this is the Sadhana Shakti. If carried out with faith, you can achieve marvellous results, get siddhi and can benefit both yourself and mankind.

6

ROSARY, BEEJ MANTRA AND SAMPUT

During meditation beads are a must. These are classified for different purposes and the beads in each rosary are different as indicated below. Padam Beej, Ruradaksh, Shankh(conch),Pearl, gem, gold, silver, root of Kush and Tulsi are used in different Rosaries. All beads in a rosary should be of equal size, free from decay and unbroken. One additional bead of a bigger size than others is put at top of the rosary.

Rosary

i) FOR SHIVA Shakti and mantras thereof as well as that of Shakti Mantra, Rudraksh rosary is best.

ii) Tulsi bead is to be used in meditation of Vishnu and Lord Krishna.

iii) Padam Beej bead is to be used in death inflicting mantras.

iv) Mantras for wealth can be recited with beads of gems, jewels, gold and silver.

v) For wealth, there should be 30 beads. For Mokash 50 beads, death Mantra 15 beads, for general desires 27, for Sex Sidhi 54 beads and for all other purposes 108 beads should be there in a rosary.

Rosary should first be cleaned with Ganges water, and be treated with incense, dhoop , deep (Jyoti) and then used as in Sadhana.

Method

The use of rosary needs special attention. Many persons do not know how to use the rosary. Check the procedure carefully. The rosary should be kept hidden while meditating and should not touch the ground. If it does so, it becomes powerless and ineffective. The Rosary is to be used with the third finger and thumb. The first finger should be kept separate. When one round of the rosary is completed, it should be rotated. Counting of Mantras can be done in any way suitable to the Sadhaka.

Asanas used during meditation should be either Padma or Siddhi Asana. Asana (carpet on which one sits for meditation) should be preferably of deer skin as this is believed to be the most auspicious. Tiger skin can also be used. In case you use a leather asana, a cloth must be spread over it.

How to Purify the Rosary

Before one starts meditation or Sadhana, the rosary must be purified. On the day, you have selected to start sadhana, get up early in the morning before sunrise, take a bath and wash the rosary in Holy Ganges water. Then the rosary should be kept near the incense or dhoop while reciting Beej Mantra 11 or 21 or 31 times over the rosary. It should then be used for Sadhana.

BEEJ MANTRA

A seed when sown grows into a fruit bearing tree. In the same way the Beej Mantra is full of Shakti. There are various Beej Mantras each with its own power. When mixed with other Mantras additional power accrues to that Mantra.

It was said that the first primordial sound produced at the time of creation was the syllable 'OM' and this became the first Mantra. This consists of three letters A U M. The sound'A' starts from the throat and comes as far as the lips and as such is the longest and fullest vowel, The letter 'M' is the sound produced when the lips are closed and thus it is the last sound. In Between is 'U'.

Thus 'OM' embraces all the sounds within it. Every sound in the alphabet is called a matruka and it represents a devata. 'OM' represents all devatas. Again 'A' 'U', 'M' represent respectively, Brahma, Vishnu and Isvara and thus they represent the trinity or Parabrahma. In Mandayuk-Upanishad a good representation of 'OM' is given. They represent the three states of the individual awake, dreaming and asleep, and are identified respectively with'A' 'U' and 'M'.

OMKAR is the basic mantra of God which is further broken into eight parts, namely Prithvi (Earth), Jal (Water), Vayu (Air) Aakash (sky), Moon (Heart), Buddhi (Intelligence), Ahankar(Ego Pride) and Angi (Fire).

Basic Beej Mantra 'A', 'U' and 'M' is further expanded into the following types of Beej , Yog Beej , Tejo Beej, Shanti Beej and Raksha Beej, which respectively are known as Aeng (Aim) Hreem, Sreem, Kreem, Kleem, Dum, Gam or Glaum, Lam, Yam, Aam or UM or Ram.

There are one word Beej Mantras which are particularly suitable to young boys and girls who can repeat them with zest and faith, to secure good results.

1.	Kshasraum	क्षौं	Narasimha bija. Removes all fear and sorrows.
2.	Aim	ऐं	This is Saraswati Bija. This enables young boys and girls to be proficient in all branches of learning.
3.	Shree	श्रीं	This is a mantra of Lakshmi. Repetition of this leads one to prosperity and contentment.
4.	Hareem	ह्रीं	This is Bhuvaneshvari Mantra. It is also called Maya bija. Its importance is described in Devi Bhagavatma. One becomes a leader of men and gets all one needs.
5.	Kaleem	कलीं	This is the famous Kamraj Beej. It fulfills one's desires.
6.	Kreem	क्रीं	This is the Beej of Kali, who destroys enemies and gives happiness.
7.	Dum	दुं	This is Durga Beej. She is the highest deity and as such can give whatever a man wants.
8.	Gam Glaum	गं गलौं	These are the Beej of Ganesa. Removes all obstacles and promotes success.
9.	Lam	लं	This is the Prithvi (Earth) beeja. It helps to secure good crops.
10.	Yam	यं	This is a Vayu (air) beeja and is supposed to help secure rains.
11.	Aam Um Ram	आं उं रं	These are respectively the Beeja Mantras of Brahma, Vishnu and Rudra.

Mantras which contain upto Nine words are termed Beej Mantra, ten to twenty words forms Mantra and beyond are Mole Mantras. Broadly speaking mantras are divided into three parts as Satwic Rajsic and Tamsic which respectively indicate Atma uplift religious and material comforts and death, Uchattan, loss or, victory over enemies and oponents.

Sadhana During Eclipse

During the period of solar or lunar eclipse the Sadhaka should not waste even a minute or second because meditation during this period is always very fruitful. During this period, one should do sadhana on the banks of a river, canal or lake. If one can one may stand in water and do pooja . Do not worry on any account and keep your mind free during this period.

This is the most auspicious period for Mantra sadhana. One gets success early if the recitation and meditation is done during this period with full concentration.

Who Can do Sadhana?

In old books, containing the instructions to a sadhaka for various mantras, it is specifically mentioned that some mantras are only to be recited by Brahmins, Kshatriyas Vaishyas and Shudras.No where is it stipulated that the mantras specified for Brahmins be adopted by Shudras or Vice versa.

The author is definitely in disagreement with these directions. In the author's views , every mantra can be adopted or recited by any body of any religion provided one has complete faith and performs the sadhana with the necessary rituals. A person can attain success and get sidhi if he is sincere and devout.

General Instructions

The repetition or Purascharnas is called Japa, which destroys sins accumulated from previous birth and frees one from the cycle of birth and death, leading to prosperity and liberation. In Patanjali Yagasutra it is stated that by the repetition of the mantra, comes the realisation of the intended deity. Constant repetition keeps the Ishta deity always before you and helps you to go further in your efforts.

When one wants to do sadhana for some special purpose, use deer or tiger skin as Asana or a Kusa grass mat, when the others are not available. The rosary while reciting mantras must be kept at the level of the chest.

Earlier it has been stated that normally the third finger be used for Pooja. But for Akarshan or attraction, use the first and third fingers, the first and fourth for good purposes and the first finger and thumb for destroying enemies.

One should sit facing East for fulfilment of desires and the North for attaining Moksha.

One should not do Japa when one feels lethargic and the mind is restless.

SAMPUT

Samput are the specified words used in Mantra. These can be used at the start, middle or at the end of a mantra. The samput has a great value in Mantra shakti or in other Mantras and must be used carefully.

The use of the mantras with samput in addition to Japa can be to write the mantra on Bheej Patra with saffron using a pen of Pomegranate (Anar) wood for specific numbers as prescribed for each Mantra. The paper should be wrapped in kneaded flour and before sunrise and breakfast thrown in running water one by one, keeping the Ishat in one's mind.

The special occasions are Diwali,. Holi or Eclipse days. This also includes Shivratri, Navratras during which they get extra power to show effects.

One should perform 'PRADOSHA KALA SHIVA POOJA' to get rid of all sorts of afflictions. Poverty, miseries, calamities, adversities, grief, debt and diseases are troubling those who forget their Lord. Pradosha means Taryodasi tithis falling in the evening of both Shukal and Krishan Paksha. When the above coincides with Saturday it is known as 'SHANT PRADOSHA'. Both placate the Three Eyed Lord SHIVA. It is said that on this day all other Gods and goddesses assemble at Mount Kailash to worship Lord Shiva. This bestows all kinds of wealth and comfort to Sadhaka.

e of Samput in Gayatri Mantra

cite the example showing the use of samput in Gayatri Mantra. atri Mantra is read as below:

भूर्भुव स्वः तत्सविर्तुवरण्यं भर्गो देवस्य धीमहि धियौ यो नाः प्रचोदयात्

er the word ॐ भू र्भूवः स्व use the following words as Samput for cific purposes indicated below and then mantra be recited.

1. ॐ ऐं कलीं सौ — This samput is used for proficiency in words
2. ॐ श्रीं ह्रीं श्रीं — This samput is used for wealth and comforts.
3. ॐ ऐं ह्रीं कलीं — Enemies are destroyed, troubles and worries vanish and the individual is blessed with joy and happiness through the use of this samput.
4. ॐ श्रीं ह्रीं कलीं — Through the use of this samput one is blessed with progeny and one enjoys sexual bliss.
5. ॐ ह्रीं — Through the use of this samput, one recovers from diseases.
6. ॐ आँ ह्रीं कलीं — This samput when used blesses the sadhaka with protection from all evil forces. His hopes and wishes are realised. Like the above you can use specified Samput with other Mantras for early sidhi and results.

In English we can pronunciate the above samput as:-

1. Om aeeng Kaleeng soo
2. Om Shareeng Hareeng Shareeng
3. Om aeeng Hareeng Kaleeng
4. Om Shareng Hareeng Kaleeng
5. Om Hareeng
6. Om aeeng, Hareeng Kaleeng

GAYATRI MANTRA: "Om bhur bhava suha tatsa vetur vareneyam bargo devasyaha dhimi diyo yona parachodyat."

Homa and Gayatri

Recitation of Gayatri Mantra with Samput is very useful. Homa should be performed daily with these Mantras. Specific samputs can be used for separate purposes and the following articles be used in the Homa.

1. For gain of wealth use fresh flowers of Jui or Red Kamal. Also you can use samdhas (portion of wood used in Homa for Agni) of Bilwa tree, its leaves, flowers, fruit or its root with ghee in Homa.
2. Samdhas of Shami, Bilwa or visheshar Aak or their flowers with

ghee be used in Homa for acquisition of God, wealth etc.

3. Dip the leaves of Bale in ghee and use in Homa. This makes the sadhaka wealthy.
4. Round balls of Gugal can be used in Homa with ghee to get good fortune.
5. One is blessed with wealth, health and prosperity when Til and barley are used with ghee in Homa.
6. Homa with Mahamritanja Mantra or pieces of Goilo dipped in milk can be used with ghee in Homa for recovery from diseases and untimely death.
7. The sadhaka or others recover from fever if Homa is performed with mango leaves dipped in ghee, for recovery from diseases. You can use Bachh which has been dipped in milk or Bachh mixed in milk, ghee, curd and honey and used in Homa for wealth and comforts.
8. Lunacy is cured if samdha of trees having milk is used in Homa. Such trees are people, Bood, Bargad, Gular, Aak etc.
9. For recovery from all diseases, use Samdhas of gular tree which can be dipped in honey and juice of sugar cane.
10. Gain of wealth can be had if during a lunar eclipse homa is performed with samdhas of Khir tree and of chandan.

7

DIVISION OF MANTRAS AND THEIR USE

Division of Mantras

The use of Mantras is divided into the following six categories:

1. SHANTIKARAN: These mantras deal with the cure of diseases and warding off the malefic influence of planets.
2. VASHI KARAN: Through these mantras, you can put under your control any woman, man, officer, minister, devta, soul, animal etc. and can fulfil your wishes.
3. STAMBHAN: These mantras deal with all the persons etc., as detailed above in para 2 to stop them doing mischief, or acting against you.
4. VIDESHAN: These mantras are used for creating differences between two or many individuals.
5. UCHCHATTAN: These mantras deal with distraction of the mind of the enemy or opponents and other persons so that they may remain away from their country, birth place, residence, home, work and family members. It is also used when the sadhaka requires a person to remain at war with others.
6. MARAN: These are death inflicting mantras through which you can kill anybody at any distance without disclosing your identity. These mantras are available in Puranas, Hindu scripts, Mohammedan and Buddhist cults. Other religious persons may follow their corresponding words, which are equally applicable and can be recited.

These basic mantras are for every day use by the sadhaka and lead to early siddhi of one's mantras.

1. Om Namo Shivaye
2. Om Namo Narayane Aye Namaha.

3. Om Namo Bhagwate Vasdev Aye Namaha

These are samadhi Mantras for Japa and Upasana.

The nefarious use of these Mantras is Prohibited.

Some Important Mantras

1. *Panch Akshari*

This mantra is SHIVA PANCHAKSHRI which is of five letters and is addressed to SHIVA. It is :-

"ॐ नमः शिवाय"

"Om Namah Shivaye".

This mantra fulfills all desires. All persons without creed and sex can do japa of Mantra. It leads all to moksha. There are no restrictions, like Homa, initiation and time. It always remains pure. The word Shiva is sufficient to destroy all sins and when Namaha is added, leads to liberation. One need not be surprised, if one is initiated by a Guru and reaches one's goal quickly.

2. *Asht Akshari*

Another important mantra is Narayana Ashtakshari, that is Narayana Mantra of eight letters.

"ॐ नमः नरायणाय"

This mantra is sought after by all the devotees of Narayana. One is blessed and can achieve anything. It is said that if a Sadhaka recites Om Namo Bhagvatel Vasdevaye continuous repetition of this mantra for a week, he will be able to see angels and talk to them. It must be uttered loudly . This mantra too can be repeated by all castes and creeds.

3. *Ganapati Mantra*

In Tamil Nadu, the lord is called PILLAYER The mantra is given under Tantra.

"ओ श्रीं ह्रीं कलीं ग्लौं गं गणपतेय नमः"

Om Sharem Hareem Kleem Glaum Gam Ganapateye Namaha.

As is well known, Ganapati is always worshipped first to remove all impediments that may come in the way of performing any act or ceremony. Hence the mantra not only removes all obstacles but also gives success in one's efforts. A simpler mantra is also known as:-

"ओं गं गणपतये नमः"

Om Gam Ganapataye Namaha.

4. *Hanuman Mantra*

Lord Hanuman Ji is an embodiment of Lord Shiva and Vishnu. The mantra for Hanuman ji is :-

"ओं हुं हनुमते रूद्रात्मकाय हुं फट् स्वाहा"

"Om Hoom Hanumate Rudratamakaye Hoom Phut Swaha."

There is no favour which he cannot bestow. Hence he is favourite of many as he is easily approachable. He is the embodiment of all good qualities which he freely gives to his devotees. One need not be surprised, if one finds more temples devoted to Hanuman Ji than any other god.

5. *Saraswati Mantra*

The goddess Saraswati bestows knowledge and without her the whole world would remain steeped in ignorance and dullness of intellect. Mantra contains ten letters.

After completing the religious rites in the morning including Pitha Nyas, Rishi Nyas is performed. Also Kara Nyas, Sarauga Nyas are to be performed. Then Mantra Nyas is to be performed in eleven places namely Cerebrum , brow, both eyes, both ears, both nostrils, mouth, rectum and feet. After all these rites, the Pooja of Goddess is to be performed with mantra:-

"ओं ऐं कलीं सौं: सरस्वत्यै नम:"

"Om aim Kleeng saum Saraswatiya Namaha".

By the Japa of this Mantra, the Sadhaka attains high proficiency in education and becomes a learned scholar.

More details are given in the following pages.

6. *Dattatreya Mantra*

ओं ह्रीं परब्रह्म परमात्मने हरि हरब्रह्मेन्द्राय दत्तात्रेयाय स्वाहा।

Dattatreya is a favourite in Maharashtra and adjoining provinces and is the presiding deity of all those who practice yoga. As such there is nothing which he cannot bestow on his followers.

7. *Maha Mrutyunjaya Mantra*

This is a mantra taken from Rudram:

"स्वाहा ओं त्र्यंबकम् यजामहे सुगंधि पुष्टि वर्धनम् उर्वारूकमिव बंघनान्मृत्यो र्मुक्षीय माऽमृतात् ओं ह्रीं परब्रह्म परमात्मने हरि हर ब्रह्मेन्द्र"

"I bow to the three-eyed, who is fragrant and who promotes nourishment. May he liberate me from death in order to enable me to reach immortality in the same manner as a cucumber is separated from the creeper."

This is addressed to Lord Shiva who is the conqueror of death. The mantra is repeated by the bed-side of a patient, who is seriously ill. It protects an individual from accident and indeed from death and keeps off diseases. It bestows wealth and ultimately immortality.

8. *Surya Ashtakshari Mantram*

"ओं घृणि सूर्य आदित्यमु"

This is from Suryapanishad in Atharvaveda. Whoever does japa of this mantra becomes a brahma vetta, a knower of brahman. If one repeats this with his face towards the Sun he will be free from sins. If one does in japa the Noon with the face towards the Sun, one will immediately be freed from sins committed just then. When done in the Morning one becomes healthy and will be able to secure cattle and will be able to know the meaning of the vedas. When one does it three times a day one will get the merit of performing one hundred yajanas. If repeated in the month of aswiyuja when the star is swati, one will be saved from the jaws of death.

9. *Mantras and Tantra*

I give below three mantras taken from Tantras. They are rated very high and as such should be taken up by sadhakas. The first two are taken from Mahanirvana Tantra. The first is

"ओं सच्चित एक ब्रह्म"

This is the Brahma mantra, "Om" meaning the trinity of the creator, protector and destroyer. Brahma is the eternal, changeless consciousness, one without parallel. This is the highest mantra which does not require the usual sanskaras (ceremonial rites) for repetition. This obviously refers to SIVA. But an initiation from a Guru is necessary, alongwith the above is the mula saktri mantra. This is akshari and consists of ten letters.

"ह्रीं श्रीं क्रों परमेश्वरि स्वाहा"

The other is the shodasi, and consists of sixteen letters. This is considered to be the highest mantra and of the greatest potency.

"ह्रीं श्रीं क्रों परमेश्वरि कालिके ह्रीं श्रीं क्रों स्वाहा"

The mantra is used in the practice of Sakti (Kali) sadhana with kulachara rites in which enter the five makaras(see Tantra for makaras). The third is from kularnava Tantra. The mantra is called Para Prasad Mantra: (Hansa) हंस

'Ha" is the outgoing breath and "sa" is the ingoing breath. This mantra is the living form of Siva Sakti, Jiva (Individual soul) utters this mantra 21,600 times day and night. As there is no japa it is called ajapa. A corresponding mantra was mentioned by Sankara in his prapancha sara. He called it soham or Ajapa Gayatri.

10. *Devi Mantra*

Mantras pertaining to goddesses are called Devi mantras. These mantras are famous for their quick and instant response. However extreme care should be taken in maintaining outward and inner cleanliness. Otherwise consequences will be bad. Hence one should consult a Guru for guidance. However I give below some mantras which do not need such extreme restrictions.

a)	Saraswati Mantra	ओं ऐं सरस्वत्यै नमः	(for learning)
b)	Kali Mantra	ओं क्लीं कालिकायै नमः	(for prosperity and liberation)
c)	Durga Mantra	ओं दुंदुर्गायै नमः	(for prosperity and moksha)
d)	Tripura Bala	क्लीं सौः	(It is a powerful mantra)
e)	Lakshmi	महालक्ष्म्यै नमः	(for wealth, prosperity and happiness)

11. *Karna Pisachi Mantra*

This enables one to hear news from other places or even from other worlds through this goddess. There are several of these but I give only one. ओं अरविंदे स्वाहा This must be repeated ten thousand times for 21 days, after which one gets siddhi. The Goddess shows herself and tells the Sadhaka about the past, present and future.

RULES AND METHODS FOR WORSHIP OF DIFFERENT GODS AND GODDESSES

Observance of time honoured usage or customs is necessary for meditation or offering of prayers. A person who practices 'Tapasya' (sadhana) and makes magnificent gifts without observances of custom cannot achieve success in any work.

A devotee (Sadhak) should perform his worldly duties, regarding them as his deity's

यतु करोषि यतु अश्रासि यज्जहोषि ददाधि यतु
यतु तपस्यषि कौन्तेय, तदूकुरूस्व मर्दपणम्

"Yatu Karoshi Yatu Ashrasi Yajjahoshi Dadadhi Yatu
Yatu Tapasyashi Kontaye, Tadookoorusav Mardapanesma"

The above sloka means this, "Oh son of Kunti offer me whatever you do eat, give and pray in meditation.By this way you can get rid of the sins due to one's karma or actions and attain God". A devotee should completely surrender himself to God. He should sing the name of his deity as many times as he can. A sadhaka will be required to perform his duties every morning for a long time in order to achieve success in his Sadhana for the attainment of the desired objects of his devotion.

Given below are methods and rules for worship of different Gods and Goddesses for the guidance of readers.

1. Durga

After completion of usual religious duties and Nyas of Rishis mentioned in Durga Mantra "Karas Nyas" is to be exercised uttering.

"ॐ दुर्गे अङ्गष्ढाभ्याम् नमः"

Om Durga Aangashtabhayam Namaha.

This is to be followed by "Anga Nyas" with the following mantra:-

ॐ दुर्गे ह्रदयाय नमः, ॐ दुर्गे शिरसे स्वाहा, ॐ दुर्गायै शिखायै वषटू, ॐ भूतरक्षा कवचाय हुं. ॐ दुर्गे दुर्गे रक्षणि नेत्रत्रयाय वोषटू, ॐ दुर्गे दुर्गे रक्षणि करतल पृष्ठभ्याम् फट् ।

"Om Durge Hirdayaye Namaha. Om Durge Shirsey Swaha.Om Durgaye Shikhaya Vashtu, Om Bhutraksha Kavchaye Hoon. Om Durge Durge Rakshni Netartaraye Vashtu, Om Durge Durge Rakshani Kartal Prishthbhayam Phut."

After this the sadhaka is to meditate on the goddess keeping his image before his mind's eyes. He should then place the 'Arghya'. Then pith puja is to be performed according to rules mentioned earlier for 'Purascharan' of his mantra. Five lakhs japas are to be performed.

Durga Mantra

This mantra is efficacious in everything and fulfils all one's desires. The word Doong (दूं) is formed by adding together Maya (ह्रीं) Adri (द) Karna (अनुश्वर) Bindu (दु:) and Pranab and Bisarga is added at the beginning of the word.

The mantra formed by adding together the word (दु:) Panchanga (ग) Pratishta (आ), Bryu (फ) Bhoutik (ऐं) Contains eight letters with Namaha(नम:). It is also written in Raghava Vatta and other treaties that Durga mantra consists of Tar (ॐ) , Maya (ह्य) ,Nijabij (दुं) and is to be uttered by adding (दुर्गा नम:) at the end.

Methods of Worship

After completing religious duties of the morning with 'Pith Nyasa' according to customory rites of Puja, a devotee or Sadhaka has to perform Nyasa of Pithshakti in the centre of the heart. Nibhandhan Grantha says Puja of Naba Sakti such as Prabh, Maya, Jaya, Sukhana, Bishuddhu, Nandini, Supra, Bijaya and the bestow of success is to be performed. Navada is the Rishi and Durga is the Goddess of the mantra.

Next the devotee is to sit in meditation of the Goddess, keeping her image before the mind's eye and utter:-

सिंहस्था शशिशेखरा मरक्तप्रख्या चतुर्मि भुजै:
शड़ ख-चक्र-धनु श्रांश्च दद्याति नैत्रै: स्त्रिभि: शोभिता

After Pith-Puja the Goddess should be worshipped with the mantras:

आं प्रभायै, ई मायायै ॐ जयायै, एं सूक्ष्मायै ऐं विशुद्धायै,
ॐ नन्दिन्यै औ सुप्रभायै, अं विजायायै, अ: सर्व्वसिद्धायै नम: ।

After this, offer Puspanjali and invoke her with prayers. After completing all these rites of Puja, Sara Anga Puja (षड़ड्गपूजा) is to be performed with the mantra:-

ॐ ह्रीं ॐ ह्रीं दुं दुर्गायै हृदयाय नम:

'Om Hareeng Om Hareeng Doom Durgaye Hardayaye Namaha"

This is to be followed by Puja on the crest of lotus petals uttering:

"जं जयायै नम: विं विजयायै नम:,
क्रीं कोर्ते नम:, प्रं प्रभायै,
श्रं श्रद्धायै नम:, श्रां श्रुत्यै, मं मेघायै नम:"

"Jaan Jyayee Namaha, Veen Vijayaye Namaha, Kareen
Korte Namaha,Prana Prabhaye Shareen Shradaye
Namaha, Shruaan Shrutayee, Maan Medayae Namaha"

After this, Indra and other Gods with their respective weapons are to be worshipped. In this way Puja of the Goddess Durga is to be completed with the ceremonial discarding of Dhup etc. at the end. Eight lakhs of Japa are necessary for 'Purascharan' of this mantra.

2. Saraswati

The Goddess is to be worshipped by uttering the following:-

"ॐ ह्रीं हेसौ ॐ सरस्वत्यै नमः"

'Om Hareeng Hesoo Om Sarwatiya Namaha".

Method of Worship

After completing the religious rites in the morning including Pitha Nyas, Rishi Nyas is to be performed according to the rules enunciated in the Shastras. Then kara Nyas is to be gone through with mantras etc. This is to be followed by "Sarauga Nyas". Then "Mantra Nyas" is to be performed in eleven places namely cerebrum, brow, right eye, left eye, right ear, right and left nostrils, mouth, rectum and foot by uttering:-

ॐ नमः, ह्रीं नमः ऐं नमः ॐ नमः,
सं नमः, रं नमः, स्वं नमः, हों गमः
नं नमः, मं नमः।

"Om Namaha, Hareeng Namaha, Aaeeng Namaha
Om Namaha, Sam Namah, Ram Namah, Hong Gam
Savam Namah, Hong Gam, Nam Namaha, Mam Namaha"

All other Puja rites and mantras are to be performed and uttered according to the rules and method of worship as explained below. These methods and rules apply also for the the worship of "BAGESWARI".

The mantra of the Goddess, who bestows knowledge and without whom the whole world would remain steeped in ignorance and dullness of intellect contains ten letters SARASWATI is formed by adding Adri (द) after Barun (व) which results in वदवद and then by putting स्वाहा after वाग्वादिनी

After completing the religious rites of the morning Pith Nyas as usual. Nyas of God is to be performed by uttering ॐ मेघायै नमः ॐ प्रक्षाय नमः etc. (Om Medayee namaha, Om Prakshaye Namaha). This is to be followed by 'Nyas of Rishi' uttering शिरसि कन्व ऋषय नमः (Shirsi Kanv Rishie Namaha) according to the rules mentioned in the Sastras. Then a devotee is to practice Kara Anga Nyas by uttering the mantra "अं कं

खं घं ङं आ अङ्गष्ठाभ्याम् नमः, इं चं छं, झं ञं ई मर्ज्ज नीजयाम् स्वाहा' and so on. After completing Anga Nyas he is to meditate on the Goddess. After this, place the conch and then perform Pith Puja of Pitha Devata, namely Goddess of intellect, meditation invocation land offering of Pancha Pushpa to the Goddess and one after another. Thereafter Puja of Japa, Satya Bimala, Jnana Buddhi, Medha and Prajna is to be performed on the lotus petas. After this, Brahmins and others and gods of all directions with their weapons are to be worshipped.

These ceremonies being over, puja of the Goddess is to be completed with the ceremonial discarding of Dhups etc. and concomitant rites of immersion. Ten Lakh Japas are necessary for Purascharan of this mantra.

3. Shiva

"ॐ ह्रीं हौं नमः शिवाय"

"Om Hareeng Hoong Namah Shivaya"

Method of Worship

After finishing the morning religious duties and pranayam first, according to the rules of ordinary puja, Nyas of Sree Kantha, Ananta, Sukshama, Trimurthi, Ambareswar, Arghysh, Bharbhuti, Hari Akrur Maheshwar and others a combined image of Rudra and his Sakti is to be performed on completion of Pith Puja according to usual rites of Puja. It is mentioned in Sarada Tilaka that Bama, Jyastha, Raudri, Kali, Kalavikarani, Bala Bikarami, Balapramathini Sarbabhuta damini are the Pith Sakti "Asan Puja" of Shiva is to be performed with mantra.

नमो भगवते सकलगुणात्मशक्तियुक्तात अनन्ताय योगपीठात्मान नमः

"Namo Bhagwate Sakalgunatmshkatiyuktate Anantaye Yogpethatman Namah".

It is to be worshipped by invoking him on the seat (Asan). This is to be followed by Nyasa of Rishis. After this Karanga Nyasa and Nyasa of Panchamurthi namely, Ishan, Tatpurusha, Aghore, Bamadeva and Sadya Jata and Panchakala Nyasa of Ishan are to be completed. Then Nyasa of the six limits of the body of Maheshwara is to be practiced . Next the Sadhaka is to meditate on the God SHIVA, keeping his image before the mind's eye. After completion of meditation Arghya is to be placed. The CONCH is not used in SIVA Puja. This is to be followed by Pith Puja according to Saiva Cult. Then Abraran Puja is to be performed after invocation and offering of Pancha Pushpa to the God. Finally the puja is to be completed with the ceremonial immersion of incense etc. and other religious rites. Five lakh japas for Purascharan and fifty thousand Homa are necessary.

4. Lord Ganesh

All human desires and ambitions are fulfilled by uttering the mantra of this God. The God is to be worshipped with the mantra Gang (गं)

Methods of Worship

After completing all religious duties of the morning including Pith Nyas all other Gods are to be worshipped by uttering.

ॐ तीव्रायै नमः ज्वालिनै नन्दायै भोगदायै कामरूपिण्यै उग्रायै तेजवत्यै सत्यायै विन्धनाशिन्यै सर्वशक्तिकमलासनाय नमः

"Om Teevaraye Namah Jawaliney Nandaye Bhogdaye Kamrupenaye Ugraye Tevatye Satyaye Vindhnashinaye Sarvashakti Kamalasnaye Namah".

The seat is to be offered to this God with the Pith mantra. This is be followed by Rishi Nyas and Karanga Nyas . After this, the devotee is to meditate on this God and at the end of Manasa Puja, Arghya is to be placed. This being over, Pith Puja and Puja of Pith Devata on the crest of the lotus petal is to be performed. Then repetition of meditation of this God is to be followed by invocation and offering of Panch Pushpa. Thereafter, Abaran Puja and worship of Panch Pushpa and worship of all other Gods with this mantra. ?

"Om Ganadipatye Namah" etc, are to be performed. Then the devotee has to perform Sarauga Puja. This God is to be worshipped on the petals of lotuses by reciting the mantra:-

ॐ वक्रतुण्डोय नमः, ॐ एकदन्ताय नमः, ॐ महादेवाय नमः, ॐ गजाननाय नमः, ॐ लम्बोदराय नमः, विक्टाय नमः, ॐ विन्धबाजाय नमः, ॐ घूम्रवर्णाय नमः

"Om Vakartundoye Namha, Om Ekdantaye Namah, Om Mahadevaye Namah, Om Gajannaye Namah, Om Lambodraye Namah, Om Viktaye Namaha, Om Vindhbajaye Namaha, Om Dhumarvarnaeye Namaha".

Thus the pooja of this God is to be completed with the ceremonial throwing away a discarding of incense etc. Four lakh japas are required to be performed for Purascharan of this Mantra.

5. Lakshmi

Mantra The one letter Bij, Shree (श्रीं) is known as Lakshami Mantra.

The worship of Goddess Lakshmi brings fortune and prosperity. All desires are fulfilled by uttering the mantra of this Goddess.

Methods of Worship

"Nyasa" of Rishi is to be practised after completion of religious duties and ceremonies of the morning including Pitha Nyasa. Then Nyasa of Nava Sakti is to be performed with the mantra:- "Shirsi Bhirge Rishishaye Namah, Mukhe Nivardaraytrichhnd Se Namah, Hirdaye Shireye Namaha, Om Vibhutayee Namaha". It is to be followed by Asan Nyas and Karanga Nyas.Then the worshipper should meditate on the Goddess uttering. "I adore her who is holding a lotus tipper in the right hand and showering blessings with her lower right hand as well as holding a lotus in her upper left hand and abhay Mudra in her lower left hand, who is seated on a lotus with a crown of jewels on her head, clad in silk cloth". In this manner, Mannas Puja and placing of the conch is to be completed. After Pith Puja of Nav Shakti on the crest of Lotus Petals is to be performed. Then he should again sit in meditation of her image and complete all of her religious rites including invocation and offering of Panch Puspa to her. At the end of these, "Abaran Puja" is to be gone through. After this, lords of ten directions, Indra and others with their weapons are to be worshipped. The puja is to be finished with the immersion of incense etc. Twelve lakh Japas are necessary for Purascharan of this mantra.

6. MahaLakshmi

Mantra and Rules of Worship

ओं क्रीं ह्रीं श्रीं ल्लीं हैसौ जगतूप्रसूत्यै नमः

'Oong Kareeng Hareeng Shareeng Laleeng Hasoo Jagtuprasutaye Namaha".

Methods of Worship

Having completed the religious duties of the morning including Pith Nyasa as mentioned in Lakshami mantra, Rishi Nyas is to be performed. Then after purifying of the hand Nyasa, Panch Bija is to be practised by adding Pranab at the beginning and names at the end while counting the joints of the fingers. Then Nyasa of the entire body from the crown of the head to toe is to be performed with the basic mantra. After the Nyaa of 'Sapta-bhatu' such as skin, flesh, blood, fat, bone, marrow and semen is to be practised by uttering the mantra.

By purifying the palm with the basic mantra, Nyasa of Pancha Bij is to be performed with Five fingers. This is to be followed by Kara Nayasa and Anga Nyasa with the above mantra.

Meditate on the Goddess after Manas Puja and conch is placed. After that Pitha Puja and Panch Pushpa etc, is to be performed. Perform Abaran Puja, then puja of Asta Shakti such as Uma and others is performed on lotus petals. After this Sankhanidhi on the right Padmanidhi on the left and Barun in the West are to be worshipped.

The twelve Rashis, nine planets and eight elephants (Asta Gaja) such as Oirabat, Pundarik, Baman and others are to be worshipped all round the Goddess, to be followed by the Puja of Indra and other Gods with their weapons. Then Puja is to be completed with the immersion of incense etc. Twelve lakh japas are to be performed for Purascharan of this mantra. At the end of Purascharan, one lakh twenty thousand burnt offerings (Homa) with lotuses are necessary.

If the Sadhaka performs the puja of Gods and Goddesses with rituals, methods and rules in soul and body, he is sure to meet with success.

Other Mantras

A few tried and tested mantras for specific purposes are provided for the guidance of readers.

1. *Eye Diseases*

Aruna mantra must be repeated 10,000 times for siddhi. Mantra reads as:-

"ओं अरूण हुं फट् स्वाहा"

"Om Arun Haem phut swaha",

Then water must be purified by uttering the mantra seven times and eye should be washed with this water. It will cure even serious eye diseases.

2. *Ear Diseases*

"ओं दां दारवासिनोभ्यां नमः"

This should be recited 1008 times.

3. *Tetanus*

"ओं यं धनुर्धरिमम्यां नमः"

This should be recited 1008 times.

4. *Throat Cancer*

"ओं चिं चित्रपटाम्यां नमः"

This mantra should be recited 1008 times.

5. *Mental Diseases*

"ओं उं उमादेबिम्यां नमः"

This mantra is to be recited 1008 times.

6. *Stammering*

"ओं सं सर्वमंगव्याम्यां नमः"

Recite the mantra 1008 times.

7. *Protection from Enemies And Thieves*

Recite this mantra 1008 times for siddhi. When anybody teases you, opposes or troubles you, recite the mantra 21 times with his name. He will stop troubling you.

"ओं ऋषमाय नमः"

Again if on the road there is any trouble, take 4 small stones and repeat the mantra 21 times and throw the stones on the four sides.

8. *Advancement of Learning of Children*

"ओं महेश्वराय नमः"

Recite this mantra 1008 times for siddhi. Take 16 gunjas weight of powdered vasa in milk saying the mantra 1008 times. This must be drunk by young boys and girls. It must be done for forty days after which they become good students, scholars and may even become poets.

9. *Getting Children*

This mantra is from santan Gopata Statra. This must be recited 1008 times by the pregnant lady the mantra reads as:-

ओं देवकी सुत गोविंद वासुदेव जगत्यते दहि मे तनयं कृष्ण त्वामहं शरणं गतः

10. *Attainment of Peace of Mind and Happiness*

This mantra is from Kama Ratna and is known as Sarvarishtan Asana Mantra.

"ओं क्षौं क्षौं"

By reciting this mantra, procure the root of white arkar or oak on Sunday in Pushyami nakshatra and bind it to the shoulder. This will remove all troubles bestowing the sadhaka with happiness and peace of mind.

11. *Securing Easy Delivery*

Recite this mantra repeatedly in the delivery room. This mantra is from kama Ratanam.

"अं ओं हां नमस्त्रिमूर्तय"

12. *Palpitation of The Heart*

When Panchakshari or ASTAKSHARI mantras (Already provided in this chapter) are repeated a few times it produces an immediate effect.

There are thousands of mantras described in Mantra Maharnava and Mantra Mahodadhi and in Tantra texts.

These mantras are very powerful. They are not to be sneered at. When properly recited, they are a boon.

Other Uses of Mantras

1. *Vashi Karan Mantra*

This mantra is used for others to be kind to the Sadhaka. It brings others under control. The mantra should be used for couples whose relations are strained, or for superiors, officers, ministers, colleagues etc. This mantra should not be used for nefarious means to control beloved, other men and ladies. No doubt it will work, but this is not the correct use of this mantra.

(i) *Mantra:* "ॐ नमों सर्वलोक वशीकराय कुरु कुरु स्वाहा"

"Om namo Sarvlok Vashikaraye Kuru Kuru Swaha"

In Pushya rakshatra, uproot the roof of Puran-rava plant. Recite the mantra 7 times and wear it on the arm. All will be kind to you.

(ii)Supari (used in betel should be infused 108 times with this mantra. Whosoever is offered this supari and eats it, will be under your control. It is best to take sweet supari packets duly infused and kept with you for use.

Mantra:- "ॐ देव नमो हरये ठं ठं स्वाहा"

"Om Dev namo Hrarye tha tha Swaha"

(iii)The mantra should be recited ten thousand times to attain siddhi. After that take any good fruit and infuse it with the mantra 108 times. Whosoever will take the fruit will remain under your control.

Mantra:- "ॐ ह्रीं मोहिनी स्वाहा"

"Om Hareeng Mohini Swaha"

(iv)Rise early in the morning and after your ablutions purify the water with 7 mantras and with the name of the person required to be brought under control. Drink this water. Repeat for 21 days. The person concerned will be under your control.

Mantra:- "ॐ चिमी चिमी स्वाहा"

"Om Chimi Chimi Swaha"

This mantra too can be used to control the enemy. Procure 7 red chillies with branch. Light a fire, recite the above mantra adding the name of enemy before the word "Swaha" and put one chilly in the fire. Repeat 7 times for 11 or 21 days. For enemy, this should be started on Tuesday or Saturday.

(v) "ॐ नमो कामाख्या देव्यै अमुक में वशकरी स्वाहा"

"Om namo kamakhaya devoye Amuk me Vshakari Swaha"

Recite this mantra ten thousand times. Replace the name of lady in the place of word Amuk in the mantra and then recite for siddhi. Use the articles by infusing 7 times with this mantra and give it to the lady to eat. She will come under your control.

(vi)This is a Mohammadan Mantra which reads as " Eena etevena shetan meri shakal ban Amuk ke pas jana oose mere pass lana rahi to turi Bahan, bhanji, par teen san teen talag"

Stand naked on the wrong side of cot, take Gur in your hand and recite the mantra 121 times. Keep Gur under the cot and sleep during the night. In the morning, the Gur should be distributed among the boys. Replace the name of lady in place of word Amuk in the mantra. The lady will approach you within 7 days.

(vii) Ladies can use this mantra to control their husbands who have gone astray, those who do not cooperate and are out of control. This mantra too can be used to control enemies, opponents, superiors and others.

"ॐ नमो महार्यक्षष्ये मम पति मे वशय कुरू कुरू स्वाहा"

"Om namo maharyakshaya Mam Pati me vashya kuru kuru Swaha"

Recite the mantra 108 times duly performing Homa. The articles used in such mantra must be infused with recitation 7 times with above mantra and given to the husband to eat to control him.

(viii)In "Aagam Tantra" this "Kam Gayatri" Mantra is provided, which is most effective.

"ॐ मनोभवाय विधाहे कन्दपयि धीमहि तन्त्रः कामः प्रचोदयात् ।"

"Om Manobhavay Vidahe Kandpye demahi Tantra Kama Parchodayat".

Recite this mantra 1.25 lacs times to attain siddhi and to appease Kam Devta. After that use this mantra for any lady who will be infatuated and remain satisfied under your control.

(ix) *Kamakhya Vashi Karan Mantra:* A most effective mantra. This mantra is to be recited one lakh times for siddhi. Replace the name of lady or person instead of word Amuk in the mantra.

"ॐ नमः कामाक्षी देवी आमुकी में वंश कुरू कुरू स्वाहा"

"Om Namo Kamakshi Devi Aamuki me Vansham Kuru Kuru Swaha".

After attaining siddhi of this mantra use any of the following methods and articles etc, which can be exorcised 108 times by the above mantra and the desired results are obtained.

1)Take out the dust from all nails of hands, feet and nose on Sunday. Exorcise and then give to lady or any person to eat in bettel leaf.

2)Make a powder of Kakjanga, Kesar, Mausil and Tagar. Exorcise 108 times with above mantra. Preserve the powder and put on the forehead of the lady or any person who will become infatuated with you.

3)Procure on Sunday flowers, leaves, root, trunk and branch of black dhatura tree or plant. Mix in them Kesar, camphor and Gorochan. Make a powder of all. Exorcise the same 108 times. Put tilak on your forehead and go before the lady or any person, who will be subjected to vashi karam.

4)Make a powder of Brahm Dandi and Ash from a cremation ground and recite the above mantra over it. Put it on the head of lady or any person.

5)The meat of an owl must be dried in the shade, powdered and exorcised 108 times with the above mantra. Put the powder on the head of a lady or any person for infatuation.

(x) " ॐ चामुण्डे हुलु हुलु चुलु वशमानय अमुकी स्वाहा"

"Om Chamunde huloo huloo Chuloo Vashmaney Amuki Swaha".

This mantra must be recited ten thousand times to attain siddhi by replacing the name of lady or any person in the mantra. After that exorcise any food or betel leaf 7 times and give to the lady or any person, who will come under your control.

2. *Uchatan Mantras*

These Uchatan Mantras are used for anybody to distract him from his path, and then wander. He will not be able to concentrate on a matter. These mantras are used for your opponents, enemies etc.

A man who has abandoned his family can best be brought back through the use of this mantra. In another case when a man or a lady has illicit relations with the opposite sex resulting in ill fame to the family and the destruction of the happiness or prosperity of the family, these mantras can be used to correct her or him. These mantras can also be used for men, ladies, enemies and friends. However, misuse of mantra is prohibited.

(i) "ॐ नमो भगवते रुद्राय करालाय अमुक पुत्र बान्धवैस्सह शीघ्र मुच्चाटय ठः ठः ढः"

"Om namo bhagvate rudraye karalaye Amuk Putra Bhandvasasyah Shighra muchchataye tha tha tha".

This mantra should be recited ten thousand times to attain siddhi. Replace the name of person in mantra in place of Amuk word.

When you want to use this mantra, procure the articles to be used and infuse them 108 times, then give the person concerned. He will be affected.

(ii) "ॐ श्रीं श्रीं श्रीं स्वाहा"

"Om shareem shareem shareem swaha"

Recite this mantra ten thousand times for siddhi. Then purify the articles 1089 times and use them for the person concerned.

(iii) Recite this mantra ten thousand times as above. Replace the name of person in place of word Amuk.

'ॐ नमो भीमास्याय अमुक ग्रहे उच्चारण कुरुकुरु स्वाहा'

"Om namo Bhimasaye Amuk Grahe Uccharan Kuru Kuru Swaha"

USE : The above mantras may be used as directed below:-

1. Take a wood of Gular tree about 12 inches long. It should be purified with any of the above mantras siddhi 108 times and buried in the house where Uchattan is required.
2. Take a bone of a male 12 inches long and use as above.

3. Homa be performed with the recitation of name of preson considered for Uchattan with above mantra using the wings of a crow and owl. Ahuties in homa must be done 108 times on Tuesday or Sunday.
4. Lemon wood, owl's bone, nail and skin of cat, Juice of Dhatura and a bone from cremation ground. All must be purified 21 times. In any house and wherever they be buried or thrown, the inmates will be subject to Uchattan.
5. A shiva linga be pointed with Braham Dandi and ash of cemetery, On Saturday night shiva linga alongwith white sarsoon can be thrown in the house of person for whom Uchattan is required.
6. Procure dust of the place where Asses relax at Noon, while facing East or West in left hand. This must be purified 108 times. Throw the dust for 7 continuous days in a house. All inmates will be affected by Uchattan.

(iv) Eye of the owl be purified for 108 times with this mantra:

'ॐ नमो वीर हुं हुं नमः"

"Om Namo Veer Hoong Hoong Namaha".

The eye be thrown in between two friends or husband and wife etc. They will be at dagger's drawn. But its use is prohibited under the Tantric law being a nefarious use.

3. *Maran Mantra*

The mantras have been provided in the author's books, "Ppacticals Of Mantra And Tantra" and have not been provided here as these can be used for nefarious purposes.

4. *Videshan Mantras*

Videshan Mantras Are Used To Create Differences between two or more persons. These are used when a person puts loss to others and cannot be controlled. These mantras are used for their home and other affaris, so that they do not find time to tease others. You can use these mantras against your enemies.

However, nefarious use is made by some persons to create differences between husband and wife, father and son, brothers, friends etc, which must be avoided. Use these mantras for good and healthy purposes. The Shastras have however premitted the use of these mantras for self protection.

We provide a few mantras for such purpose.

"ॐ नमो नारदाय अमुकस्य अमुकेन सह विद्धेषणं कुरु कुरु स्वाहा"

"Om Namo Nardaya Amukasya Amuken Seh Vidheshna kuru Kuru Swaha".

Recite this mantra one lakh times, use the name of persons between whom differences are to be created in place of words Amukasaya and Amukan in the mantra. When you attain siddhi of this mantra, it should be used. Infuse the articles used for Videshan with 108 mantras and use them.

"ॐ नमो नारायणाय अमुकस्य अमुकेम सह विद्धेषण कुरु कुरु स्वाहा"

"Om Namo Naryane Amukasaya Amukem Seh Videshan Kuru Kuru Swaha".

This mantra be recited 10 lac times in 21 days.

Change the words of person in place of words Amukasaya and Amukem in the mantra. Then purify the articles of Videshan with 108 mantras and use them.

"ॐ विस्वाय नामगंर्धव लोचनी नामो लौर्सात करनै तस्मै विस्वाय स्वाहा"

"Om Visvaye Namgandharv Lochni Namo losart Karne Tasmey Viswaye Swaha".

Recite this mantra one thousand times while standing and perform homa with 1000 mantras.

Procure in Punarvasu nakshatra four inches long wood of Chitavar tree and infuse it 7 times with above mantra. Bury it in the house of enemy. They will leave the house and will be subject to Uchattan.

5. *Stambhan Mantra*

Stambhan mantras are those through which you can stop your enemy, opponents from creating trouble. Through these mantras you can control the activities of others which are not in your interest.

We provide a few mantras for the same.

"ॐ नमो भगवते शत्रुणां बुद्धि स्तम्भनं कुरू कुरू स्वाहा"

"Om Namo bhagvate Shatrunam Budhi Stambam Kuru Kuru Swaha".

Recite this mantra ten thousand times. Infuse the articles 108 times with this mantra and use them. The intelligence of the enemy will become nil and he will not be able to do any mischief. Replace the name of enemy or person with the word "Shatru" in the mantra.

6. *Shanti Mantras*

Shanti mantras are used to cure diseases, to remove the influences of souls and planets etc.

1. *For Good Health*: The following mantra be recited three times and infuse the water; the water to be drunk by the patient or Sadhaka. One will be benefited.

Mantra

"ॐ अहं वैश्वानरो भूत्वा प्राणिनां दहमाक्षितः प्राणापान समायुक्तः पचाम्यन्नं चतुर्विधम्"

"Om Aaham Veshvanye Bhootva Praneenam Dahmakshiet Pranapan Samyukta Pchamyananm Chaturvidham".

2. *To Prevent Abortion* : (i) If a woman does not conceive or is aborted due to some reason or other, then the use of this mantra is very useful.

"पुमांसं पंत्र जनय तं पुमाननु जायताम् भवाति पुत्राणां माता जतानां जवयाश्यं यान् ।"

"Pumansam Patram Janey Tam Pumananu Jayatam
Bhavati Putranam Mata Jatanam Jamyashyam Yan"

This mantra is from *atharva veda* 3/23.

At the time of prayer daily in the morning, take a vessel full of pure water, keep it before your Ishat or God. After finishing your daily prayer, take a few drops of water and reciting this mantra, shower the drops on the lady. A small quantity of water may be taken by her.

(ii) When a lady does not conceive after the birth of child or there are continuous abortions after that such state is called "KAKVANDYA". In such a case, when she wants one more child, the following mantra be recited 108 times daily for 21 days.

Mantra :

"ॐ नमः शक्तिरूपाय यम ग्रहे पुत्रं कुरू कुरू स्वाहा"

"Om Nama shaktirupaye Yam Griahe Putram Kuru Kuru Swaha".

In addition to the above mantra, the following be also followed.

Bring the root of Ashavgand on Sunday during Pushya nakshatra and mix it with milk of Buffalo. Make powder of it. This be taken by the lady with milk one or two tolas daily. After seven days, She will conceive.

3. *For Birth of Son:* This is a very strong and TESTED mantra, which is said to have been desired by LORD SHIVA to PARVATI for securing a son

"ॐ ह्रीं ह्रीं ह्रूं पुत्रं कुरू कुरू स्वाहा"

"Om Hareeng Hareeng Haroong Putram Kuru Kuru Swaha".

Thee lady should recite this mantra on a branch of a mango tree or under the mango tree at a lonely place. The mantra be recited before lord SHIVA and PARVATI 108 times daily and for 21 days continuously.

4. *To Cure Piles :* The mantra reads as :-

"खरामान की टेनीशाह खुनी बादी दोंनों जाय उमतो उमतो चल चल स्वाहा"

Infuse water with mantra thrice and wash the private place with this water. Take a red cotton thread and put 7 knots in it. Infuse this thread 21 times with the above mantra and tie on big toe of foot. Piles will be cured.

5. *Cure From Epilepsy* : When one suffers from the fit of epilepsy. Write this mantra on Bhooj Patra with Ashot Gard and put it on the neck of the patient. One will be cured.

"हाल हर सरगम मंडिका पुडिका श्रीराम फूंक मृगी वायु सुखै ॐ ठः ठः स्वाहा"

"Hal har sargam Mandika Poodika Shri Ram Phoonk mirgi vayu sukhe om the tha Swaha".

8

SPECIFIC MANTRAS

We will provide a few very important mantras for various purposes. These effective mantras must be recited as per directions with full faith and rituals to gain one's objectives.

1. For Sarv Sidhi

Mahamritanje Mantra is the most auspicious mantra in the Vedas. Daily recitation of this mantra is very useful to the Sadhaka and saves and helps man in the many difficulties and hurdles of life. It is a tested mantra of the author.

However, in mantra shakti samphut is added. The Sadhaka should recite this mantra one lakh times. It bestows the person with health, wealth and power. It saves the Sadhaka from Akal Mritayu or untimely death.

The mantra with samphut is as below: This mantra is known as Amrit Sanjivni Nidya Mantra.

To attain desires and Vidya or education, recite the mantra and pour sweet milk water on the SHIV LINGA.

Mohamri Tanje Mantra

"ॐ हौं जूँ सः भूर्भवः स्व त्र्यम्बकं याजामहे सुगन्धि पुष्टिवर्द्धनम नम्, उर्वा रुक्मिक बन्धनान्मृत्योभूक्षीय मामृतात् । भूर्भवः स्वरो जू सा हौं "

" Om Hoong joon Sah Bhoorbhava Swaha
Tarayambakam yajyamaha Sughandhim Pushtivardhanam.
Urvarukmev Bandhnan mritiyo bhukshaye Mamritat.
Bhoorbhva Sawaron joon sa Hoong Om"

Another way to use Samphut in Mahamritanje Mantra is as:-

"ॐ हौं जूँ सः ॐ भूर्भवः स्व ॐ त्रयम्बकंयजामहे ॐ तस्यवितुवरिण्य ॐ सुगन्धि पुष्टवर्धनम् ॐ भर्गोदेवस्य धीमहि ॐ उर्वारुकमिव बन्धनात् ॐ धियो यो नः प्रचोदयात् ॐ मृत्योर्मुक्षीय ॐ माऽमृतात् ॐ स्व भुवः भूः ॐ सः जूं हौं ॐ"

"Om Hoong joon Sah om Boorbhava Swaha om Tarayambakam yajyamaha om Tasyavitur Varaneyam om sugandhim Pushtivardhanam om Bhargo Devasya Dhimahi Om Urvarukmev Bandhnat Om Diyo yo na Prachodyat Om mrjtiyomukshaye Mamritat Om Swaha Bhoova Bhoo Om Sah joon Hoong Om".

2. For Education

Another strong mantra for education, intelligence and wealth is given below . This must be recited one lakh times.

'ॐ क्रीं क्रीं क्रीं' "Om Kreeng Kreeng Kreeng".

Another powerful mantra for the above purposes can be recited one lakh times also.

(i) "ॐ सच्चिदा कैमं ब्रह्म ह्रीं सच्चिदेकानेक ब्रह्म"

"Om Sacheda Keem Bharm Hareeng Sachedakanek Bharm".

(ii)"ॐ सच्चिदा कैमं ब्रह्म"

"Om Sacheda Keemam Bhram".

One rosary of the above mantra should be recited daily for 41 days.

3. For Attaining Moksha

To attain Moksha, one should recite one rosary of the following mantras daily. These are very powerful mantras.

ॐ नमो भगवते सर्व भूत आत्मने वाररिवाय सर्व आत्म संयोग योगपद्म पीठ आत्मने नमः

"Om Namo Bhagwate Sarv Bhut Atmaney Varrivaye

Sarv Atam Sanyog Yogpadam Pith Atmaneye Namah".

(ii) "ॐ श्रीं ह्रीं क्रीं कृष्णाये स्वाहा"

"Om Shree Hreeng Kreeng Krishnaye Swaha".

4. Lakshmi Mantra

Recite this mantra one lakh times five times daily. One is blessed with wealth.

This is TESTED MANTRA.

"ॐ नमो धनदायै स्वाहा"

"Om Namo Dhandaye Swaha"

This same mantra holds good for Shri Vidya, Bhuvneswari, as these are the other names she is known by in other parts of the country.

The mantra bestows, wealth and happiness and is also recited in case of troubles and turmoils.

5. For Success In Election

Success in election depends upon intelligence, connections with public and the workd one does for the people of the area, sharing their sorrows and grief. In order to be successful in politics one must be close to the people.

To achieve all the above objectives, one should recite any one of the following mantras with full confidence 11 times a day for 41 days. One will be crowned with success and occupy high office as a minister etc.

(i) ॐ इममिन्द्र वर्धय क्षत्रियं म इमं विशमेक वृषं कृणु त्वम्
निरमित्रानक्षणु हास्य सर्वास्तान् रुधयास्मा आहमुत्तरषु

"Om emminder Vardhaye shteriyame ma emam Vishmek virsham Kirinu Tawam,

Nirmitranakshanu Hasye Sarvastan Randyasma Ahmutrashu".

(ii) अयमस्तु धनपतिर्धनानाभमं विशां विश्वपतिरस्तु राजा
अस्मिन्द्रि महि वर्चासि घेह्यवचसं कृणुहि शत्रुभस्म

Aayemastu Dhanpatidharnanabhayme Visham Vishwpatirastu Raja

Asminndera Mahi Varcharsi Ghehavchasam Krinuhi Shatrubhasam".

"युनिज्म त उतरावन्तमिन्द्र येन जयन्ति न पराजत ते
यस्त्वां करदेकवृषं जनानामूत्त राज्ञा मूतमं मानपानाम्"

"Yunijam ta uttravantminder Yana Jayanti na Prajat Te,

Yastavam Kardekvarsham Jananamutam Manpanam".

6. For Yash Prapati

Yash Prapati means, you may do any good to a person or persons, but they will not realize it and will not be thankful to you. Instead they will criticise or demand such favours as their right.

By the Japa of these mantras all people will be indebted to you. You will be respected and others will acknowledge the good done to them. These mantras must be recited 11 times a day for 41 days continously.

"ॐ गिरावरगराटेषु हिरण्ये च गोषु च
सुरायां सिचयमानायां कीकाले मधु तन्मयि"

"Om giravargrateshu Hirnye ch goshu cha.

Surayam Sicheymanayam kekale madhu Tanmeye".

7. For Having Progeny

In case the couple does not have a child, one can acquire progeny through mantras, provided one does the Sadhana with full faith following the prescribed rituals.

(i) "ॐ श्री ही हीं कली गली" (Mool Mantra)

"Om shree Hareeng Kaleeng Galeen".

"ॐ देवकीसुत गोवन्द ! वासुदेव जगत्मये"

"देहि ये तनय कृष्ण ! त्वामहं शरणं गतः"

"Om Devekisut Govind Vasudev Jagatpite"

"Dehi ye Taney Krishna Tawamahem Sharanam Gata"

This mantra should be recited 3 lakh times continuously.

(ii) ॐ नमो भगवते जगत्रसूतयै नमः

"Om Namo Bhagwate Jagatprasutaye Nam"

This mantra too must be recited 3 lakh times continuously.

(iii) ॐ कलीं गोपालवेषधराय वासुदेवाय हूं फट् स्वाहा

"Om Kaleeng Gopalveshdhraya Vasudevaye Hoong Phut Swaha".

This is a Tested Mantra

Recite the mantra one lakh times and then perform Homa with sugar, curd, ghee , rice and five types of dry fruits (Mix them with water and boil. This is known as Khir in Hindi). Before Japa is started perform pooja of Lord Krishna sitting inside the blooming flower of Lotus कमल के मध्य में विराजमान भगवान बालकृष्ण Kamal You will surely be blessed with a son.

Important: A client approached this author with the above problem. He was advised to do the above Sadhana. He came back after six months without any result. On being questioned the client replied that he had entrusted this task of Japa to a Pandit.

The author disapproved his action and invited his attention to the warning already published in the famous book. "Saturn A FRIEND OR FOE"?

"Hired persons do not pay. Your own Karmas will pay you What you want to get done. Do it yourself and then feel the results. Do not waste money on false hopes."

After that the couple did Sadhana themselves and were blessed with two handsome sons within a period of 3 and a half years. They had a daughter earlier.

So dear readers do the Japa and prayer yourself.

8. Karodh Shanti Mantra (to Reduce Rash Temper)

This mantra controls one's anger. When one suffers due to anger and there is constant bickering in the family, this mantra should be recited 21 times and water be infused with it. The water should be sprinkled three times on the face of the person.

Mantra: "ॐ शांते प्रशान्ते सर्व क्रोध पशनोन स्वाहा"

"Om shante Parshante sarv Karodh Pashnon Swaha".

9. For Successful Completion of All Jobs

A TESTED mantra is given below. It must be recited ten thousand times to obtain Sidhi of the mantra. When you are to start any work or have a meeting with any important man for some specific work, etc recite this mantra 108 times. You will succeed in obtaining your goals.The mantra reads as:-

Mantra: "ॐ नमो सर्वार्थसाधनी स्वाहा"

"Om Namo sarvarthsadhni Swaha"

10. To Attract All Or Anyone

This mantra is called "SARV AAKARSHAN MANTRA".

Mantra: "ॐ चामुण्डे तरुततु अमुकाय अकर्षय अकर्षय स्वाहा"

"Om Chamunde Tarutatu Amukaye akarshaye Akarshaye Swaha".

Recite this mantra one thousand times daily for 21 days. Replace the name of the person in place of the word "Amuk". One will be infatuated. This is a TESTED mantra . Every male or female can use this mantra.

11. To Appease Devas, Ishat

Mantra: "ॐ ह्रीं नमः" "Om Hareeng Nama"

Wear red clothes and a rosary of Red Kum Kum and recite the mantra for Seven day, 5000 times daily .The sadhaka will have the blessing of his/her God. Whoever one desires will also become infatuated.

One should recite this mantra all the time for comforts etc.

9

ARTICLES USED FOR PUJA

In the previous chapter, we have written at places that articles be infused for a specific work and homa be performed with articles for specific purposes. In the absence of details of such articles, the Sadhaka gets baffled, so given below is a list of such articles required to be infused and used in Homa.

Articles For Homa and Infusing

1. *For Vashikaran*

The articles are Beel leaves, wings of crows, Jasmin (Chandi) flowers, Kaneer flowers, Rae and salt . The Deva is Saraswati Devi.

2. *For Shanti Karan*

Use milk, til, ghee, leaves of peepal and mango tree and also samdhas of these trees. The Deva is Rati (wife of Kam Dev) Devi.

3. *For Stambhan*

The articles are Beel leaves, barley, Kamalghati, curd and ghee. The Deity is Lakshmi Devi.

4. *For Uchattan*

Use hair of the person for whom the mantra is used, seeds of cotton and Neem and Crow wings.The deity is Durga.

5. *For Videshan*

The articles are Beel leaves and Chirozi. The Devi is Jyeshtha.

6. *For Maran*

We have deliberately not provided any mantra, Yantra or Tantra for this nefarious use. However, the articles are Dhatura leaves, poison mixed with blood, milk of goat, ghee, cotton, flesh and bone of man, nails of Sadhaka, Sarsoon oil, wing of crow owl and other birds, Bilwa, Sarsoon, aak milk, pepper, chilly and peepal tree milk. Deva or Deity is Bhadra Kali Devi.

Other Purposes

For birth of girl Kheel for wife and women with Mamal, Homa is to be performed.

For Siddhi, use curd and Ghee.

For Officers, Ministers etc., use fruit, ghee, bilue leaves and til.

For longevity use, ghee , til, mango leaves in Homa etc.

For fever, use mango leaves.

For rain, use sandha of beet and its leaves.

To attain proficiency in speaking, use ghee, and gugal.

For Saraswati Siddhi, use Malika flowers, Jatu and Punag and fruits of Nagkesar.

Use only the articles prescribed for a particular purpose.

Tithis and Days

1. Santi Karan should be performed on 2nd, 3rd, 5th, 7th tithies. The particular days are Monday, Wednesday, Thursday and Friday. This can be permitted on any day or on any tithi but is best if carried out during an auspicious moment, as it gives success speedily.
2. Vashi Karan is to be performed on 10th, 11th, Amavas, 9th and 1st tithis . The auspicious days are Sunday and Friday.
3. Stambhan Karan is to be performed on 5th , 10th and pornima tithies following on Monday and Wednesday.
4. Uchattan mantras are to be performed or recited on 8th, 14th, 6th tithis. Rikta tithi of Sunday is also good. All days are auspicious except Saturday, Rikta tithi means 4th, 9th and 14th.
5. Videshan Mantras are to be recited on Poornima, Rikta tithis of Sunday, Saturday, Sunday are auspicious.
6. Maran Mantras are to be recited and Used on 14th, 8th and Amavas tithis. The days are Saturday,Tuesday and Sunday. They

can also be performed when malefic planets are rising.

Time

A day is divided normally into 4 parts from sunrise to sunset. In the first part of the day, Vashi Karan is to be performed, the Second part is good for Videshan and Uchattan Mantras. The rest of the day is useful for Shanti Karan, Uchattan, Stambhan and Maran.

Nakshatras

The following nakshatras are auspicious for various purposes.

1. Shanti Karan can be performed in any nakshatra.
2. Vashi Karan and Stambhan, auspicious nakshatras are Jyeshtha, Uttrashada, Anuradha, and Rohini.
3. Videshan, Uchattan and Maran Mantra are to be recited during swati, Hast, Mrigasira, Chitra, Uttraphalguni, Pushy, Punarvasu, Aswini, Bharni, Aridra, Dhanishta, Sarvana, Magha, Vaisakha, Krittika, Poorva phalguni, and Rewatinakshatras.

Auspicious Lagnas

1. For Shanti Karan, Vashi Karan, Maran and Uchattan Karan are to be performed during Aries, Virgo, Sagittarius,and Pisces Lagnas.
2. Stambhan is to be performed during Leo and Scorpio Lagnas.
3. Videshan and Uchattan are to be performed in Cancer and Libra lagnas.

At the end of this part, the author again requests the readers and Sadhakas that practice of Mantra siddhi be started confidently and using the precribed rituals. Do not use the mantras for any nefarious purposes. Start under the guidance of a competent preceptor or guru.

Your Own Sadhana will lead you to success. The author is in no way responsible for your failures.

Lord SHIVA will bless you with success.

Part III

TANTRAS

10

THE TANTRA AND ITS DIVISIONS

Definition

The word "Tantra" is composed of two words, viz तन्त्र is तन and त्रै. It means that through Sadhana Pooja, Bhakti and other methods one can mould nature and God according to one's desires. All methods of Sadhana are also called Tantra. The word in Shastras is defined thus:-

सर्वऽर्था येन तन्यन्ते त्रायन्ते च भयाज्जनान्
इति तन्त्रस्य तन्त्रस्वं तन्त्रज्ञा ! परचक्षे ते

If one knows in detail all mantras and their uses one can use it to protect the people from fear etc. and do good service for them.

According to others, Tantra is a Shastra through which we deal with various aspects like Pooja of SHIVA SHAKTI and others, administrative methods, rules, methods of dealing with others and Shastras which deals with the articles connected with the above points.

Tantra is a Sadhana, a method, a technique or a path and is available in all religions. One may have faith in any religion. One can practice or do Sadhana as it does not touch one's religion and faith, rather it strengthens it by way of Puja and prayer to God. One may be Hindu, Jain, Buddhist, Muslim, Christian or connected with any other religion. Tantra is a regulated path to bring God, the deities and others under one's control through worship and prayer as it contains various methods of Sadhana and use of materials in specified forms, under set rules and directions. People in general understand Tantra as magic or mysticism, a misgiving which is very deeply rooted in their minds. They feel that as a magician performs, miracles so too Tantra and its practitioners indulge in magic. In this material world every one has numerous desires and people are very egoistic. They forget that the law of nature denotes that if one wants anything one has to struggle for it . People want short cuts, that do not pay with Prakiriti or nature. The path is straight but one has to traverse through it safely and methodically, not casually.

In modern society every one is too busy. People have no time either for self-realisation or their immediate families. They seek help from astrologers, preceptors and religious guides who will perform their duty in return for money. One is ready to pay because one wants relief from evils, worries and turmoils. But how many have got so far? Hired persons do not help . One's own karmas will pay. Whatever one wants one should do wisely rather than waste money on false hopes and charlatans.

The above paragraph is from the author's famous book,"SATURN A FRIEND OR FOE"? This is applicable to Tantra also as people become distracted from Tantra when they do not attain the desired objects because they do not do Sadhana themselves and depend upon others. This is another reason that people have lost faith in our old age Tantra techniques.

The second name of Tantra is Aagam (आगम)) . These two are interconnected. Aagam is described in the sloka as:-

"आगम शिववक्रत्रेभ्यो, गतं च गिरिजामुखे
मतं च वासुदेवस्य, तत अगन उच्यते ।"

Aagam are the words which Lord SHIVA told to Parvati and which were accepted by Lord Vishnu. So the origins of Tantra can be traced to Lord Shiva, with the sanction of Lord Vishnu and which has further come down to mankind through Devi Parvati. Thus the way for Moksha and worldly affairs are contained in Aagam and Tantra.

Since tantra is not practiced scientifically and tantrics misguide others for their own gains, the public has lost faith in this system.

Tantra and Mantras are interconnected. Tantra cannot be successful without Mantra Siddhi. Unless both are practiced simultaneously success cannot be achieved in Tantra. On the other hand one can attain success and sidhi only in Mantra.

So readers, one should clearly understand that Tantra is a Sadhana and not magic. Tantra is a Sadhana, Shastra, consisting of a religion's treatise compiled by Lord SHIVA containing mystical formulae for the attainment of supernatural powers. It is NOT a religion.

In Mantra, Tantra and Yantra, one makes offerings to an image. This has been misunderstood and therefore needs some explanation. In the act of offering, the Tantrik identifies his or her own self with the image focussing that self upon it. The things offered are flowers, light, bells, ghee, incense, food etc, which are sensory symbols. One washes the image, touches it with coloured powders known as gulal, sindoor etc, and garlands it with flowers to honour it. Actually the Sadhaka, in the above process, welcomes the image into his or her home and into himself or herself. The offerings are made to different images in different ways. One of them is the Devi's image. Other's may be diagrammatic Yantras. Some images are in permanent materials, others are made of wood, mud or paper to be destroyed after use. However, it is often believed that the images gain power and value by being used in worship over long periods or by highly developed Tantriks. This has proved to be true.

Use of Mantras

The use of Mantras as already explained is the most important feature of Tantra. These mantras are syllables, single or strung together, most of which are without obvious meanings. They end in a nasal humming sound represented by m, k, or L. There are"seed mantras" otherwise called "Beej Mantras" which are forms of particular energies known to the Tantrikas. Although they are not identified with any worldly objects, they are associated with functional deities. Mantras are used continually in Tantrik rituals, and are whispered or chanted in different combinations and contexts. It is important that one must learn to speak them properly and to activate their meanings. The mantras may be written in Sanskrit letters on ritual objects, or on the yantra diagrams, or are painted on the yantras themselves.

Mantras uttered during the rituals are so designed as to create appropriate vibrations within a psychic field. The Tantrika utters beeja mantras, seed syllables of one pointed thought activity directing them towards different parts of his and his Sakti's body. During all these processes, he meditates on and repeats the Sanskrit mantras: "Om Harim Kling Kandarpa Svaha", "Om Ananda Bhairavyai Namah" or "Om Harim Krom Svaha", The male and female psyches are always atuned to the vibrations a powerful mantra can create. The seat is first sanctified with mantras for Asana shuddhi and then one takes the seat, made of grass, deer skin or a raw wool or cloth carpet.

Light and sound play an important role in the Panchamakara rite. Dim lights are required.Violet and red lights are of importance. In purifying themselves sadhakas make use of different colours such as red, violet or pink colours. The cosmic rays of colours that strike the body are incorporated within by the process of Pranayama. Corresponding vibrations are set up, as each breath has its own characteristic colour rays which penetrate various chakras, being absorbed and rediffused through chromatic colour breathing.

Asana and its Use

Tantriks often practice in a cremation ground, a rite known a Savasana. Meditation on a certain kind of corpse stresses the truth of transcience, consequently such a place is ideal for meditation. Thus the sadhaka or yogi's heart itself becomes a cremation ground–pride and selfishness, status and role, name and form all are burnt to ashes. Since a cremation ground and the midnight hours are best for undisturbed meditation, an explosion of Psychic potential occurs. The atmosphere is charged with powers that can frighten the aspirant. He first overcomes the terrifying images and temptations that confront him before an awareness of tranquillity can be established.

Asana is actually a step by step dissolution of the body into the subtle elements, a process of gradual involution whereby the body is identified with the sense of smell, water with taste, fire with vision, air with touch, ether with sound. These five elements are merged one by one into their sources with the potentials of the energies(Tanmatras) and ultimately ego(Ahan Kara), is dissolved into mahat, the great one. Shakti or pure consciousness is constantly coming down in a shower on human beings, but on account of cosmic bombardment, it is immediately trasformed and diffused throughout the body. In reuniting SHIVA SHAKTI, the adept can reach out and enjoy the benefits falling from the Sahastara Chakra, the centre of communication directly between the individual being and the infinite consciousness above.

Sj.Ajit Mookerjee in his book TANTRA ASANA has also said that the attainment of the state of perfect bliss is the ultimate aim of Tantra. Our ordinary pleasure experiences are of an extremely limited nature as they afford only fleeting glimpses of supreme joy. This ephemeral quality will always put us back, preventing the advance towards self realization.

Tantra Asana is one of the means of this realization. Asanas, the science of psychoyogic poses, are based upon a concept of the universe and of man's role in it. The asanas aim is to make one aware of one's potential and to realize and experience joy in being one with the cosmos. It is a yogic practice of transcending the human condition. Tantra itself is unique for being a synthesis of bhoga and yoga, enjoyment and liberation. There is no place for renunciation or denial in Tantra. Instead, one must involve oneself in all the life processes which surround us. The spiritual is not something that descends from above, rather it is to be discovered within. Tantra asana is a method of uniting the individual self with the Absolute Infinite (Atam and Brahman) in the cosmic conscious state known as Samadhi. Here there is only Pure Existence, SHIVA SHAKTI , where the formed and formless are united and merged. It is the state of Sat-Chit-Ananda, that is , pure Existence-Consciousness-Bliss.

A Study in Tantric Physiology

In the human body, there are several energy centres containing latent psychic powers. These are called chakras. If activated, they hold potential for reaching cosmic planes of existence. They can be portals to a new existence and the realization of inherent powers.

The Six main chakras of the human body are the Muladhara Chakra (at the base of the spine), Svadhisthana (near the generative organ) Manipura (near the naval), Anahata (near the heart) Visuddha (near the throat), and Ajna (between the brows). A seventh Chakra, situated four fingers above the cerebrum, is Sahasrara, symbolically represented by the thousand paralled lotus. Sahasrara is said to be the abode of Lord SHIVA, Cosmic consciousness, and Muladhara the seat of Shakti, from whom originates that Cosmic force known as KUNDALINI. Ultimately, Tantra asana aims to arouse Kundalini Shakti to unite with SIVA, realizing the highest, most intense joy Mahasukla.

The human body also contains Five sheaths of "Koshas".According to Tantra, only a third of the human body is in evidence – the rest is invisible. The five sheaths are

1.Anna Maya, 2. Prana Maya, 3. Mano Maya, 4. Vijnana Maya, 5. Ananda Maya.

The physical sheath of the body is called the Anna Maya Koshan, with earth, water and fire elements having their functions in the Muladhara, Swadhisthana and Manipura Chakras.

Para Maya is the sheath of the Vital Air. It holds the life force "Prana", which expresses itself in the form of air and space. These elements control the Anahata and Visuddha psychic centres.

Mamo Maya and Vijnana-Maya koshas are identified with the congnitive principle, the Ajna Chakra is their centre. When it is revealed, one sets the inner vision, a simultaneous knowledge of things as they really are and the third eye opens in the centre of the forehead.

All the six centres (Sat-Chakras) are located with the Meru Danda (the vertebral Column) not in the gross (Sthulasharira) but in the subtle body (Linga Shashira). As the repository of psychic energies, they govern the whole condition of being. However in man's normal state, these chakras are dormant.

Through planned meditative asanas, Kundalini Shakti, the great power within the human body, usually latent, lies awakened. This force is compared to a snake lying asleep in the body. Once released from the Muladhara Chakra, it uncoils and begins to rise upward, breaking open and transforming each energy centre as it ascends until Shakti enters the magnetic sphere of SHIVA consciousness.

In yogic practice, discipline of breathing is absolutely essential. Prana, the life force, or vital air, enters the human entity through these psychic centres and nadis getting diffused throughout according to different functions. These are known as Vayus (Vital Airs) which are important to the Tantric practitioner.

Need for a Guru

The Guru is a preceptor and a guide in the performance of puja and puja practiced and performed by a person who is uninitiated by a Guru becomes ineffective or fruitless. In Hindu shastras it is laid down that neither a visit to a place of pilgrimage nor the practice of meditation and observance of ritualistic vows by a person becomes successful unless initiated by a Guru.

One should perform all religious duties after being initiated by a competent and honest Guru. Just as a Brahmin is not entitled to the study of Vedas etc, relating to Satkarma unless and until his thread ceremony is performed, so also an uninitiated person has no right to worship gods and utter mantras. One is therefore, required to be initiated by a Guru according to Tantric rites.

Various kinds of initiation by a Guru have been mentioned in the Tantra Sastras. They are Sakti, Sambhabi, Mantri, Anabi, Kriyabati, Barnamoyee, Kalatma, Bidhanmdya etc. Despite different kinds of initiation, all produce the same effect and lead to liberation from bondage.

Division of Tantra

Tantra is an independent Shashtra, which indicates the way to bring situations and people under one's control in order to obtain one's desires through puja, sadhana and other methods. Sadhana Shastra contains the various methods of Sadhana which can be divided into FIVE parts.

1.PATTAL: (पटल) This part details the importance, of jaap for various desires, Homa, Mantra and Homa articles for a particular Deity or Deva. Use of mantras if any are also indicated in this.

2.PADDATI: (पद्धति) The methods of Sadhana indicated in this part, includes the methods of taking bath from morning to puja Jaap mantra, their use and methods of Sadhan for particular occasions.

3.KAWACH: (कवच) The method which we adopt to appease each devta through their names and pray for protection etc, is known as Kawach. It is a way through which Sidhi of Devtas is obtained. So in case of Sidhi, the Sadhaka cures the diseases. Kawach is used after japa. Kawach is written on Bhooj Patra, water and other articles and are infused with Kawach. Talismans are made through it and clothes etc. can also be infused for use in Tantra.

4.SAHASTRA NAM: (सहस्त्रनाम) Means thousand names. The verses contain the thousand names of the deity for which pooja is performed. These are worshipped through various methods and articles, Home etc which are indicated therein. This Sahastra Nam indicates the various detail of different deities etc. Specific mantras for sidhi of these deities are detailed therein.

5.STOTRA: (स्तोत्र) Stotras are the verses of Pooja, prayer of deities. Also methods are indicated for use of Mantra, method of making Yantras, use of medicines, and other details have been provided in the stotras.

The above five parts constitute Tantra Sastra. In Kaliyug, Tantra Vidya is more successful because Vedic mantras are like sleeping snakes due to bad Karmas of the people and are not so effective unless a Dharam-Atma or pious man obtains Sidhi for them.

Tantra and Religions

As already indicated above Tantra is being practiced since ancient times in all religions.

1. Jain Tantra

There are many old treatises in the Jain religion which deals with Tantra. In the second century we find Swayam bho Stotra by Samant

Bhadra, in 3rd century Shanti Satav by Mandev and in 4th Century Mahavir Stuti by Dish Sain. In 5th Century Shantyashatak by Pujepad and in 6th century Awasghar Stotar were written. Likewise in 7th Bhakatamar stotar in 8th Viswaphar Stotar , in 9th Shanti Satav, in 11th century Aakrishman dal stotar, Ekibhav Stotar and in 12th Century Kalyanmandir Stotar were written. Navgarah Stotra, Saraswati Stotra, Jawala Malini Kalp, Mantra Raj Rahas, Tantra Leelavati, Bhairon Padmavati Kalp, Chintamani Kapal and Mantradhi Raj were published in different centuries upto the 12th Century.

These stotras and books are known as Navkar Mantra Kalp, Loksas Kalp Namo Thun Kalp, Chander Pragyapti Kalp compiled by Jain munies and contain valuable material on Tantra vidya.

In Jainism Padmavati, Chakreshwari, Ambika etc, are held in high esteem as these deities are worshipped by them. Before the 5th century there were three main religions Vedic, Tapas and Bootak Vadi. People were attracted to Japas through the use of Mantra. Yantra and Tantra, Panch Agni Tap, Hathayog etc., were also included by them. Pasharvanth gave importance to Dhyanyog. Panch Namaskar was in vogue already but Beej Mantras were introduced in the namaskar and these mantras were used to cure diseases.

Saraswati and Devi Padmavati are worshipped by Jains. Saraswati Kalp is held in high esteem by them. So Shakti pooja was also done by them.

During the Jain period Pandrehiya, Beesi, Teesi, Chauthesia, Paastheia etc, six sided triangle (फट्कोण) Trivarat Ardh Varat, Hastakar, Istri shastar Kriti mulak, Parush Kriti etc., dealing with Yantra were compiled.

In addition Rishi Mandal Yantra, Namaskar, Chakar, Vijay Yantra, Sarvtobhador Yantra, Vijay Pataka, Arjun Pataka, Ravana Pataka, Hasti Yantra, Ashav Yantra, Sani Yantra were some standard works which were published. In Bihar today Vijay Raj Yantra, Vijay Pataka, Sarv to bhador Yantras are being used.

In Jainism Aarsh Vidhannushasan, Tantra Prakash, Koshtak Chintamani, Panchmaskriti, Deepak, Rishi Mandal, Yantra Vidhan etc, were standard works on Tantra which dealt with its different aspects, and have thus contributed a great deal. It now stands established that in Jainism, Yantra-Tantra and Mantra have been practiced for centuries and Jain Rishies have given us valuable knowledge of the subject much of which is still available and being practiced today.

2. *Buddhist Tantra*

Before 251 A.D. during the reign of Emperor Ashok the third conference of the Buddhist community was called in Patliputra. Many Bhikshus were expelled by Mogliput Tip who resided near Nalanda. Emperor Kanishka called the 4th conference in 78 A.D. The Mahayan Buddhist sect developed by that time. After King Harsha, Nalanda became the centre of Mahayana Buddhism. After 500 years of Buddhism this sect stood fully developed. During 4th and 5th century Tantric Vidya was being practiced by the mahayana sect. Before 6th A.D. Tantra was being preached widely in spite of the fact that Mantra, Yantra, mednal, Mudra, Shakti Tatav, Panchamkar etc, Tantric ways were already being practiced by Mahayan Bodh sect.

Between about 400 to 700 A.D. Tantra was practiced secretly and after that it was practiced through competent persons. Between about 4th and 5th century, the end era of Mhayan, Tantra was not being practiced openly and for 300 years Pancham Kari Sadhana and Mantras were practiced secretly, although it remained in existence. Through this Vajaryan and after that Kalchakaryan and Sahajyan came into existence. The Bodh Sahjyan era came to an end in the 12th century. Vajarayan was in existence between the 7th to 10th century, after being practiced in secret for 300 years. After that it was made popular in public through sermons and songs. So during 7th, 8th and 9th century Tantra and Mantra became popular and was used widely. Shakti Sadhana was introduced in Buddhism through Manjushri Mool, Kalp etc. which were standard works. Bodhvihar of Nalanda made great efforts to propagate the cult of Tantra. They preached Tantra in China , Mongolia, Lanka, Burma, Tibet, Indonesia, Bhutan and Sikhim amongst other countries.

Buddhist Tantra was translated into Chinese and Tibetan languages during the 9th to 11th century. Mantras leading to Siddhis were popular during 7th century to 12th century. Tantric Buddhist Sadhana was made popular through scholars of Buddhism. The period between the 7th to 10th century witnessed the propagation of Shakti sadhana and the compilation of standard works.

Dhakshena char and Vama char are two parts in Hindu Tantra and likewise Kriya Tantra and Charay Tantra are two parts in Buddhism. In Yog Tantra the lady is the focal point. Body control is achieved through this sadhana. Dhakshanachar Sadhana was practiced during the 7th century. The main stress was laid at that time on Kriya Tantra and Charay Tantra . Standard books during the 7th and 8th century indicate the use of Vama Char. At the end of 7th Century or in the beginning of 8th century and upto 11th and 12th century, Sanskrit books of Vajarayan were written. Despite objections raised by the Muslims who were ruling then the treasure of books on Tantra in Tibetan and Nepali were preserved.

Guhe Samaj Tantra and Guhe Siddhi Sadhana are two standard works. In these books Siddhi have been classified as two types–ordinary and special siddhis. In ordinary siddhis, antardhan, Anima, Lagia etc, are mentioned and detailed, whereas special siddhies cover Buddhism. Guhe Samaj does not accept methods and ways of siddhi through which one's body is put to any difficulties as they believe in Sadhana where the body is not put to any hardship. They believe in Shakti. They have categorised 84 siddhies and practiced these during 633 to 1200 A.D. Upto 11th century Shive Tantra and Buddhist Sadhana became very popular and was being practiced freely along with the words of Hindu Tantras also.

From the above we may conclude that Buddhist Tantra can be traced as far back as 2nd or 3rd century.

3.*Brahmin Tantra*

Brahmin Tantra has been divided into three categories Viz Vaishnav, Shaiva and Shakti Tantra. Vaishnav is called Sahita. Shaive Tantra Aagam and Shakt Tantra is known as Tantra. Vaishnav Tantra includes religious mantras, mantras, yantras and yog sadhana. Ishwar Samhita, Poskhar Samhita and Gyan Amrit Samhita are the main works in Vaishnav Tantra. Gyan Amritsaar Samhita and Narad Pancharatar are famous works. Shaiva Tantra has its own ancient history, Sidhant Shaive, Vir Shaive, Jangam Shaive, Tudra, Pashupat, Kapalik, Vam etc, are the standard works included therein. The main amongst them are 10 satwick agam, 18 Rudragam and 64 Bhairvagam. These deal with mainly Shakti Siddhies and due to this were divided into many branches. Tantra has been divided into three parts namely Satotar Peeth and Amanaye, Stotar Vibhag pertains to Shaive, Peeth vibhag to Bhairvas and Kauls and Amanaye Vibhag to Shaktis. Shakt Tantra has been explained in detail and is widely known. A few tantras have been divided into three parts and it has been laid down that they be followed accordingly, these are known as Rath Karant, Vishnu Karant and Ashav Krant. These include many tantras and standard works among them are Vam Kashwar Tantra, prapach Sar and Parshu Ram Kalp Sutra. Dhyan Yog and Hathayog have also been detailed and are not so different from the Tantrik Point of view.

Satyandar Nath and Gorakh Nath were well-known religious preceptors. They obtained Sidhies due to their sadhana. They showed the way to the general public in very simple words and ways. Their directions contain no Beej Mantras nor Sanskrit words. Their language is very simple to understand and the mantras are very powerful. Sabar Mantras are very powerful for Sidhies.

Tantra shows the way of Moksha by first indicating difficulties and then showing the way to overcome or cross them. There are different ways such as Vam Marg and Dakshin Marg. Both indicate different paths but both lead to Moksha. Acharyas and other learned persons had indicated that Tantra contains Shakti or Shiva Karm and Vigyan. Also Istri and Man, Upasana and Anand are contained therein. To attain Mokash is very difficult and one has to do an intense Sadhana.

In Kularnav Tantra it is laid down:-

"कौलाचाराः मुरमकठितः योगिनामप्यगम्य"

"Koolachara Muramkathita Yoginamapayegmyah".

This means that keel Marg is very difficult and to attain perfection in it is an awesome feat.

In Kali Mantra it is stated that:-

सदयं भांसच मीनं च मुद्रा नैथुन से वच
एते पंच मकारा स्यु मोक्षदाः कलौयुगे

This means that in Kalyug wine, fish, meat, women and wealth leads to Moksha.

In Mahanirvan Tantra it is said.

पौत्वा पीत्वा पुनः पीत्वा यावत् पतति भूतले
पुनरुत्याय द्यै पोत्वा पुनर्जन्म ग विधते

This means Drink, keep drinking, drink continuously and drink till the time you lie down on the ground. Stand up and then again drink and after that one will be free from Punarjanam i.e. to take birth again and again, he will attain Moksha.

In Bhirva Chakra, caste and creed, Varun etc., have no limits. In the above stanza wine has been used in good sense. Actually one should drink for sadhana. Those who drink for the sake of intoxication are not given Guru Mantra. This is performed through Vir Bhav and Deviya Bhag. Deviya Bhag is a superior method for Sadhan. In this method one must eschew pride anger, greed and money. One must give up sex. One should treat all as equal with no difference between enemy and friends, mud and chandan, palatial building and hut etc. The devotee does not believe in anything in the world except God. This is Divaya Bhog and the Yogi attains Moksha through this way. The Sadhaka through meditation becomes a learned man after understanding the guide lines.

In Divaya Bhog the Panch Kareya (Five points laid above) changes its meaning. Pooja and Sadhana have replaced these words. For women and sex it indicates Yog. Women are treated as Shiva's Parvati and Lord SHIVA as Lord of Universe . All these things no doubt are very difficult in Kalyuga.

4.*Muslim Tantra*

The Holy Quran of the Muslims does not order for Mantra upasana. The only directions contained therein are to Pray to God (Aallah) for all one's desires. Sabar Mantras are found in Nath Sampardye and like that there are Sabaṛ Mantras in abundance in Quran. In this system the pir or wali, Fakir or religious guide is only requested to bestow the Sadhaka with success.

Use of Tantra

Tantra is used to rid people of their troubles, diseases , worries etc. One can attain Moksha through Tantra. Tantra must be used for constructive reasons and should not be used for nefarious purposes.

Tantra and Yantra are interconnected. But according to Tantra principles Yantra - Tantra and Mantra all are interconnected. All the three are part of Mudra Kariya which leads to the awakening of Kundalini through which one can attain the fulfilment of one's desires. Mudra is not confined only to figures but also to Maha Mudra, Yoni Mudra etc. Tantra is the method through which we can discover and use the hidden powers of various types and Shakties in Yantras.

Tantra Granths

Granth means a book or a work on specific subject. The various specific Granths such as Vaishnav Tantra, Shaive Tantra, Shakt Tantra, Ganpatya Tantra, Budh Tantra, Jain Tantra etc. are explained below.

1.*Vaishnav Tantra*

The main theme of this Tantra is PANCH RATAR about 200 in number, out of which many are available while others are not. These were published between 4th and 12th century as detailed earlier. The important Granth is Ahirbudhaaneya Samhita. (अहिर्बुध्न्य संहिता) In this Granth important topics have been detailed, such as Dharma, Darshan

, Meanings of words, Vanarashram, Dheksha-Varnan, Mantra, Yantra, Chakkar, Yog and methods and rules for victory over enemies.

In addition to the above, Ishwar Samhita, Poshkar-Samhita, Param Smhita Atwat Samhita, Bhrahdhu-Bharm Samhita, Gyan Amrit Saar Samhita etc., were published in the past Gyan Amrit Sarr Samhita has been published with the title NARAD PACH RATAR which contains details of Krishna and Radha. By the Sadhana of Panch Ratri or "five nights" one can attain Sidhi, hence its name. There are a total 64 granths in the Tantra.

2. *Shaiva Tantra*

Shaivagam Samhita is quite detailed.This includes Sidhant Shaive, vir Shaive, Janam Shaive, Roodar, Kapalik, Vam, Bhairva etc. Ten Shaivagam, 18 Roodragum and 64 Bhairva gaman are famous. 22 Mohan Tantras are most important as they contain details of Buddhist Tantra, Jain Tantra etc. Shava Tantra includes the famous works as "UDHOTKAR", "Bhas Varg", "Gan Karika", "Pashpat Darshan", "Mrigaandra", and "Puskar" etc. These Granths are detailed with subjects like Sarishti in a Tantric way.

In Agam Pramanye,Shiv Puran and Agam Puran many more methods of Tantra have been included which are quite effective. In the olden days Tantra was divided into two parts. Vam and Dakshin. The main granth for these details are Moolavtar Tantra, Swachhand Tantra and Kamik Tantra etc.

3.*Shakti Tantra*

This tantra has been divided into three parts Saroto Vibhag of Shaiva, Peeth Vibag of Bhairon and Kaulmarg Anuyatiano and Amanaye Vibhag of Shat. Out of the three, Shakti has been more detailed in Tantra than the other two.

Different aspects of Shakti have been given in Tripur Sundari and Saundria Lahari which are two main Granths of Shati Tantra. Saundria Lahari is divided into three main parts namely Kaulmant, Mishratma and Samiamat, Kaulmat contains 64 Agams, of which 1 to 5 are known as Panch Tantra which are Mahamaya, Shambar, Yogni, Jalshambar and Tatav. 6 to 13 are Swachhand, Karodh, Unmat, Ugar, Kapali, Thandkar, Shekar and Vijay or the eight Bhairon Tantras. 14-21 deals with Shakti, whereas 22nd is Gyanarnav.

A few Tantra Granths have been divided into three parts viz Rath Karant, Vishnu Karant and Ashav Karant. These parts contain 64 granths. Ashav Krant also contains 64 granths.

All these Granths have been written by great Acharyas and scholars.

4.*Ganapatya Tantras*

These Tantras contain the details of Ganpati Puja. There are different methods and aspects of puja. These methods are also available in Mishar Granth of Tantra. In different parts of India Ganpati Pooja is done in different forms. "Ganpatia tharv shirshak" is another name given under the influence of the Acharyas of Southern India. More details can be taken from Prapanch Sar, Shards Tilak, Mantra Mahadadhi etc., which are famous granths.

5.*Buddhist Tantra*

These have already been detailed earlier. These are many granths not all of which are available. These are being practiced in some parts of the country.

6*Jain Tantra*

These too have been described earlier. In Jainism Nagarjun is treated in high esteem. The name of the Granth by Nagarjun is "Kakshputi".

In this granth use of herbs and medicine have been outlined. There are many more Granths in Jainism which are quite important on Tantra.

11

YOGA AND TANTRA

Yoga

There is at present a great interest in the study of Yoga and particularly of Hatha Yoga, not only in India, but also in the Western countries. But to many, the aim and purpose of Yoga is not clear. Most people think that Yoga consists of few asanas and pranayams or that it is a magic or occult science by which one can secure some miraculous powers or siddhis.

The word Yoga comes from a Sanskrit word 'YOJ', which means to join, to unite, to synthesise and so on. Its ultimate aim is to join the individual self to the universal self. But the self is not gained by weak persons as laid down in Mundak Upnishad. In the initial stage, the building of a healthy body and training of the mind are the principal aims of Hatha Yoga. This training leads us to identify with the universal self or atman in us. In between there are several stages.

Various books by various learned authors clearly indicate that Yoga was studied in India from very ancient days. In Upnishads, four Yogas are mentioned viz, Hath Yoga, Laya Yoga , Mantra Yoga and Raja Yoga. At present, Yoga is generally understood as a combination of Hatha Yoga and Raja Yoga. This combination is known as STANGA YOGA, i.e. the Yoga with eight limbs or parts. There are Yama, Niyama, Asana, Pranayam, Pratyahara, Dharna, Dynana and Samadhi Yogas which will be explained briefly.

1. *Yama*

YOGA: It contains practice of ten qualities.

1. **Ahinsa** –(Non Injury) committing no injury or violence.

2.	Satya	–speaking the truth under all circumstances.
3.	Astayam	–Not stealing.
4.	Brahmacharya	–Celibacy and leading a sexual life according to injunctions.
5.	Ksama	–Spirit of equanimity in all circumstances.
6.	Dhurti	–courage.
7.	Daya	–Kindness to all beings.
8.	Arjavam	–maintenance of the same relations with friends and foes alike.
9.	Mitaharm	–Moderation in Eating.
10.	Vratam	–Doing of permitted acts.

2. *Asana*

It means a posture in which a person sits, stands or lies. It has a particular purpose in preserving the body and health.

3. *Pranayama*

Means control of prana or vital air. Actually it means the control of breath in several ways.

4. *Prathahara*

In Hatha Yoga, it means Nada Yog. It is also considered as the powerful control of the " indriyas" or organs of the body which naturally and freely tend towards the enjoyment of physical pleasure. Restraint and constraint of motion of air from one part of the body to another is also called Pratyahara. For some it means indifference to the pleasures of life.

5. *Dharana, Dhyana and Samadhi*

All belong to Raja Yoga. Dharma is considered as concentration of mind and Dhayana is meditation for long periods. Samadhi is the complete absorption of the mind in an object, where only the object remains and the subject disappears.

Laya Yoga is the complete suppression of the mind and its fixation on the self. Some consider it to be the rousing of the Kundalini in the Sushuma. It is also considered to be part of TANTRA.

6. *Mantra Yoga*

This consists of repetition with concentration of words consisting of what we call BIJA AKSHARAS, which are symbolic representations of the cosmic powers or Devatas. Then there are principal Yoga,

KARAM YOGA, BHAKTI YOGA AND JNANA YOGA as mentioned in the Bhagwat Gita.

Tantra for Kaly Yuga

The votaries of Tantra assert that the ultimate aim of Tantra is the same as that of Veda, namely, the attainment of God or truth, knowledge, bliss which are the attributes of the Absolute. According to Kularnava Tantra, it was believed that the Vedas or Sruti which literally means what was heard from Paramatma was intended for the Krita Yuga and Suriti that is what is remembered by the Rishis for Treata Yuga. Purnas or epics which incorporate the above two for easy understanding and assimilation for.

Dowapar Yuga

Lastly Tantra was specially allotted for Kaliyug. They say in Kali Yuga, it is not possible to adhere to the elaborate rituals and austerities prescribed by the Vedas, but it is possible to practice Tantra which leads to the same goal and at the same time contributes to man's physical needs.

Veda and Tantra

It is said that Veda and Tantra runs on parallel lines which converge at the end. Still there are certain important differences. Vedic initiation is somewhat restrictive, as it shuts out women and persons of certain castes, while Tantra opens its doors to all and excludes none.

Indeed Maha Nirvana Tantra says that it is incumbent on a Brahman to initiate even low caste people in the Tantra. Women are as eligible as men. Again for Vedic Study, one has to undergo strict discipline, develop mental discrimination and detachment involving study and meditation. Tantra is not so exacting. It divides people into three classes viz Pasubhava or animal type corresponding to Tamas, Virabhava or hero type corresponding to Rajas and the third Divyabhava, divine type corresponding to Satava. These divisions are flexible and one can pass from a lower state to the higher one.

Tantra – A Practical Science

An important aspect of TANTRA SASTRA, is that it is a rational science, which can be verified at every step and which requires no faith. There is always stress on the practical side. It provides a graded system of sadhana depending on the competence of the sadhaka.

There is puja or workship done with flowers, incense etc. Then repitition of mantras. After this dhyana and ultimately the attainment of brahaman. It absorbs more vedic rites. The most important point about Tantra is that it takes into account the physical needs of the individual in this world, which are considered as very real not illusory.

Tantra contains both subjective and objective science. Thus Tantriks made contributions beginning with miracles, socery and ending with the science of herbs, mentallurgy, medicine, Astrology and Astronomy etc. In brief, Tantra enables man to act through dharma or virtue, artha or (wealth) Kama (Desire) and Moksha (Ultimate liberation).

All that is mentioned above can be achieved by Mantra, Yantra,Tantra and Devas, through the help of a preceptor or Guru. Tantra proclaims without hesitation that Mantra can produce any desired effects. Yantra and Tantra are powerful and the Devas (both high and low) exist. Through them an aspirant can secure siddhis (great powers) and ultimately reach brahman. In kularnava Tantras seven rules of conduct are laid down. They are Veda, Vaishnava, Saiva, Vama, Siddhanta and Brahman. The first three come under Pasubhave, the fourth and fith under Virabhava and the last two under DIVYA Bhava. Similar stages are also mentioned in Yoga Vasistha.

Vamchara

Five articles are used in the worship of Devi these are madya (wine) Mamsa (Meat) Matsya (fish), Mudra (grain) and maithana (Women-literally copulation). These are known are Five M's or Pancha makaras.

Some Sadhakas took these five M's literally in their physical sense and indulged in them in the most revolting manner bringing Tantra into disrepute. People began to look at it with horror as people of this cult indulged in physical excesses. In Kularnava Tantra, it is stated that wine is the intoxication produced by the meeting of Kundalini Sakti with SIVA in Sahasrara. The flesh is that of the animal of duality which is cut by the knower of Yoga with the sword of knowledge and Yoga. Eating of fish brings the senses under the mind's control and reigns in the self. Maithina is the ananda produced by the union of the supreme Sakti and the supreme self.

Yoga is another technique of transformation, an important part of Tantra. Yoga used in Tantra is based more or less on Hatha Yoga, with an extra dimension. The bodily attitudes, contractions and pressures which make up Hatha Yoga are designed to specifically work upon the inner mechanism of the human body.

To perform Hatha Yoga without doing any inner work on the subtle body is a pointless exercise from the Tantra point of view, though it may help the outer body's health and stamina. A person practising Hath Yoga will easily recognize the relations between its pulls, twists, contractions and pressures and various centres of the subtle body. However the extra dimensions in Tantrik Yoga comes from the bodily actions which are performed during sexual intercourse. These are meant both to enhance the physical sensations and to transform them into a vehicle for blissful insight, which can be experienced only with a sexual partner, under the guidance of a Guru, though in fact one partner may be the teacher, very often the woman.

Buddhist Tantra lays little stress on the lowest lotus in the subtle body, knows no Kundalini and prefers to omit the lotus behind the genitals. It does, however, identify the ascending consciousness–energy with the sexual vitality, symbolizing it by the male, borne by the female figure. But at the level of heart, Tantrik Buddhism envisages its most sweeping and characteristic set of the sphere of energy which is far more elaborate than the heart lotus in the Hindu system.

The famous mantra of Tantrik Buddhism is "Om Mani Padme Hiun Om","Mani Padme" means jewel in the lotus or Male within the female organ, the state of completeness, energy infusing wisdom. HUM is the sound of power forcing the mantra into realization. The energy is often symbolized by an implement called VAJRA, double ended with ornate curved prongs enclosing a central straight prong. All tantrik Buddhists own one, which serves each person as a reservoir of personal power. Vajarapani means he who holds the Vajra. In order to help his meditation the Tantrik monk may also use a bell, whose rim is gently and continuously rubbed with a stick so as to produce a sustained gentle and entrancing hum.

This sound is the symbol for the remotest expression of the subtle Tantrik truth. It is the audible form of the most ancient and potent Indian mantra 'OM' .

The Tantrika may find in this sound the consummation of his meditative and devotional activity, his sexual Yoga and mantra pratice. He may finally learn how to send the harmonizing "OM" resonating up the crystal cavity for his spine, and open his whole body to that root energy, which will then flood in through the crown of his head from the reality beyond time.

To make this experience real and permanent, to live and be continuously aware of it constitutes the whole aim of Tantra.

The Vajra and Bell

A Buddhist monk, visited the office of the author. Satisfied with rare predictions sbout him and after obtaining a 'SHRI YANTRA' to wear, the monk invited the author to his temple at Delhi.

The author was escorted by Buddhist monks into their temple as a monk of their respect and regard for him.

After discussing Astrology, Yantra, Mantra and Tantra with the Head priest of the temple, some rituals and Puja of Lord Buddha was performed. The priest then purified a few Yantras. The Head of the temple presented the author with their most sacred emblems duly purified the 'VAJRA and BELL' which is shown at figure 2.1 For details refer to the author's book, "THE PRACTICALS OF YANTRA". (Revised Edition).

The VAJRA as directed by the Head priest is being used along with a specified mantra very successfully to detect the influence of an evil eye, souls, Masan (Ash of cremation ground etc) given to anybody for bad purposes.

The VAJRA is touched to the body from head to Toe with the Tantric rites, gives vibrations to the author enabling him to trace out the afflicted body part. It has also been used with success to locate any tantric articles thrown in a house. It is really a very useful emblem for Tantrikas to detect the above evils. The VAJRA and BEEL are being used in meditation by the author with great success by grace of Lord SHIVA AND LORD BUDDHA.

As explained earlier these emblems are really a reservoir of personal power and hence help during meditation.

12

PRACTICAL USE OF TANTRA

It is difficult to determine the number of Tantras available in our country. In Kaliyuga, some factors are very important to the householder or common man. These have already been described in both earlier parts of this book viz "Vashi Karan" which means subordinating another to one's will, "Akarshana", attracting others "Stamblan" means making some one immobile or helpless, "Videshan", or creating differences and dissensions among others, "Uchattan" or creating distraction in the mind of any body and finally "Maran" means causing death, specially to one's enemies.

Tantra is an Indian cult and is practiced by Hindus, Muslims, Buddhists and Jains alike. There are Symbols in the Vast natural coverns of Palaeolithic Europe (C-2000 BC) which can be accurately matched with symbols still used today by Tantriks. Tantra is not a religion or "Jadoo Toona" magic, but a way of thought and action which works for the benefit of people. The old texts, as far back as the sixth century, consist of prescriptions for actions including mental action. If one does not act according to what Tantra prescribes, one cannot achieve one's aims.

Tantra is fundamental and total. Its real importance is that Tantrik plunges straight to the heart of the problem. The methods provided in Tantra as given below are to be practised methodically and with full faith and respect so as to achieve success. Directions whenever specifically provided must be obeyed carefully. Homa where indicated, should be performed with the correct material and appropriate mantras. Directions must be followed implicitly in order to get the right results.

There is an Indian saying, 'GHAR KI MURGHI DAL BARABAR'

means that everything found at home is worth nothing. As Yantras, Mantras and Tantras contained in this book and other famous books of seers and the author (namely PRACTICALS OF YANTRAS & PRACTICALS OF MANTRA AND TANTRA) are of Indian origin people in our country treat them as hoax and do not respect them with full faith. However, in foregn countries these are being practiced and used with full faith and people are greatly benefitting from them.

To cite a concrete example, 'Inspiration House Deptt., F-25,3435 Motor Avenues, Los Angeles, C.A. good 4 USA' is the house which propagates Indian Yantra and Mantra and sells them on white printing paper for the benefit and use of the public at large. These include Yantras and Mantras for power, love, money, career, health, good luck and peace of mind. People use them with full faith and get maximum benefit out of them. They have termed the mantras as Magic words. These yantras are Shri Yantra, Lakshmi Yantra, Hanuman Pooja Yantra, Vyapar Vaidhi Yantra , Surya Yantra, Nav Garah Beesi Yantra and Yantra for peace of mind etc.

We in India should follow them in this respect in order to gain the benefits by reviving our culture.

Vashi Karan Tantras

1. *For Every Body*

To enchant anybody , the following few Tantras should be employed. This is called SARV JAN VASHI KARAN. This also includes Mohan or Aakarshan etc.

Mantra:

"ॐ नमो आदिपुरुषाय अमुक अकर्षण कुरू कुरू स्वाहा"

"Om Namo adipurushaya Amuk akarshan kuru kuru swaha".

(i) The above mantra must be recited ten thousand times to attain siddhi of the mantra . Purify the articles 108 times and use for the person by replacing the name in the mantra for the word AMUK.

(ii) Juice of leaves of black thorn apple (called Dhatura in Hindi) and Gorochan should be mixed. Write the name of the person to be controlled on Booj Patra with a pen made of white Kaneer branch. Arrange or make yourself, coal of Khair tree (Catechu). Put Booj Patra over the fire of coal of Khir wood and recite the above mantra 108 times. The person concerned will become infatuated and will approach you of his or her own accord.

"ॐ नमो भगवते ज्वालाग्नी शय्यादिष्ठा विनाय स्वाहा"

2. *To Enchant Someone*

"Om Namo Bhagwate Jawalagni Shayadhishtha Vinaya Swaha".

METHOD: Recite this mantra 12,500 times facing North after Sunrise with rosary of Red coral on an auspicious day and Lagna to attain siddhi of the mantra. — —

The mantra should be recited 21 times on Vashi Karan articles and given to anybody to enchant him/her.

(i) Root of Gular tree should be ground, and purified as detailed above. Use it in betal leaf and whosoever takes the betal will become enchanted.

(ii) Supari used in Betel leaves should be purified 108 times with the above mantra. Whosoever will eat this, will be fully enchanted.

(iii) During Shukul Paksh on Sunday, take ash from cremation ground, mix your semen and ash of your twenty nails. This powder should be purified 108 times and preserved.As and when required, the man or lady may be given a pinch of it in the food so that the person becomes subject to Vashi Karan.

(iv) Procure the clothes of girls who had been in their first periods. Make a wick from the cloths, burn the wick in lamp containing Arindi Oil and collect the Kajal and preserve it. During Swati nakshatra, put a pinch of this Kajal on anybody. The person will be infatuated.

"ॐ नमो कामाक्षोदेवी अमुकी नारी में वश कुरू कुरू स्वाहा"

3. *To Gain Siddhi*

"Om Namo Kamaksho Devi Amuki Nari me Vash Kuru Kuru Swaha".

The mantra should be recited ten thousand times to gain siddhi. Replace the name of the person with the word Amuki Nari and purify 108 times the following articles and use as directed below:-

(i) On Tuesday or Sunday bring dust from a place where Asses relax and burn the same. It should be well screened to get the powder. Mix a pinch of powder in eatables of lady or ANY BODY who will be enchanted.

This has been TESTED in many ways several times and has proved successful.

(ii) Meat of oil be dried in shade. Any body on whose head a pinch of it is put will be enchanted.

(iii) Mogra flowers should be purified 7 times with "OM HIRANG SWAHA", Anybody smelling it will be enchanted.

(iv) Obtain dust of feet of Washerman during Pushya Nakshatra. Put a pinch of it on the head of anybody on Sunday evening. The person will become infatuated.

(v) Obtain a bone from cremation ground and rub it in the milk of sheep (भेड़) Sprinkle a pinch on a person, who will become enchanted.

"ॐ नमो महायक्षिष्ये मम पति में वश्यं कुरू कुरू स्वाहा"

4. *For Inpatuation*

"Om Namo Mahayakshisaya Mam Pati me Vashayam Kuru Kuru Swaha"

Recite this mantra 1008 times and perform Homa to gain siddhi and use as below after purifying it 21 times.

The lady can use this to control her husband or to infatuate anybody.

The lady should weigh flour equal to weight of her left shoe. Make four chapaties on Sunday or Tuesday. The chapaties eaten by any man will come under your control.

5. *For Fulfilment of Desires*

A thick root of white arka (H-Oak T.Jilledv Gigantic Swallow Wart) should be taken with devotion by one who should be celibate on a Sunday in Pushyami nakshatra. The root must be made into an image of Gaanpati. The image must be worshipped uttering the following mantras.

"ॐ हरी पुर्वदया ओं हीं फट् स्वाहा"

"Om Hareeng Poorvdya Om Hareeng Phut Swaha"

Red Kaneer flowers (Raktesvamara) should be offered in the fire along with ghee and honey. This must be continued for a month for fulfilling one's desires. One's desires are always fulfilled.

6. *To Cure Stammering*

Bramhi (Manduka Pernit. Saraswati Indian Penny wort), Mundi (T.Bodararam sphaesarhus Indicus Vacha) orris root (Sunthi), dried ginger (Pippali), long pepper taken in equal quantities be finely powered. If a pinch of this is taken with honey, stammering is cured.

7. *For Becoming A Scholar*

Take two kinds of Turmeric (S.Kushta orris root) Vasa (T.Atimadhuram Kuth pippli)(Long pepper), sunthi (dried ginger), Jeera (T.Jelakrra, Cumin Seed), Ajmod,(Tomam, Haubaiu), Mulaithi

(Lequorica, sushti medhura T.Atimadhuram) all in equal quantities. Dry them and make the mixture into a fine powder. If one takes a Pinch of this powder with ghee for a month, he becomes equal to Brihaspati. This is particularly recommended for young men and women.

8. *To Become A Poet*

In Pushyami Nakshatra, root of white oak should be taken dried in shade and powdered finely. A pinch or two should be taken every morning with butter milk or ghee, uttering the mantra.

ॐ महेश्वराय नमः

"Om Maheshvarye Namah"

This must be done for seven days. Food should be only rice with milk.

9. *For Snake Bite*

Curd, honey, butter, long pepper, Ginger, Black pepper and Kuth (Rastur Acaniesu) should be mixed and a small amount of rock salt added. If this is taken, even those bitten by a most poisonous snake recover.

10. *To Become Popular*

(i) Take the root of Punaruar and tie it to one's hand.

(ii) Make a paste of Gorochan and of sehdevi plant and put it as a tilak.

11. *For Success*

On the full Moon day of the month of Margasira take the root of Mayura sikhi and put it around the shoulder (in war or when in Pushya Nakshatra) take gunja and tie it around the right arm. There will be success.

12. *To Be Free from Fear of Beasts*

(a) On Sunday, in Pushyami nakshatra, take the root of white arka and tie it around the right hand.

(b) On an auspicious star, take the root of dhatura and tie it around the right hand.

13. *To Control One's Life*

Obtain the horn of a bull which died on Sunday. Dust from under the feet of a man or woman should be filled in the horn. Purify the horn with smoke of Gugal. Horn must be fixed in the houses of man/lady, who will come under your control.

Tilaks

There are several types of Tilaks for Vashi Karan of men, ladies ministers etc., a few of which are mentioned as follows.

(i) Kakri Singhi , Bach, Koot and chandan should be ground well. The powder should be put on your body and incense applied on one's clothes. Tilak of powder be applied on your forehead. Go to the desired person or lady who on seeing you will be infatuated.

(ii) If Horochan and Kum Kum is ground and mixed with the Juice of a Banana and applied as Tilak, the lady will be enchanted as and when the man approaches her.

(iii) Mix ash of cremation ground and Brahm Dandi Powder. The woman on whom this is thrown or who puts a tilak on her forehead will be enchanted. Be sure that powder touches her body parts positively in order to bring her under your control.

(iv) On Sunday, ground Tulsi seeds in juice of Sehdevi should be put as tilak in order to infatuate any person.

(v) Bel Patra should be dried in the shade. Make pills after mixing it in milk of kapila cow. As and when required the pill should be mixed with water and applied as tilak. All will be infatuated.

(vi) Gorachan and Liver of Fish (पित्ता) must be mixed equally. Apply tilak on your forehead. All will be infatuated.

(vii) Excreta of Peacock and teeth of snake be grounded to make powder. Put a tilak of this, and whereever one goes there will be videshan.

Kalp of Owl

Each part of an Owl's body (Symbol of wisdom) is used both for good and bad purposes . We provide a few.

1) The eyes of owl be mixed with Kasturi. Put it on anybody and he or she will become your friend.
2) The flesh of owl be dried and preserved . Give a pinch of powder in eatables to anybody, who will become worried.
3) Anyone on whose Head Pinch of the above powder is put, will be much enchanted.
4) Burn the bone of owl, the ashes be put on the head of any body who will become a vagabond.
5) Burn the feet of an owl. The ash if administered to anybody in eatables will remain worried on some account or other.
6) Mix the powder of owl's bone in milk and saffron and give to drink, on Pushay nakshatra on Sunday to anybody, who will become insane and die.

7) The excreta of owl should be dried mixed with supari and whosoever will take it will become insane or become an imbecile.

8) Put the eyes of an owl in water, one eye will remain open and the other will remain shut.

If the closed eye is kept under the pillow, the person will become dull and will not like to get up.

The other eye can be fitted in a ring and be kept on the body, the person will not sleep.

9) Feet of owl be purified and kept in a cash box. The person will not suffer any financial difficulty.

10) Procure the eye of an owl on Sunday. Put it in smoke of Gugal and make small pills of it. On Tuesday, the pills should be purified 108 times with the proper mantra and kept at a place where the two persons live. There will be quarrels between them.

11) On Sunday procure blood of an owl and crow. Mix the used clothes of both persons in that during Krishna Pakash on the night of Chaturdesi and purify them with proper mantra 108 times. Put them between the friends. Soon both will be at daggers drawn.

12) Hold wings of owl and crow in either hand and tie them with black bare thread (सूत) Hold these wings again in the hand and perform Tarpan 108 times with Anjli. This will cause Videshan. Take care to recite the Mantra while binding the two with thread.

13) On Sunday take the ash of the wings of a crow and owl and purify with proper mantra 108 times. Put this ash on the heads of two persons. Enmity between them is assured.

14) On Amavas, Sunday or Tuesday when the moon transists in Scorpio Sign, procure the head of Gugu, nails of owl, cheel and crow which should be mixed and made into powder . Put them to the smoke of Gugal turn it all into ashes. Purify the above with a mantra 108 times.

Put a pinch of it in the house of persons, which will cause quarrels, bickerings and separation.

15) Homa be performed for 108 Ahuties with wings of Black owl with the name of enemy. Use Uchattan or Vidashan Mantra. The enemy will be subjected to its effects.

16) Make powder of Owl's head. Purify 21 times. Throw it on the head of enemy or anybody.One will subjected to Videshan or Uchattam.

17) Eye of owl be purified 108 times with this mantra:-

"ॐ नमोवीरहूं हूं नमः"

"Om Namo Veer Hung Mung Namah", and throw it between two friends they will be at dagger's drawn. This can be used between couples if there is reason to break up a romance or infatuation.

Videshan Tantra

Videshan Tantra is that through which differences are created between friends opponents and other adversaries.

These Tantras are used when a person or persons create obstacles, troubles for another man and creates an unhealthy atmosphere at home or in the office putting others to mental strain. In order to stop them from doing so, these Tantras are used so that the victim gets relief.

When there are acute differences between husband and wife, friends, partners, brothers and with other people etc. These Tantras are used in self-defence to get relief as these are allowed under the Shastras.

We provide a few Tantras in this regard.

Mantra

"ॐ नमो नरायणाय अमुकाकेन सह विद्धेषणं कुरू कुरू स्वाहा"

"Om Namo Narayanay Amukaken Seh Videshanm Kuru Kuru Swaha"

This mantra must be recited for 21 days. Change the word AMUK with the names of person. Then purify the requisite articles with 108 mantras and use them as directed hereunder:-

1. Fix the pointed wings of Sae (सई के कांटे) on the door of house of the person between whom you want to create differences after purifying them 108 times. There will be quarrels and separation between the two.
2. Collect the dust from under the feet of persons between whom the differences are to be created. Make idols of this dust. Purify the idols with above mantra 108 times. Bury them in the cremation ground. Differences will be created between the two and they will have no compromise.
3. Collect the dust of the place where Asses and Rams (भैंसा) relax on Sunday noon. Purify with the above mantra. Wherever the dust is thrown, Videshan will start . This is a Tested Tantra.
4. The wings of the owl and crow can be purified with the above

4. The wings of the owl and crow can be purified with the above mantra is recited 108 times. Tie both the wings with black thread. Fix them in the house of enemy or where differences are to be created. Take them out, when effect is to be stopped.
5. Hairs of horse and Ram (भैसा) should be purified 108 times with the above Mantra. Wherever these are burnt differences will be created.
6. Clothes of the man and hair of lady should be burnt on Tuesday. Purify the ash 21 times with the above mantra. The ash can be given to them in eatables or thrown on the heads of both. They will be at dagger's drawn. This is a tested tantra.
7. Light the hair of woman in a cup, which may be filled with water. This be given to her husband, paramour etc., for drinking. When the water is being poured in cup or glass, purify the same 21 times with above mantra. There will be differences and quarrels between the two.
8. On Saturday procure the hair of a cat and rat. On Sunday bring wood of crow nest from a Neem Tree. All these should be burnt. Put the ash in a cloth and throw in the houses of the enemy etc. There will be quarrels and bickerings in the house and they will leave the place.
9. Procure hair of elephant and lion and dust of underfeet of persons for whom videshan is required. All should be mixed and buried in the ground. Light a fire at that place. Put 108 Ahutics in fire with flowers of chameli (Jasmin) with the above mantra. There will be Videshan between the two and they will become of each other.
10. Prepare a paste of IVORY (Teeth Elephant) and Teeth of Lion and grind both of them. Mix them in butter. Put its tilak on forehead. Go to any meeting. There will be Videshan and meeting will disband.
11. Excreta of Bilowa and rat should be grounded and made idol of it. Wrap it in blue cloth and purify 108 times with above mantra. There will be Videshan between the two causing quarrels and separation.
12. On Sunday procure the hair of rat and Bilav. Purify them with above mantra. Bury it in the house where you want to create videshan. There will be quarrels and separation in the house.
13. Procure wings of Gugu and crow on Saturday and burn them at midnight. Purify with above mantra. Put it on the heads of persons who will fight with each other.

Uchattan Tantras

Uchattan Tantras are methods through which persons, animals, birds etc., are driven away from their place of habitation and profession etc. Actually these methods of Videshan and Uchattan are used for enemies, either of the country or personal.Through these methods the enemies are directed to actions which are against the interest of others. Suppose a man has deprived another man of his wife, children, land, house, Jewellery, vehicle, wealth etc., in an unauthorised way he is surely to be punished. Tantra allows uchattan to be performed is self-defence.

However these rites should be applied in a constructive way and used only at the time of urgency, such as in evicting an illegal tenant.

In Tantrik sadhana, there are rites dealing with ladies, men, enemies friends and other people which should however be used cautiously because they are very effective if performed with due rituals and faith.

Uchattan means separation, extirpation, uprooting, dejection, sadness, indifference, distraction in one's mind by the help of incantations.

On the basis of the above, we provide a few Tantras for the use of sadhakas and readers.

Mantra :

"ॐ नमो भगवते रूद्राय करालाय अमुक पुत्र बान्धवैस्मह शीघ्र उच्चाटय ठः ठः ठः"

"Om Namo Bhagwate Rudray Kralaye Amuk Putram Bhandvasaymah Shigar Uchattaya the the tha".

"ॐ श्रीं श्रीं श्रीं स्वाहा"

"Om Sharee Sharee Sharee Swaha"

Recite any of above mantras ten thousand times to attain sidhi. Replace the name of person in mantra in place of word Amuk.

Purify the articles as below before use with above mantra 108 times.

1 Take wood from a Gular tree about 12 inches long. It should be purified with above mantra 108 times and buried in the house where Uchattan is required.
2 Take a bone of male 12 inch long and use as above.
3 Homa with 108 ahuties be performed with the recitation of nameof the person considered for Uchattan with the above Mantra usingthe wings of crow and owl.

4 No mantra is required in this case. A shiva Linga be painted with Braham Dandi and Ash from the Cemetery. On Saturday night Shiva Linga and white sarsson should be thrown in the house of person for whom Uchattan is intended.

5 White sarsoon and idol of Lord SHIVA in repose should be purified 108 times with the above mantra and on Saturday be buried in the house of the concerned person for Uchattan.

6 A Crow's nest should be burnt and the Ask purified 21 times with the above mantra. The person on whose head or the house on which this ash is thrown will be subjected to Uchattan. All members of the house will be afflicted.

7 Lemon wood, owl's bone, nail and skin of cat, juice of Dhatura and a bone from the cremation ground should all be purified 21 times with the above mantra. In any house and wherever these be buried or thrown, the inmates will be subjected to Uchattan.

8 Drive a nail of Umri tree 12" long in any house after purifying it 21 times. All inmates will be subjected to Uchattan.

9 Peepal wood 2.5 feet long should be purified 21 times and buried in any house during Aswini Nakshatra. Uchattan will take place.

10 Prepare a powder with excreta of owl and sarsoon and purify it 108 times. As and when it is thrown on the head or applied on any person he or she will be subjected to Uchattan.

11 The dust of the underfeet of a She Ass should be purified on Tuesday Noon 21 times. In any house, where it is thrown the people of the house will be subjected to Uchattan. Dust collected from left foot on Sunday will have the same effect.

12 At Noon bring the dust from a place where asses rest, while facing East or West in left hand. This can be purified 108 times. Throw this ash for 2 continuous days in the house. All will be subjected to Uchattan.

13 Wood of kum kum 21 Inches long be procured in Uttra phalguni Nakshatra. Purify it 21 times. Bury in any part of the house where Uchattan is required.

14 The root of Kalchari should be purified 21 times and be buried in the house of the enemy or any person for effective Uchattan.

15 Make an idol of Seedia salt (Pakistani salt). Write the name of the person over it. Purify with the mantra 21 times. The idol should be put in water for bathing daily. As idol shrinks in size the enemy will be subjected to Uchattan.

16 Seeds of Hartal, Dhatura and Lehsan should be poured. Purify

it 21 times. Put on the head of anybody who will become shameless. He will become allright when given milk and sugar to drink.

17 Homa for 108 ahuties with above mantra be performed with wings of black owl with the name of enemy. One will be afflicted with Uchattan.

18 Make a Powder of an owl's head purify it 21 times. Throw it on the head of enemy or anybody, who will be subjected to Uchattan.

19 Eye of Owl should be purified 108 times with this mantra "ॐ नमो वीर हुं हुं नमः "Om Namo Veer Hung Hung Namaha" Throw it in between two friends or a couple who will be at dagger's drawn.

20 Procure the root of white kandyari. Purify with above mantra 21 times. Bury it in any house. All inmates will be subjected to Uchattan.

21 Bring water from a well or tap found on roadside during Mrigasira Nakshatra. Purify 21 times. Put on the forehead of anybody for Uchattan.

22 Bring one empty jute bag on Sunday from enemy's house. Sitting on that bag recite this mantra daily for 3 days.

ॐ ह्रीं कलीं श्रीं फट् गुरूडाय जपाय स्वाहा"

"Om Hareeng Kaleeng Shareeng Phut Gurudaye Japaye Swaha".

Then recite this mantra 24 times, the bag be sweeped (झाड़ दो) All inmates will be subjected to Uchattan.

Tantras for Various Uses

In this section, we provide Tantras for various uses. These Trantras are very important and useful.

1 When in extreme happiness a man or woman cries, these tears should be sucked by one who has worries. The worries will vanish.

2 The milk teeth of a child when it falls should be picked up before falling on the gound. If a lady childless ties it on her left hand in silver or copper talisman, she will be blesssed with a child.

4 If the abovea teeth are tied around the waiste of a woman in silver talisman, She will not conceive and will abort.

5 If the teeth are kept by anybody with him or her and uses it in a silver talisman the person will be respected everywhere.

6 The string chord of the first male child should be dried and kept in safe or cash box or in purse. The man is respected and blessed with wealth.

7 In case a man or woman has six fingers in both hands and both feet or on one hand and one foot, she or he can cure disease simply by touching the whole body of a patient.

8 The teeth of lion be used as Yantra in the neck of the child. The child will not be affected by these evil eye and effects of souls. Also there will be no trouble in taking out teeth.

9 Excreta of elephant be used as above factors.

10 If the woman uses above yantra as per serial no.10, she will abort.

11 Excreta of horse be burnt and mixed with Til oil. Rub on the head, the hair will grow and also become longer.

12 Leech be roasted in oil and make ash of it. Hot sarsoon oil be put in it. Apply it on the head, hair will grow.

13 The teeth of mule if kept in one's pocket, ensures wealth.

14 The shoe of mule should be burnt and mixed in linseed oil. Apply it on the bald head, hair will grow.

15 Bring the dust from the place where Asses relax on Sunday without telling anybody. The dust should be put to the smoke of Gugal. If this dust is then applied on the forehead of anybody or is thrown in any house, there will be constant quarrels.

16 The Umbillical chord of cat commonly known as "Billi Ki Jeer" is kept in cash box or purse, one is blessed with wealth.

17 The teeth of rabbit can be used as Yantra around the neck or kept with a person it gives spiritual strength.

To Prevent Abortion

1. One piece of Balka and dust from the ear of a man should be put in pashmina cloth. The lady should wear it around the neck, she will not abort.
2. The root of khairanti herb should be wrapped in kacha thread woven by a virgin girl and be tied around the waist of a lady. She will not abort.

Birth Of Child Or Son Especially For A Barren Lady

Given below are a few Tantras for the birth of child or son. Also these are effective for Vandhya or barren women.

For Sure Birth Of Son (tested)

1. The Monday falling after the monthly period of a woman, the husband should keep fast on Monday. The lady should go to Lord SHIVA'S TEMPLE. After performing pooja and offering water, one seed of the SHIVLINGI should be cleaned with water. Bring

it home and wrap in old gur, which the lady should swallow. Repeat for 11 days. Keep a fast on Monday and avoid sex for eleven days. One will be blessed with a son.

2. This is from Nityananda's Kama Ratna.
   i) Take tender leaves of palasa plant (Butta Frondosa Tel Moduka) with milk for seven days during and after menstruation. The lady should take light food. She must not have any fear or sorrow in her mind. Sleeping during the day is prohibited. This is considered very effective for ensuring the birth of a son.
   ii) Take seh devi (CONYZA CINARAE) plant on Sunday in Pushyami nakshatra. Dry it in shade inside the house, and grind it to make powder. The powder should be given with milk of single coloured cow. The lady will become pregnant and give birth to a son.
   iii) The plant Nagkesara (Messusa Ferrera) should be powdered. If taken with ghee of a young cow for seven days by a lady along with food, she will be blessed with a son.
   iv) Powder the seeds of Gokshura and take it with the juice of Nirgundi. If it is taken for five or eight nights after menses, pregnancy comes within a week.

   It is good to repeat the following mantra :

   " ॐ मदन महा गणपतै रक्षामृतं मत्सुत देहि "

   "Om Madan Maha Ganpate rakshamritam Matsutam Dehi"
   v) Make a powder of Borex (Suhaga) and excreta of pigeon, add water to make a paste. Paste be applied on male organ before coitus. One will be blessed with son.
3. Root of castor plant should be taken during Sharavan nakshatra and worshipped, and worn around neck. Pregnancy will take place.
4. Sehdevi and Yashtima Dhukum should be mixed in cow's milk and sugar. It should be taken during menses. The woman will surely bear a son.
5. Take the plant Vishnukrant (S. Aparajita) with roots and make a paste with buffalo milk and butter. If this mixure is taken for seven days during menses, the woman becomes pregnant.
6. The roots of Aswagandha should be secured on Sunday in Pushyami nakshatra and grounded with buffalo's milk and a quantity equal to black grain seed (about twenty mashas) be

taken for seven days regularly. The woman will become pregnant.

MANTRA: The following mantra be recited for 108 times for 7 days to get better results.

"ॐ नमः शक्तिरूपाय अस्यागृहे पुत्रं कुरू कुरू स्वाहा"

"Om Namo Shaktisrupaye Asyagharhe Putram Kuru Kuru Swaha"

Ladies Having Only Daughters Birth of Son

Ladies having only daughters, may use the following for the birth of son.

i) A peacock feather is taken and the central eye is carefully cut and made into a ball with some Jaggery. Three such balls be prepared and should be taken in the morning after three months of pregnancy. A son will be born.

The word Jaggery means 'SHAKAR' made of old Gur. It is known by different names in other parts of the country.

ii) After two month's pregnancy, tender leaves of Vasaka (A Vasica nees; Justicia Adhatoda) should be mixed with milk and drunk.

To Prevent Birth of Children

Our old texts provide Tantras to prevent the birth of children for BIRTH CONTROL or for any other reason.

i) On Krishna chaturdashi (14th day of dark half) secure a whole Dhatura (Dhatura, T. Ummetta) plant and tie it around the waist of a woman at the time of union with her husband. There will be no conception. If the plant is removed, one can have children.

ii) If the powder of above plant is placed in private female organ it completely stops the birth of children.

iii) If a mustard plant is tied to the head of woman, and if she enjoys sex, there will be no child birth. But if the plant is removed, child birth is possible.

iv) The following yantra can be used for this purpose also. Write this Yantra with blood of ring finger or with Cat's faeces (Excrements of

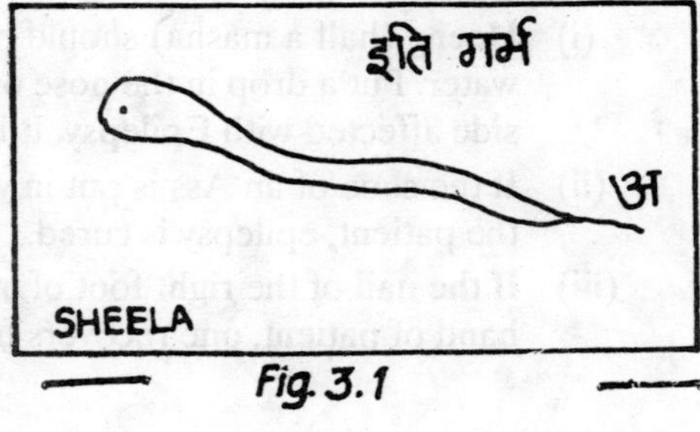

Fig. 3.1

Bowels or excreta)

Write the name of lady in place of word 'SHEELA'. Yantra be then buried underground. There will be no children.

You can write this yantra on Bhooj Patra or plain paper.

v) The root of orange tree (T. Narinja) which is running East on a good day (Preferably on Thursday, day of Jupiter) and grind it with black pepper and drink it with water. There will be no more children.

vi) During menstruation, if one takes castor seed in the morning for seven days, the lady becomes barren.

vii) If during menstruation, a lady takes cow's ghee and also after she enjoys sex with her husband, there will be no fear of pregnancy.

viii) Podina leaf be dried in shade and ground into powder. During sexual act weight equal to nine black seed grams (Mashas) should be taken with water. As long as this is being done, there will be no conception.

ix) Before the sexual act, smeer the female organ with Til oil (seasame). There will be no issue. This is very simple and cent percent success is claimed for this.

For Removal Of Troubles (tested)

Measure the thread of Mauli (red thread used in rituals) equal to the length from foot thumb to head. Wrap it on a coconut which contains water. Stand on a bank of river, lake or canal at the time of sunrise facing East. The coconut be thrown in the river over your head. This will remove all troubles.

For Cure of Epilepsy

Epilepsy is a disease of the brain causing fits and convulsions. Convulsion is a state of being coiled.

In this disease hand and feet twists also. The following are a few useful Tantras:-

(i) Heeng (half a masha) should be mixed with a few drops of water. Put a drop in the nose on the side of nostril, than the side affected with Epilepsy. It is a tested cure.

(ii) If the shoe of an Ass is put in water and the water taken by the patient, epilepsy is cured.

(iii) If the nail of the right foot of an Ass is used as ring in right hand of patient, one recovers from the disease.

(iv) Ring of left horn of cow should be worn on Tuesday in 4th finger of right hand to get cured from Epilepsy.

(v) Ten grams of Heeng should be put in cloth and worn around the neck to have cure from Epilepsy.

For Sexual Strength

1 3 mashas of onion seeds should be mixed with 3 mashas of Mishri (condensed sugar) and ground well. During winter take this three or four times with milk. This will increase your sexual power. IT IS TESTED.

2 Tulsi seeds, Kamal Gata and Konch each 2 half tolas and Meneka without seeds 1/8 seers (125 grams). Should be ground well. Add a small quantity of Kasar, mix it well and make pills. As and when required, take a pill with water. It has been TESTED on patients.

3 The fat of chicken mixed in Murdasinghi be applied on private part of man to increase sexual power.

4 Procure private parts of a bear (RICHCK KINDRI) rub it in Jasmin oil for 15 to 20 minutes. The paste be applied on Private Part of man for 7 days without any sex during these days. After that you will find more sexual power. IT IS TESTED ALSO.

5 If a piece of Alum or root of Langra Mango tied around the waist or bone of camel is placed on the head side of the cot and one enjoys sex, the retention power is increased.

6 A rope of camel hair tied around thigh, one will not discharge till removed.

7 Procure on Sunday, root of Lajwanti plant in Pushy nakshatra. It should be kept in a ring made of silver, to increase the powers of the wearer.

8 If one indulges in sex after applying paste of Kesu flowers under the feet, one will enjoy more.

9 After sex act, rub your semen with left hand on left of underfoot of lady, she will be much infatuated to enjoy more sex.

10 Grind Kamalgata in honey. The paste be applied on upper side of the umbillical. One will not discharge till the paste is removed.

11 Gorochan can be mixed with dried tongue of an owl. This should be preserved in copper talisman. As and when required, keep this talisman in mouth. One will enjoy more.

12 Seeds of Dhatura be ground in honey and use as per 10 above.

13 Bitch, koot, kesar and Gorochan be mixed in equal quantity. Mix with ash of cremation ground and make powder of all. The powder be applied on the forehead of lady who will be responsive.

14 Juice of leaves of Lajwanti plant if applied on private part of lady will lead to greater satisfaction.

To Remove Malefic Effects of All Planets

The roots of Aak, Dhatura, Upamarg, Bargad, Peepal and shami plants, leaves of gular and mango trees, dhoob grass, ghee, milk, rice, gram, moong, wheat til, Honey and Matotha, should be procured.

To Cure Excessive Bleeding–(Tested)

This Tantra has been given to the author by a Devi Saint and has been Tested on many ladies suffering from excessive bleeding during menses or due to tumour etc. It is a simple and effective Tantra.

Sandoz Calcium Lactate powder, white burnt alum, malathi and Majoo phal each 35 grams be ground together. Take one doze equal to teaspoon with curd daily in the morning after breakfast, four times a day. Bleeding will stop.

To Get A Good Husband–(Tested)

To get a suitable and good boy for one's daughter, is a cause of worry for the parents. Parent sometimes take too long. The following Tantra, worship and method is quite effective. It stands *TESTED* and many have been benefited.

"ॐ कात्यायानी महा भागे महा योगिन्य धीश्वरीं नंद गोप सुत देवि पतिं मे कुरूते नमः"

"Om Katyayani Maha bhage Maha yoginya dhishvrim, Nand Goop Sutam Devi Patiam me Kurute Namah".

The girl should recite the above mantra facing East and West in the morning and evening with clean clothes while sitting on a Asana at a lonely place.

Three rosaries be performed at every sitting. If one can perform five rosaries, it will bear early result. After 41 days of continuous recitation and on Friday or Monday in Shual Pakash, Puja of mother Parvati be performed. The girl should offer meals to Nine girls who are minor and three small boys. Donate Dupatas and clothes to girls and boys according to one's capacity. Also give donations to a Brahmin. She will be successful in her desires.

1. When excreta of lion is mixed in wine and given to anybody, he will leave the habit of drinking.
2. On Tuesday, or when Moon is in Scorpio sign, the excreta of black chicken is put on the door of anybody, there will be constant quarrels in that house.

3. In Aswini Nakshatra, if smoke of shoe is given to any person affected by souls, the person will become free from such effects.
4. If the roots of Lemon tree is taken by a lady with water who is blessed with sons and wants daughters, she will give birth to girls.

To Abort

Use the following Tantras for effective results.

(i) If the root of the Brahmi herb is worn on the body of a lady, she will abort.

(ii) First teeth of child be used as talisman in silver on left arm she will abort.

(iii) Procure root of Dhatura in Pushy nakshatra on Sunday. Wear or tie it on the neck through raw thread woven by a virgin girl. One will abort.

(iv) Give smoke of excreta of horse to private part of lady, who will abort.

(v) Make a powder of Soure Tumbi (Groud) in water and apply on the private part of lady, who will abort.

(vi) Apply paste of the excreta of an elephant on the private parts of a lady, or if she keeps the teeth of a snake with her, she will abort.

1. To get relief from HYSTERIA, take a louse from a sheep and wrap it in wool of blanket, and wear in a copper talisman, one will recover from the disease.
2. In case of irregular menses and pain, the lady should tie rope of reed (Moonj ki rassi) around her waiste during the night. In the morning, the rope be thrown where four roads meet. Pain will go and regular menses will start.
3. Make a bangle of black female horse and nail of a boat after mixing the metals together. Perform Pooja of bangle with Dhoop, lamp etc., and wear on right hand. One will recover from Windy or gastric complaints. Also one is protected from the effects of souls. This too will increase the sexual power of the wearer. It is A TESTED powerful tantra. Refer 57 serial also.
4. Wearing of Rangaa metal on right hand second finger to reduce fat in the body. One will become lean.

To Cure Piles

(i) The ring of skin of rhinoceros if worn will cure the piles.

(ii) Tie around the waist about six mashas of root of black thorn apple. It controls piles and night discharge.

(iii) Specially made ring with stone is provided to patients by the author.

1. Make powder of Kesar, chandan, Camphor, Tulsi leaves, which are mixed in cow milk. Apply this tilak on your forehead and appear before an officer, lady or anybody who will be kind to you. this is TESTED tantra.
2. The seeds of Tulsi and Zamikand when taken in betel leave will enable a man or woman to enjoy the sexual act for long.
3. Burn the wing of crow on Sunday night between 11 and 12 O'clock with a few clothes on your body. This ash be mixed with sugar in equal weight. Whosoever is given this ash to eat will remain under your control.

For Transfer

When anybody wants his transfer from a place, he should take a bath before sunrise and change the clothes. After sunrise he should pay Surya Namaskar and take 21 seeds of Red chilly and offer to Sun with a prayer of your transfer at a particular place. Repeat this process for three days. You will receive your transfer orders at the earliest.

For Vashi Karan

1. A plant known as ANJEER is generally found in Hilly areas. Its fruits are very sweet. This plant or tree has one dried branch always, which is called, "BEEDA ANJEER".

   Cut this Beeda Anjeer to 4-6 pieces. To control a man, the piece be used for beating or patting the bitch for 4-5 times or in case of woman, use it on dog. Keep the name in your mind while beating, Burn the piece afterwards and the ash be given for eating to the person, who will be infatuated.
2. Grind Braham Dhandi or the root of a bargad tree and apply the tilak on your head. Go before person who will be infatuated.
3. The root of pomegranate, its flowers and leaves be mixed and ground with yellow sarsoon on Sunday. Keep this powder. Apply tilak and appear before anybody, who will be infatuated.
4. The flower of Jasmin (Chameli) should be wrapped in cotton and a lamp lit in chameli oil. Collect Kajal in skull of man. Put Kajal in eyes, and go before anyone, who will be enchanted.
5. Tick or Louse from body of dog, Bhanware, Lajwanti or Sehedevi be ground together on Sunday and preserved. Apply tilak for Vashi Karan.
6. The sting of Scorpio, nails of crow and dog all be put in skin of

camel. Make a talisman of it. Put on the neck of insane man or woman who will recover.

Cure From Souls

Take a nail of boat and horse shoe, make a bracelet by mixing both metals. Put this to smoke of Dhoop and infuse the bracelet with following mantra and wear it on the right hand for the removal of effects of souls. Many diseases will be cured. Refer serial no.44 also.

Mantra

"ॐ नमः शमशान वासिने भुतादिनां पलायं कुरू कुरू स्वाहा"

"Om Namaha shamshanvasiney Bhotadinam Plaem Kuru Kuru Swaha".

Recite this mantra daily 108 times for 41 days facing East in the morning to attain siddhi of mantra. This mantra is to be used for removing effects of souls.

1. Mix and grind Gandhak, Gugal, Lack, hairs of forehead, Elephant's Nails and skin of snake. Infuse with above mantra and the affected man be given smoke of this. One will be cured.
2. Turmeric and the juice of flowers of kashiphal should be ground on stone. Infuse with the above mantra. This water should be used as eye drops by the patient. One will be cured from effects of souls.
3. Procure meat and skin of Gugu on Saturday. Grind them separately. Mix them on Sunday and infuse with above mantra. Whole house be infused with smoke of this mixture. All effects of souls, Ghosts etc., will be removed.

For Gain In Business

1. Procure on Sunday the Navel chord of cat (Billl Ki Jeer) and with due respect, place it in the articles which will have good sale. Alternately use this in the cash box. You will not remain short of money.
2. Recite this mantra 108 times on black horse beans (Black Urad called in Hindi) and spread them in shop or office. Repeat this for four Sundays after reciting the mantra 108 times.

Mantra

" भंवर वीर तू चेला मेरा, खोल दुकान कहाकर मेरा उठे जो डन्डी बिके जो माल, भैवर वीर सोखे नहीं जायै ॥"

All the scattered pieces of Urd be collected during sweeping of shop next day and all these placed on four cross roads or keep them in cloth and preserve in the shop. The business will be boosted.

13

HERBAL PLANTS IN TANTRA

Tantra deals with the medicinal and other uses of plants. This is called KALPA TANTRA.

Uprooting of Plants

There is a definite procedure to uproot a plant on a specified day and in a specific nakshatra. Plants taken out without the prescribed procedure do not serve any purpose. Plants grown in forests have intrinsic strength. Plants grown on ant hills, pits, on the roadside, under trees, in temples and burial grounds should be discarded.

One must get up early in the morning, bathe, worship Lord SHIVA and go to the plant. Sprinkle water on the plant. One must then fold one's hands respectfully to the tree or plant and after offering prayers can then begin uprooting the plant.

The plant must be dug on a specified day and nakshatra. Before digging one must utter the following mantra.

Mantra

"ॐ हरीं चण्डै हूं फट् स्वाहा"

"Om Hareeng chande Hoong Phut swaha"

Finally while cutting or uprooting roots, plants or tree one should say the following mantra.

Mantra

"ॐ हरीं क्षौं फट् स्वाहा"

"Om Hareeng Kashong Phut Swaha".

According to the above procedure procure the plant and use as directed.

Plants in Mountains

There are many plants found in the mountains which are very rare and beneficial to mankind and have medicinal value. The same plants are very useful in Yantra and Tantra as well. Given below are a few plants and their uses which should be noted carefully by the sadhaka.

1. *Amar Kantki*

This plant is available in India between Ranikhet and Bhuwali and the upper region and of the Himalayas along the course of the river Yamuna. The plant is four feet in height and two feet wide. Its roots are 6 to 8 inches deep, and its leaves are pointed and thorny. In winter, the plant has good growth, whereas in Summer the leaves wither away. It is green in colour.

In case one takes the juice of the root of this plant, one is cured from Bronchitis, Palpitation of heart, bodily weakness etc. If one takes this medicine or juice for six months continuously, weakness in sexual power is removed in males. This is specially useful for old age. In Russia, this is used very widely. When the roots are put in water it discharges a yellow colour. This water, if taken cures many diseases and is also used for Achaman and Sadhana purposes. Another use of the leaves of this plant is the extraction of the juice of its leaves, which can be passed through the process of calcination. This extract, if used as medicine results in rejuvenating men within one week !

2. *Mayura Sikha*

This plant is known by many names such as Mayur Kand, Siki, Sikha or Mayura Sikha and Celosia cristata. It is found in Kulu Manali. The People of this area worship this plant, it's roots, trunk and leaves all of which are used in many ways. It cures Rheumatic pains, Cancer, Brain fever, and other diseases. It is being used widely in China. White hair can turn black again through its use. This Plant is three to four feet in height and looks like Tulsi plant. If the plant is taken in Pushyami nakshatra and tied around neck of a child, it keeps off ghosts and evil spirits. If the child is suffering from fever due to an evil spirit and if it is exposed to smoke coming from the burning plant, the person is cured immediately. If a man sets out in the night with the root of plant in the hair of his head he is free from the fears of ghosts and serpents.

If its roots are powdered and taken regularly for two months, the skin's dark hue is removed automatically and a fresh red skin appears, which removes all signs such as old age wrinkles. The juice of its leaves if mixed in wine (about two to three drops) in the case of a man's sexual power, it increases and makes him look younger. If the juice of the plant is mixed in oil and milk the plant is mixed with four times its weight of snuli powder (T. Chemudu, M-Sehuna Milk hedge) and an equal amount of butter and cow milk along with five black grams seeds, it cures stomach parasites. Women can use the juice of its root to enhance one's beauty, it make the skin shine and removes dark circles from under the eyes.

3. *Rudra Vanti*

The root of this plant is very useful. The old root of this plant has specific use, and the older it is, the more effective. It is said that the old root of this plant costs five thousand rupees a gram. The Juice of the root is specially useful for Diphtheria, cough, Cancer, diseases of the semen, weakness of organs, Gastric and other diseases connected with the stomach.

The juice of its roots also helps diabetic persons. The paste of its leaves if applied on head for 3 days cures baldness and black hair grows again . The growth of ordinary hair is increased, specially for ladies, whose hair is falling. The root and leaves can be used for any pain or problem in the joints and bones.

NOTE: In these and other paragraphs in this book the letters T-stands for Telegu, H-for Hindi and S for Sanskrit and L the last is the botanical name.

4. *Vajara Danti*

The plant is well known and so is called T-Uttareni, H-Apamarga Chirat, L-Chyyranthes Asper.

Its roots are used for cleaning the teeth. If the root or skin is kept between teeth for 21 days, the teeth become strong. If milk of roots is taken in, it increases the semen. If drunk for 21days, one is cured of all diseases.

Flowers of sesame, with lotus flowers and juice of leaves of this plant, in equal quantities should be mixed and warmed in the sesame oil. The oil must be used for 7 days, the hair becomes thick and black. The plant should be plucked on a Sunday in Pushyami Nakshatra.

5. *Aam Tari*

This plant is found around Dehra Dun and in the Lal Tiba area of Mussorie. It is barely four or five feet in height and has small leaves, which shine during the night. Its leaves dipped in water for three days and then ground to a paste, if applied on the face, hands and body all wrinkles will go and one will look young.

The powder of its roots if used for one month will make white hair black again. It is also useful for ladies who do not conceive, have irregular menses and have frequent abortions, all of which are cured through its leaves.

6. *Kali Tumbi*

In jungles of Rajasthan, mountains of Manipur and near Gangotri, a tree like ता ड़s found known as TUMBA. Its fruits are like coconuts, which fall after they become ripe. Out of these fruits, one black fruit is rarely found. Actually this is used for Tantrik Sadhanas.The seeds of Kali Tumbi is rubbed in ten-year-old gur which becomes a paste. At the time of Sidhi many Tantriks offer their tongue and body parts by cutting them to Ma-Kali and after that restore them in position through the paste.

7. *Black Turmeric*

It is known as Kali Haldi and is used in Tantrik Sadhana.This plant is found around the Narbada river in Madhya Pradesh, in Makwan Pur Dist of Nepal, and in the plains of Vastor.

It is used as a paste in medicines for Bronchitis.The paste is also used as a Tilak by Tantriks on the forehead of Kali-Ma.

8. *Aparajita or Giri Karnika*

T-Vishnu Kranta, H-Sanka Pushpi, Evolulus Aloinoides are the names of this plant.This small plant has violet flowers and grows wild on hedges and fields.The time for plucking the plant is the 8th and 14th tithi of dark fortnight in pushyami or Hasta nakshatras and during a solar or lunar eclipse. The flowers or the roots should be powdered and made into small pills and dried in the shade. This should be done while thinking of Lord SHIVA after bathing and donning white clothes.

If the paste is applied on the forehead, a person is able to bring others under his control. In war, before a strong army if one wears this on the forehead, the enemy is subdued. If one rubs this Paste over the body or applies it on the arms, one lives a long time.When the dried leaves are made into a beedi and smoked; it cures cough and asthama.

9. *Nagada Mani*

It is known as (S. Visarpini, T-Isdvari, H-Irvari mool A indica).The plant can be identified by its blue trunk. Its leaves are like betel leaves and has yellow flowers. It is a creeper.

The name implies that it is inimical to serpents. In the three worlds, it is the plant that develops quickly auspiciousness (Mangal Yam). Purity (Pavitra), prosperity, steadiness, memory knowledge, intellect, knowledge of scripture (sruti smriti).

It gives peace of mind and strength. A king should wear this plant before going to war around the ear, neck or hand. When worn around both the elbows or around the waist, it increases beauty and virility and brings all under Vashi karan.

If kept in a house it averts deaths. If one wears it around the neck, one has no fear from fire, oceans, wars, Tigers, demons, lions and of enemies.

As medicine it destroys the poison of snakes and other land animals. Other poisons of living or non-living bodies and minor poisons are destroyed at the mere sight of it, including the poison of scorpions.

It cures Goitre, wounds, stomach and Heart troubles and if taken for a year with ghee and honey, a person gets rid of all ailments, and is free from wrinkles and white hair. One becomes strong, free from all diseases and longevity is increased. If taken with ghee by ladies it will cure barrenness. This should not be given to pregnant ladies as it leads to abortions.

10. *Black Rice*

Its growth is natural in small quantity in Assam hills during the rainy season.When chewed, the colour of the mouth become red. It is also called Bloody Rice. The red water made through its powder is used in Tantrik sadhans and particularly sidhi of Durga-Mato to whom this rice is offered.

11. *Danwantri*

The plant is available in Jammu-Kashmir area and being called as Dhanuri by the local people. The plant is about three feet in height and its growth is about two feet.This plant shines and twinkles like a fire during the night. Its leaves are pointed and some thorns are found with its roots. The trunk, leaves and its roots are very valuable and are used to cure many diseases. One does not feel hunger and thirst for 24 hours if one takes just one leaf. One leaf taken with honey by a woman prevents her from getting pregnant. Fresh leaves made into a powder if taken with milk cures eye diseases.

Its root if mixed in vegetables and cooked removes the blackish hues from the body and face. The powder of its root processed through calcination, if applied as a paste removes the black colour of the body and a new good colour of body appears and one looks beautiful. One becomes lean if its roots are taken, weight is also reduced by this plant.

Dry its leaves in the shade and make a powder. This powder when mixed with honey and taken for a week removes sexual incompatibility. If taken for a month, one feels fully invigorated. For ladies, the plant acts like magic. The powder if taken by them for a month makes them beautiful and the body becomes lean and attractive.

If its root is cooked with dal, and taken for 15 days, it clears the skin of blemishes and body becomes attractive. The powder of its root mixed with hair oil and if rubbed on the hair, removes white hair and leads to a luxuriant growth. The juice if applied on the face for three days removes all marks of small pox and the face becomes clear.

12. *Sveta Punar Nava*

This plant is known as Tella Galiyeru-T, Gadabani-H, Decandra Dimi-I.

This is a well known plant, used by Ayurvedic physicians as a remedy for eye diseases. It has two kinds of flowers white and red. The white variety is discussed here.

The root when rubbed with cow's ghee and applied to the eyes destroys all eye diseases and when the root is taken with milk, it cures flowers in the eyes, with honey cures watering of eyes, with kanji, night blindness. If taken with cow's ghee the powder of the whole plant (dried in the shade) cures Gastritis and disorders of the spleen. When taken with crystal sugar continuously in the morning, increases longevity.

When taken with Jyotishmati (T-Maneru or Malkingni L-Mountana) it increases sexual potency in men.

When the paste of roots is taken with water and applied to the eyes many eye diseases are cured. When taken with honey it keeps off old age.

Chronic Jaundice is cured by taking few of the slender leaves of the plant with milk for one month.

When the plant is taken with rice cooked in milk, it cures diseases of head and fevers.

The plant as a whole can be plucked from its roots on a Sunday in Pushyami nakshatra. It should then be dried in the shade and powdered. The powder should be put in a mixture of ghee and honey and kept for one month. In Vasant Ritu (Spring season) in early

March-April, one teaspoonful should be taken after a bath. It makes the hair become black and also makes one very wise.

13. *Ankola*

T-Udhugu, H-Thera, L-Sage Leaved Alangiam. This tree has four colours – White, red, green and black. The roots running towards East are to be taken on Thursday in hasta nakshatra. They are to be mixed with camphor and honey and are to be applied to the eyes in the evening. Disease of the eyes including blindness are cured.

If the seeds are taken with honey for 21 days and one looks at a serpent, it dies immediately. If the powder of the seeds is taken during the bright fortnights (before full moon), one is relieved of old age and is rejuvenated.

The fibres of lotus stem are soaked in the oil of the seeds and made into a wick and lit. The soot formed from the flame is collected. If the soot is applied as Anjan to the eyelids, the person cannot be seen by others.

14. *Kakajangha*

(T-Velama Sandhi, T-Eseasptinta). The plant as a whole should be uprooted on a day in Pushyami nakshatra. It must be dried in the shade and ground to a powder. A pinch of powder should be mixed (karsh) with crystal sugar and the root of Sara Panka (T-Vempali, L-Parapurea Linn) and ghee. If taken for six months it protects a man from weapons. The body becomes very strong, the powder can be with milk also. If taken for 45 days, an old man becomes young. When taken with cooked rice and curd, it protects a person from weapons. This should be taken so long as there is free urination and excretion. Otherwise it should be stopped.

The juice of plant mixed with the root of ISVARA is a good cure for wounds.

The root with juice of Bringa and Amalaka (Embic Myrobalan) is heated in seasame oil. If this oils is applied on head, baldness is cured.

If the root is taken with hot water, it stops the ejection of semen. If taken with ghee, it cures stomach troubles. When taken with cold water, vomitting is stopped. If taken with milk bleeding stops. If the roots are tied to the ear, eye diseases are cured. If the root is ground in water with Gorochan and applied as Tilak, all people will give respect and become obedient. With Hingul Mercurie Sulphied (mineral) cures enlargement of spleen. With mustard oil it cures bile (Pitta) and Gout

(Vata). Taken with Gur (Jaggery) and hot water phelgm, is destroyed. If drunk with gur and butter mild, pain during Urination is cured. If taken with buffalo's milk, tuberculosis is cured.

If the root is taken by a barren woman with cow's milk from an animal having one colour at the time of her menses, she will bear sons. If the root is eaten with cashew nuts, it destroys Leprosy.

When plant is uprooted in krittika or Rohini nakshatra, one will have wealth and corn. In Revati, all actions will be good. If a Ultrabhadra and all five parts (Bark, flower, fruit, root and leaf) are put on the head, there will be all round success. If the root is placed between teeth within crevices, the worms come out.

15 *Karanja* (T-Karuga, Indian Beach)

This is a big tree. Sticks of the branches are used for cleaning the teeth. The nuts are used in medicine. The tree which grows on a soil other than white should be chosen.

If the roots are taken with milk, it cures anaemia. If the root is taken with butter milk or if the powder of the root is taken with ghee, Leprosy is cured. The leaves when formed into a paste and applied cures chronic wounds. If the powder of five parts of the plant is cooked with oil and applied on the body it cures Rheumatism.

When the young leaves are ground into a paste and applied it cures bleeding piles. If the juice of the root is applied, Fistula is cured. If the same is mixed with castor oil and applied it helps the cure of paralytic arms and legs.

16. *Manduka Brahmi* (T-Saraswati, Centella Asiatics)

The plant should be taken during the bright fortnight in Pushyami Star. The whole plant has to be powdered. If a Pinch of powder is taken with Cow's milk, within seven days all stomach troubles cease and after a fortnight the body becomes strong. In one month all diseases disappear. By using it, yakshas and rakshasas (evil spirits) are kept at bay. A barren woman gets children after taking this. If the root is taken with honey and ghee, dropsy and enlargement of spleen are cured.

With the help of this mantra, the powder can be purified.

"ॐ अमृतोदभवायामृतं कुरू कुरू स्वाहा"

Mantra : "Om Amrotidhabhvayamritam kuru kuru swaha."

17. *Sveta Gunja* (T-Telle Grivinda, H-Safed Funja, Abrus Practorious)

On a day of Uttrabhadra nakshatra and facing the north, the root of this plant should be taken. If a white thread is dipped in the juice and burnt and the black powder is mixed with cow's ghee and if applied to the eyes, it removes all eye troubles.

If the body is smeared with the plant, over all parts for seven months, the body becomes very strong. One does not get burnt even in fire.

The following should be recited, when one wants to be saved from fire.

"ॐ बजकिरणे अमृतं कुरू स्वाहा ॐ नमो महा माया वहि रक्ष स्वाहा"

MANTRA : "Om vajirkirney Amritam Kuru Swaha"

"Om Namo Maha Maya Vahir Rakshak Swaha"

18. *Dev Adali* (T Davaradangi, Bristulfia duffa Echinata)

The juice of this plant with an equal amount of Amalaka juice and twice the amount of ghee is taken in an iron vessel and slightly heated with dried stems of Amalaka. It may be taken twice a day. Milk or milk and rice should be taken. This cures epilepsy, Tuberculosis, Leprosy and Rheumatic diseases.

If a pinch of Devadali and mustard is taken with ghee and water from Oudumbar (wild Fig tree) diseases of liver and spleen, Fistula, Jaundice and anaemia are cured. If the powder is taken with the powder of Aswagandha (T-Penneru-Phsyalisfiex nosa) and ghee, it makes a man more virile and gives him a long life.

19. *Brahma Dandi* (T-Balarakkisa, H-Shialkanta, Argemore Mexicane)

This plant must be taken during Aswin or Kartik months. (15th Sept. to 14th Oct. and 15th Oct. to 14 Nov.). Mix juice of this plant with gugal (Badalilium) and apply it on the skin. It removes itches, pimples and other skin troubles. If it is taken in dark fortnight and tied to the hand, it drives away evil spirits. If the bark of root is taken with a decoction of palas (T-Madugu-Butea Enondora) it increases the semen. If taken with curd, it cures woman's menstrual troubles, and helps in child birth. If the roots of this plant are rubbed in water and taken diabetes is cured.

20. *Saha Devi* (T & H Sahadevi, Conyza Cinerac)

The plant should be taken on 8th or 14th Tithi of a dark fortnight. If tied with a thread to the hand, it facilitates easy delivery and also keeps off evil spirits. If tied around the neck of a child, it cures stomach troubles. If the powder of the plant is taken with ghee, it cures indigestion. If the plant is heated in oil and applied to the head, it cures headaches and removes whiteness of hair. If the juice of plant is heated with ghee and milk and taken, it cures leprosy.

NOTE: Only 25 medicinal plants have been listed, out of which 14 plants with abbreviations have been taken from the book, "Yoga and Tantra" by Shri J.C. Kamesvara Rao and their TANTRIK Remedies. Mr Rao has not given the specific areas of the country where these are available to facilitate the sadhaks in finding these plants. The author is grateful to Shri J.C. Kamesvara Rao for the preceding information.

Tantrik Remedies

Under KALPA TANTRA a number of remedies were considered for different diseases of which a few are given below:-

1. *Lunacy*

a) Two tolas of Juice of Manduka Parni and two tolas of honey should be taken twice daily for some days.

b) Akasavalli (T-Nulutiga, H3/4 Amarbali, Casytha Filiformis Linn). Juice of 2 tolas, Honey 2 tolas, ghee two tolas. This is to be mixed and taken for three days only.

ii) EPILEPSY: Brahamdandi Plant with roots should be taken and a decoction of it prepared. About two ounces should be taken.

Haritamanjari (H-Kuppi, T-Kuppenta) Juice of Mundka Parni leaves, taken with milk is a good remedy.

2. *Stammering*

Leaves of Manduka Parni should be dried in the shade and powdered. This powder should be taken with crystal sugar twice a day.

3. *Improving Memory and Intelligence of Boys and Girls*

Keep Vasa powder in Amalaka Juice for one day. Take a pinch and mix it with cow's ghee and give to the boys and girls or to anybody. If one takes the powder with milk and utters the following Mantra, one develops a sharp memory and intelligence. The diet should have ghee, milk and rice. The mantra is from Rasa ratanakara.

ॐ हूं रं हयशिर वागीश्वराय नमः

Mantra: "Om Hoong Roum Heyshiar Vagishvaraye Namha"

Turmeric, Vasa Kusht (H-Kuth)Pipali, dried ginger, Jera, ajmod, yakshi, Madhukam. All should be taken in equal quantities and powdered. If taken with ghee 6 mashas for a dose, one will become very intelligent.

This is from Kama Ratna.

Only a selection of remedies for the use of the reader has been included so that both they and their children are benefited. The above remedies should be tried in the case of children who are dull and backward.

Some More Remedies: Given below are few remedies secured from some Tantric texts and old manuscripts. These are particularly useful to poor people and villagers.

4. *Asthma And Cough*

1) Vajradanti plant should be dried and burnt into ashes.If the ash is taken with honey, it cures both asthna and cough. 2)Pepper, dried ginger and Ajwayin (T.Omamu) when taken with honey cures cough with phlegm. 3) The bark of a tamarind tree and vajravalli (T.Nallern, H.Hedjora) taken in equal parts is burnt into ashes. If the ash is taken with honey it cures Asthma 4)Pepper powder mixed with Jaggery and ghee cures cough. This is a well known remedy. 5)Vasaka (T.Addasaram, H.Dulasa) Juice 1/4 tola,Kantakar (T.Vakudu, Solanum Jaquini) Juice 1/4 tola and Vajradanti leaf juice 1/4 tola mixed with honey one tola and taken every morning will cure all sorts of cough. 6) Seeds of Agasthya -mundidrum (T.Avisa -H.Basna sesvania gracdiflare) are fried and powdered. If taken with honey in the morning for two or three weeks it cures asthama.

5. *Cut and Burns*

1. Vajradanti leaves made into a paste and applied to the cut, stops bleeding and heals the wound. 2. Juice of betel leaves should be applied to the cut smoothly and covered by a leaf and bandaged.In one or two days the two parts of the cut are joined and the wound heals quickly. 3. Camphor mixed with ghee should be put over the cut and bandaged. Even big cuts get joined.

6. *Diabetes*

1. The root of Brahma dandi (T.Balarakkisa H.Shial Kanta) must be rubbed with water on a smooth stone and the paste taken. This is a reliable remedy. 2. Tender leaves of Hema Pushpi(T.Tangeti,H.-Tarwar country soma) must be dried and should be taken with pepper and sugar. 3. Ragi (broken or Powder)must be cooked in hot water and the Kanji should be taken with butter milk. It cures diabetes. 4. Seeds of kasa mardhana (T.Kasivinda,Cassia sophona)should be powdered and taken with honey.

7. Diarrhoea and Dysentery

1. Decoction of Coriander seeds when taken with honey cures dysentery. 2. One can also add dry ginger to the skin of pomegranate fruit with twice the amount of jaggery.This mixture should be taken thrice a day.It cures the ailment in a single day. 3. Mango bark should be made into a paste with milk curd and applied round the navel to stop watery motions. 4. Jambu, Mango and Amalaka leaves are taken and the juice extracted. If the juice taken with honey, motions with blood will stop. 5. Barks of Bilwa (T.Maredu) and mango are taken and juice from them is extracted. If the juice is taken with honey motions and vomitting are stopped.

8. Cholera

1. Six mashas of Vajradanti root powder taken with water is a good remedy.
2. Juice of Sun flower plant when put in the ear, removes pain.

9. Eye Diseases

a) Redness and pain in eyes:
   i. Juice of leaves of Kinkirata (T. Nandivaradhana H. Chandrey Taberuoemontana) when ripe clears the eyes. The flowers also can be used.
   ii. Sesame oil mixed with lemon juice and put in eyes, removes redness.

b) Flowers in Eyes:
   i. Cowrie burnt to ashes and powdered, when applied with butter to the eye cures this problem.
   ii. If one eats pepper, tamarind and betel leaf all made into a paste, flower in the eye is removed.

c) Night Blindness:
   i. Tender leaves of Castor (4 or 5) taken every day cures night blindness.
   ii. Tender leaves of Jivanti (T Manubala of Palachethi-Dend robium mawasi) should be fried in ghee and eaten.

10. Fevers

1. Nirgundi leaves (tender) with five pepper seeds when taken cures malaria.
2. On Sunday secure the roots of Nirgundi and Sahadevi and tie them round the waist of the patient, the fever disappears.
3. The root of Arka should be taken on a Sunday and if tied to the ear of the patient, fever is cured.

11. *Fistula*

1. Leaves of Lajavati (T.Attipatii sensitive plant mimosa) when made into a paste and spread over the region cures fistula.
2. Vidang (T-Vayuvidangam) skin of haritaki (T. Karakkaya) (Myrobaiam), amalaka, long pepper should be powdered and mixed with honey and the paste spread over a piece of cloth. The cloth should be tied over the fistula.

12. *Jaundice*

1. Take the whole plant Bhuneyamalaka (T. Nelavisirika Phyllanthes Neruri) with roots and with 5 or 6 pepper seeds make a paste and make three pills 4 or 5 mm in diameter. One is to be taken at night before sleeping, one the next morning and the third at night. The diet must be strictly followed and should consist of boiled rice with curd (cow's). With three doses the disease will be cured. The colour of the urine becomes clear. This is an excellent remedy which has saved the lives of many. If the disease has become chronic, a few more doses can be taken but the diet should be strictly observed. At least three hundred cases were treated without any failure by this method.
2. Juice of Castor leaf, one tola and cow's milk of the same quantity should be mixed and given in the morning for three days. Cow's milk should be given to drink and cow's milk and rice should be eaten.

13. *Hydrocele*

1. Punarnava (T.Gatjeru, H. Sant) leaves should be ground, warmed and applied.
2. Kuberakshi (T. Gachą H. Karanjuva, Molucca bean) leaves should be warmed and applied with castor oil.

14. *Piles*

1. Three parts of the juice of bitter gourd (T. Kakara) and one part of sugar should be taken for four days.
2. Long pepper and myrobalam (harithaka) should be powdered and fried in ghee and taken with jaggery.
3. Fresh Mullangi (one root) if taken twice a day cures piles.
4. NAGAKESARA, butter and crystals of sugar should be mixed and taken for forty days at the rate of one tola per day.
5. Tender leaves of Karanjeka (T. Kanuga, Indian beach H. Karanj) when ground and applied cures bleeding piles.

15. *Skin Diseases*

1. Juice of hartiamnjari (T. Kuppente H. Kuppi, Acalyph indica) leaves when applied to the skin, cures all skin diseases.

2. Oil from Karanjaka seeds when applied cures all skin diseases.
3. Tender leaves of Udumbura (T Medi H. Gular) and pepper when ground should be applied to boils which are suppurated.

16. *Toothache*

1. Two or three drops of juice of Sitaphal leaves, when placed in the crevices of the teeth, kills the worms and removes the pain.
2. Milk of arka when placed in the damaged tooth, kills the worm and pain is lessened.
3. Leaves of Vajradanti when put in the ear removes the pain.
4. Leaves of Jambu should be dried in the shade and powdered. Add Khadirasara (T. Kaviri - Catechu _ and put between the teeth.
5. Fine powder of Harithaki (Myrobalam) should be mixed with honey and warmed in a copper vessel and applied to the teeth. The pain disappears immediately, (Kamaratnam of Nitya Natha).
6. Root of chitrika (T. Chitra Mulam H. Chitrak) should be pressed between the teeth, the pain is lessened.

17. *Tuberculosis*

1. Four parts of juice of Nirgundi plant and one part of ghee should be heated and given to the patient. He will escape from death.
2. GOKSHURA (T. Peddapalleru H. Gokhuru, Tribalus Terustris) unripe fruit 1/4 tola, ghee 1/4 tola and honey 1/2 tola. Three doses suffice.
3. Kakajanga plant (T. Velama sandhi) with roots and made into a paste with cow's or buffallo's milk should be taken.

18. *Ulcers in the Mouth and Tongue*

1 Cardamom Seeds and betel nuts should be broken into pieces and carbondised by frying. The powder should be applied to the tongue and palate.

2. Kala Jeera (T. Nalla Jeelakarra Black Cummin) should be ground and applied to the tongue with honey.
3. A particularly good remedy for children is to take half a cup of water and the juice of two lemons and little salt and a little sandal wood paste. It should be taken before meals morning and evening for two months.

Fig. 4.1

14

TANTRIC ARTICLES AND THEIR USE

Nature has created many rare things, the use of which is auspicious for health, wealth and happiness. These may raise the spirituality of the user give protection from enemies and give victory in law suits, vashi karan etc. The author has tested these on many persons and found them very effective.

A few of them are provided below and can be used in Tantra and for puja. These rare Tantric articles, are available with the author for the use of sadhakas and can be obtained from him.

1. Shvetarak Ganpati

In Sanskrit it is called Ark and in Hindi or Rajasthan is known as Aak.

This Aak plant has green and blue leaves. Its flowers are of small size but without any fragrance. The Aak plant has a rare white plant which also has white flowers. This is a rare plant and cannot be found easily.

The root of this white Aak must be taken out carefully. When the bark and thin wood over the root is peeled off, one will see an image of Ganpati below it. This is called SHVETARAK GANPATI.

Some people take the root of a white Aak to the carpenter and get a Ganpati made. This too can be useful after doing sadhana according to Tantra shastra. Yogis use it mostly for sadhana.

The Shastras say that in any house which has a white Ganpati remains free from all evils and the possessor is blessed with immense wealth. This is used for pooja. When once Ganpati is awakened through Sadhana, nothing becomes immpossible for him.

In addition, Green Topaz's Ganpati and Ganpati made of Crystal glass are very valuable. These can also be used as detailed above as it is not commonly available.

2. Parad Shivlinga

This Shivlinga is made of Mercury and silver and is very solid and heavy. Normally Mercury neither dissolves in water nor does it stand at one place when one puts ones hand on it. Yogis of high calibre with their spiritual power heat Mercury to its boiling point viz at 321 degrees Centigrade and mix silver in it. It solidifies in the form of SHIVLINGA, called PARAD SHIVLINGA. It is a very rare Tantrik article.

This SHIVLINGA when kept in the sun radiates rainbow colours. Tantriks use it for Sadhana.

3. Safteek Shivlinga

This SHIVA LINGA is made of crystal quartz or lens glass. The author has seen this in Raghunath-Ji mandar Jammu (J&K). It bestows on the possessor all comforts of life, wealth, health and keeps one free from worries and offers protection against all trouble.

4. Parcarshi Saligram

Lord Shiva too has a form of Saligram. This Saligram is of round shape and of black colour just like a lemon. The speciality of this is that you can see an image of waving serpent in it.

It is also made of PARAS stone. To the author's knowledge there is one in India in temple of Petowa Distt Kurukshetra (Haryana) and the second is in Nepal. It is rare. It may also be found near Gangotri or its branches. The author got garlanded with one from the riverbed at Badrinath.

The sadhaka is blessed with various stypes of siddhis and blessings of Kali Ma. One remains free of any trouble. It is a rare and costly item.

5. Abayukat Saligram

This Saligram is an incarnation of Lord Vishnu and is commonly available, but the round saligram is rare. The test is when one see's the Saligram in Sun, whether one can see a red light. This is best for family comforts.

6. Dakshineye Sankh

The seashell which opens towards the left hand are commonly available but the shells which open towards the RIGHT HAND are rare.

The right hand sankh or right hand Conch is found in three sizes small, medium and big and correspond to male, female and eunuch. The male sankh gives the sound of OM when put near the ear. The male sankh gives a sound when it is used by blowing through the lips. The female conch does not give any sound. A conch which is eunuck is always solid but gives no sound. A male conch is rarely available. The place or house where this shell is placed and its pooja is performed brings good future to all. It can be used in many ways in Tantric Sadhana. Puja is performed by placing it on a silver plate everyday. It is a tested article which brings wealth and the comforts of life.

7. *One Eyed Coconut:* This coconut is attributed as third eye of LORD-SHIVA. A coconut is normally available with two eyes. The coconut having one eye is rarely available and is an emblem of wealth.

On Diwali day, this can be used in many ways for Tantric purposes.

After attaining sidhi of it, the Yogi or other persons keep it in temple and at the time of sadhana, they can see all things around them or any person approaching them through the one-eyed coconut.

8. Lagu Coconut

This coconut has three eyes and is rarely available. It is of supari size and too small. This bestows wealth and all comforts of life. This is also a TESTED ARTICLE.

9. Siyar Singhi

Siyar means Jackal, which normally has no horn but when it hoots facing downwards, a small bunch of hair with a horn emerges from his body at the forehead. This is taken for and is called Siyar Singhi. It may be of small, medium and big sizes.

In Tantra and Mantra, this can be used in many ways.

It is always kept in vermillion (Sindoor), and its hair grows automatically.

If one keeps a Siyar Singhi in the house, one is blessed with wealth, one remains fearless of beasts and it provides protection, from enemies and evil spirits and gives success in law suits.

Medium and big size Siyar Singhis are kept in the temple or on the body. The small sized one is put as a talisman around the neck of adults and children. It is tested article which enables a person to accomplish all his or her goals.

10. Hath Jori

In Madhya Pradesh on Amar Kantek hills and in the Lumibani valley of Nepal, there are thick forests. In these jungles one can find a plant known as 'BIRVAH' which has blue and white coloured flowers and which is similiar to the Dhatura plant.

If one digs carefully on Sunday, the earth near the roots of this plant will reveal two small sized branches. At that place one will find branches which look like a hand having five fingers or those which look like two hands joined together in prayer. This branch is cut and separated, and is called HATH JOR in Tantra. It is small in size about 2" to 3" and equally broad. One can see two hands joined together distinctly.

After taking it out, it is immersed in Til oil. It is said that it absorbs about one kilo Til oil in a month whereas its weight remains the same. When it stops to absorb oil, it is taken out. After performing Puja, it is kept in Sindoor (Vermillion). After this, it is used in Tantric sadhanas.

In addition, there are many uses of this. This wonder of nature blesses the possessor with wealth, Vashi karan of others i.e. other people remain kind to the Sadhaka, one has victory over enemies, accidents are averted and one remains free from any Tantrik effects.

Its sidhi is very difficult. It is widely tested article.

11. Cat's Chord or Billi Ki Jeer

When a cat gives birth to children she eats away the umbillical cord. This cord if preserved is very useful in tantric sadhana. It is kept in Vermillion. It is kept after puja in the cash box and blesses the sadhaka with wealth. It is also used for Vashi karan. It gives protection from enemies. This too is used for Anusthan. By keeping it, desires are fulfilled. A widely Tested Article.

12. Kam Rup Mani

Kam Rup Mani is not normally available. This is nature's rare gift. If available and worn around the neck, the effects are that all works of users are completed as per his desires, difficulties are removed. Prosperity, success, respect, wealth, becomes permanent with him during life.

13. Shukar Teeth

Shukar or wild boar is a fierce, wild animal. His front teeth are not easily available. These teeth are used in many ways in Tantric Sadhana and Mahavidya sadhana. Tested many times.

These teeth are used as Talisman around the neck of a child, who weeps too much, urinates at night and saves children from the evil eye.

14. Kasturi

In the umbillical of deer, this round shaped piece covered with hair is found. A very soothing smell always comes out of it. It is a rare piece, used in many Tantrik sadhanas. The possessor should keep it in the cash box or on the body, so that all people remain kind to him (used for Vashi Karan). It bestows wealth and comforts. In the house where this is kept, peace prevails and one is always safe from the effects of evil spirits.

NOTE: There are other Tantric articles like leaf of Banna Ram Nami, Satawar Leaf, Meen Mukta, Chitavar wood, Nag Chandra, Khappar and deer's skin etc etc.

15. Rudraksh

Generally Rudraksh trees are found in Nepal and countries of North Asia. This tree is of medium height , its fruit is called 'Rudraksh'. The rudraksh is found in a cover similar to the walnut. When the cover is broken or cut, the rudraksh is found inside. These have from 1 to 21 faces. Faces are natural lines found across the Rudraksh. Every Rudraksh has a specific purpose. More details about rudrakshas have been provided in the author's famous book 'COMPLETE ASTRO PALMISTRY'.

16. Gauri Shankar Rudraksh

It is a rare one in which two rudrakshas are joined together. It is attributed to lord SHIVA and PARVATI. When Three rudrakshas are found, it is called, 'GAURI SHANKAR PARVATI' . These are to be worn around the neck or are kept in the temple or on the person. These bestow on the user good luck, wealth, intelligence, spiritual power and all the comforts of life. Given below are some details about rudrakshas.

Rosary Or Bead

A bead is the right instrument for offering prayers to god. The best bead is of the HOLY RUDRAKSHA in addition to other beads as mentioned earlier. The Rudrakshas have between one to fourteen faces. Other beads are of chandan, Tulsi, Saftic etc. Rudrakshas are of 38 types but upto 21 faces are available in India.

A brief account of HOLY RUDRAKSHA rosary is given below for the guidance of readers, as it is not commonly known.

How to Purify the Rudraksha Rosary

On Monday morning, one should take a bath before Sunrise, and the beads should be well washed in Cow's milk. After that the rosary should be washed in holy Ganges water. The rosary should then be put in the smoke of dhoop and after reciting the mantra "OM NAMA SHIVAE" eleven times, the rosary may be worn.

Importance of the Bead

Holy Rudrakshas are of 38 types and upto 21 faces. This rosary is very auspicious and draws man near to the Almighty. All religions, have prescribed or recommended the use of a bead. According to Hindu mythology, the use of Rudraksha rosary signifies that Lord SHIVA has bestowed all his blessings upon the user. It has miraculous effect on our body, mind and soul, and can be used for propitiation of advice on planetary positions. There is an old story about the creation of the Rudraksha. It is said that once there was a Datiya named Tripura Sur who was unconquerable. Brahma, Vishnu, and other deities were tired of him as they were being teased by him. They approached Lord Shiva and requested him to help them get rid of him. LORD SHIVA thought of using special fire-weapon named Aaghor. This weapon destroyed everything. It is believed, that it was like the Atom bomb of today. Lord Shiva used that weapon to destroy Tripura Sur. During the use of this weapon, Lord Shiva could not open his eyes and when opened, the eyes became watery, and few drops of water fell on earth. These drops later appeared in the shape of trees and the fruits of 38 types appeared which are called Rudrakshas. Lord Shiva is known as Rudra and tears called Ashak. Hence the name Rudrakshas. Of these 12 types have been assigned to Sun, 10 to fire and 16 to Moon.

Faces of Rudrakshas

It is believed that the smaller the size of Rudrakshas the more auspicious is the importance of Rudrakshas have been detailed in all the puranas of the Hindu Religion, such as Devi Purana, Shiv Purana, Sikand Purana, Padam Purana, Ling Purana etc.

The details of faces of Rudrakshas are detailed below as has already been provided in the author's famous book 'COMPLETE ASTRO PALMISTRY'.

1. One faced Rudraksha is very rare and is ascribed to Lord Shiva. On this rudraksha the figures of Shiva Linga, Serpent Om, Trishul and other auspicious marks are not found. Such rudrakshas are not genuine. The use of this rudraksha around the neck blesses the wearer with power, authority, wealth and all the comforts of life. Above all the sadhaka will have darshan of his Deity. The place where its puja is performed, wealth remains in abundance, all troubles vanish and people of that house lead a comfortable life. It bestows sarv siddhi and Moksha.

The sadhaka gets Bhakti, Mukti and peace of mind. This is the most auspicious and sacred Rudraksha.

A one-faced rudraksha can be round, flat or moon shaped. In the market fake rudraksh is found, in which one will notice figures of serpents, conches, trishul, Om or Shiv Linga etc. inscribed artificially. Sometimes two-faced rudraksha is made into one-faced by joining it so skilfully that only an expert, distinguishes it.

Mantra for Wearing

"ॐ ऐं हं श्रौ ऐ"

"Om Aeeing Hareeng Shreeng Aeeing"

2. Two-faced beads are believed to be of LORD SHIVA and PARVATI. Its use blesses the wearer with the blessings of both Deities. For SHIVA Bhakti this is termed as best. To end Tamsic habits this is beneficial. The use of this is also good for the concentration and peace of mind and for uplift of spiritual nature. Pregnant ladies should wear it around their waist or arm for the successful birth of a child. One rudraksha may be kept under the pillow. It is also very useful for vashikaran.

Mantra for Wearing

ॐ श्रीं ह्रीं क्षौं ऊ ॥

"Om Shareeng Hareeng Kashroong Vareeing Om"

3. Three-faced rudraksha keeps one free from all types of bad luck. The use of it is best for wealth and education. A fever which starts is cured by its use after three days. Persons born in Aries, Leo and Sagitarius ascendents must wear this.

Mantra for Wearing

ॐ रहूं ह्रीं हूं ओं

"Om Reeng Houng Hareeing Houng Om"

4. Four-faced is ascribed to Brahma. The use of this blesses a person with wealth, good health. One becomes spiritual and achieves the final goal in life. Its use increases the intellect and power of speech. This is also used in Vashi Karan, Akarshan and for sexual purposes. If one boils it in milk and takes the milk for 20 days it stimulates the mind and removes worries. Dull persons should use it.

Mantra for Wearing

ॐ वां क्रां तां हां ई

5. Five-faced rudraksha is believed to be more auspicious and is ascribed to KALINGAN or PANCH BRAHMA, and the use of the same leads to the blessing of Lord Shiva. It indicates Moksha and fullfilment of all desires and keeps the wearer away from diseases. To remove the constipation, one should place one bead on the umbillical and should count upto 108 and then again count 108 in reverse manner

for 21 days and keep the bead in a mandir. It is known as "Sarv Kalyankari and Mangal Data."

Mantra for Wearing

ॐ ह्रां आं क्षम्यौं स्वाहा

"Om Hareeng Aung Kashamon Swaha "

6. Six-faced is ascribed to Kartik. A few ascribe it to Lord Ganesha. Both were sons of Lord Shiva. The male should use on right arm. Its use blesses the wearer with all comforts of life. It is specially useful to attain siddhi and success in business etc. The students should use this. It is also useful for hysteria, fainting fits and other diseases of ladies.

Mantra for Wearing

ॐ ह्रीं श्रीं कलीं सौं ऐं

"Om Hareeng Shareeng Kaleeng Soueng Aeeing."

7. Seven-faced is termed as Aanat its lords are SAPT RISHIS. Its use blesses the native with respect, wealth and spiritual power.

Persons involved in Gold smuggling, frauds and other such sins should use this rudraksha. It is especially useful for the birth of a son.

Mantra for Wearing

ॐ हं क्रीं ह्रीं सौं

"Om Harang Kareeng Hareeng Soueng"

8. Eight-faced rudraksha is ascribed to Ganesh and its use is considered very auspicious. It blesses all comforts of life and removes sins arising from having illicit relations with women.

Mantra for Wearing

ॐ ह्रां ग्री लं अं श्रीं

"Om Hareeng Gareeng Ling Aeeing Shareeing."

9. Nine-faced is ascribed to Bhairon, Yam and Kapil Muni. It should be used on the left arm during Navratras for blessings from Durga. The native enjoys wealth and family comforts, Children's welfare and fulfilment of all hopes and desires. It also denotes MAHESHWARI DURGA who has nine faces.

Mantra for Wearing

ॐ ह्रीं वॅं यॅं रॅं लॅं

10. Ten-faced rudraksha is ascribed to Lord Vishnu or Janardhana. The user is protected from the malefic influence of all Planets, evil

effects of souls etc. In Tantrik rites it carries a special importance. The person who wears it is safe from all Tantrik attacks of Maran, Mohan and Akal Mritiyu (Alap Ayu death) etc. If it is used after rubbing it on stone, whooping cough is cured. The user is benefited from all directions.

Mantra for Wearing

ॐ श्रीं ह्रीं कलीं श्रीं अेम्

11. Eleven-faced bead is ascribed to Lord Indra. It is believed to be highly powerful possessing eleven strengths of eleven deities. It should be kept in the house, place of puja and in the cash box. It is specially useful for ladies, as it blesses them with a husband whose lifespan is long and one who is progressive and wealthy. It is used for Mohan purposes in Tantrik. It is said that after purification, if a lady wears it, she is surely blessed with a son.

Mantra For Wearing

ॐ रूं मूं यूं औं

12. Twelve-faced rudrakasha is ascribed to Lord Vishnu. Twelve devas are termed its lord. Its wear and use indicates comforts, employment and blessings of all the deities. The fear of thieves and fire and other obstacles is removed. All roaring animals do not harm, rather they protect the wearer. It is the best sin remover and is called 'Aditya Rudraksha'. Its rosary consists of 32 beads, which is equal to the number of teeth.

Mantra For Wearing

ॐ ह्रीं श्रीं धृणि: श्री ॥

13. Thirteen-faced rudraksha, if available and used is very auspicious. It is ascribed to Vishva Devas. The user gains moksha, conquers all his desires, ambitions and is endowed with good health, wealth, property and the comforts of life. It gives many types of siddhis and one can attract anybody.

Mantra for Wearing

ॐ ई यां अप अेम्

14. Fourteen-faced Rudraksha is ascribed to Lord Shiva. It is also believed and devoted to Hanumanji. It cures diseases. It bestows all comforts of life and a high rank in service and politics. It should be boiled in milk and drunk for 20 days the man gets relief from all worries. It also removes evil effects of SATURN, and victory over enemies.

Mantra For Wearing

ॐ स्फे खव्के हस्त्रौं हसव्य ॥

NOTE: The user of rudrakha should be free from Vices. He can be non Vegetarian, but should keep a fast on full Moon Amavas and Sankaranti days.

Importance of Rudrakshas

In the modern scientific age, everything is subjected to test. Unless and until the test is completed and results obtained, nothing can be accepted as scientific. Yet there are thousands of natural articles which are not subject to any test yet are result-oriented. These include Shavetarak Ganpati, Dakshineya Sankh, Siyar Singhi, Hath Jori, Safteek Shiva Linga, Parad Shiv Linga. Pardarshi saligram, Kam roop Mani, Abayakat Saligaram and The Lagu Coconut. All these things are very rare but when found give health, wealth and happiness.

Likewise, nature has created Rudrakshas. Rudraksh trees are found in Nepal, Tibet, Indonesia and Malaysia. The trees bear flowers and then the flowers turn into fruits which are called Rudrakshas. These are generally found with Yogis, Sanyasis and foreigners who use them around their neck as beads or as a rosary.

The rudraksha brings good fortune. Out of the series of Rudrakshas One, Five, Seven, Nine, Eleven, Fourteen and twenty-one faced ones are termed very lucky, and are rarely available. This also includes Gauri Shankar Rudraksha which is the most auspicious for wealth, family and comforts.

The one-faced rudraksha is termed very auspicious as it bestows wealth and happiness. It helps in attaining moksha and nirvan. The wearer has inclination to do good deeds and it helps in getting the power of intuition.

The Seven-faced bead is auspicious for the birth of a son. The Eleven-faced is good for religious purposes such as Bhagwat Darshan of one's deity. For property and gains the fourteen-faced rudraksha is good for wealth, the 21 faced bead is very auspicious. Panch or five faced rudrakasa is worn as it is auspicious and is a result giver rudraksh. It bestows on the wearer comforts and peace of mind.

These are often helpful in curing diseases. Those having blood pressure should wear it on the right arm. Fatal diseases, epilepsy and fainting fits are cured by rubbing it in honey. They are being used in many Ayurvedic medicines and in its capsules.

Normally one to 16 faced rudrakshas are available with the author but are costly as explained above, whereas 17 to 21 faced are rarely available. All are genuine. These should be worn after performing due rituals to gain maximum benefit out of this rare natural fruit.

Methods of Wearing

Detailed methods for wearing the rudrakasha is provided below. The person who has to wear Rudraksha should take a bath early in the morning should wear clean clothes and sit on Asana and keep with him Puja Samagri and Ganges water and the rudraksh which he wants to wear. The Rudraksh should be kept on a wooden piece before him. One should apply tilak on his forehead with chandan, sandoor and Bhasam. One should keep towel etc., on the head.

Pooja be started with three Achmans reciting each time the following mantras:

"ॐ केशवाय नमः स्वाहा"

Om Keshvaye Nama Swaha

"ॐ माधवाय नमः स्वाहा"

Om Madhvaye Nama Swaha

"ॐ नारायणाय नमः स्वाहा"

Om Narayanaye Nama Swaha

After performing Pranayam and paying respects to Lord Shiva, Ganesha Vishnu and to one's preceptor one should then do Sankalpa. In case one does not remember Sankalpa, then one should utter in one's mind that purpose for which the rudraksh is being worn. This should be done with complete faith.

After sankalpa, perform pooja of various lords and wash rudraksh in Panch Amrit and finally with Ganges water. Put a black thread in the rudraksh and wear it on the arm or around the neck.

This method is for all types of rudraksh, whereas mantras for each faced rudraksh are different.

Rudrakshas and Planets

Different Nayasas: Before starting the puja of rudrakshas the performing different nayasas like Rishi Adi Nayas, Kar Nayas, Ang Nayas, Hiradeye Nayas are to be performed one by one with fingers of the right hand to different parts of the body.

Rishi Adi Nayas: Karnyas means Sathapan. In this fingers of the hand palms, and back of the hand are to be treated and cleaned through mantras with water. Likewise in Angnayas or mantras which makes the body pure, One gets geace and the sadhana becomes fruitful and beneficial.

The mantra is read as:

वामदेव ऋषिये नमः शिरसि पंलि छंद से नमो मुखे। ऋ ऐं नमः हदि। हं बीजाय नमों गुह्यो। औ शवतैय नमः पादपो।

Hirdeye Nayas: In this vidhi all the five fingers of right hand are used in Hirdeye Nayas with the following mantra

ॐ ऊँ ह्रीं ह्रदयाय नमः

ॐ ऐं ह्रों शिर से स्वाहा

ॐ हं हूं शिखाये वषट

ॐ औं है क्वयाय हुँ

ॐ एं ह्रौं नेत्रयाय वौषट्

ॐ उं हः अस्त्राय फट्

The above mantras are to be recited 108 times at the time of wearing one-faced Rudraksha on Monday before the idol of Lord SHIVA after performing the above rituals. In the end perform Puja of the rudraksh and wear it around the neck or on the arm with a black thread. Panch Amrit should be taken by the Sadhaka.

The wearer should generally recite the mantra 54 or 108 time daily in the morning or any time during the day. The mantra is

'ॐ ह्रीं नमः"

The controlling planet is the Sun and it can be used against the evils of Sun such as disfavour, from the goverment, headaches, eye troubles, bile and liver complaints. Gives rise to status and power.

Two Faced Rudraksha: This rudraksh is worn for fulfilment of desires and for Mansik Shakti. Its main Mantra is

ॐ ह्रीं क्षौं व्रीं ॐ

ॐ अस्य श्री देवदेव मन्त्रस्य अत्रिऋषि गायत्री छन्दः देवदेवशों क्षीं बीजं क्षौं शक्तिः रम चतुवर्ग सिद्धिये रूद्राक्ष धारणार्थे जपे विनयोगः।

After that Rishi Adi Nyas, Karnyas and Hirdeye Nyas are to be performed the rudraksh worn as per directions detailed above.

The wearer should recite mantra during day or in the morning. It is effective against cough, cold, mental troubles, unhappiness and poverty. Its ruling planet is the Moon.

Three Faced Rudraksha: By wearing this all sins are removed. It protects the sadhaka against accidents, troubles and increases intelligence.

Main Mantra

ॐ रं है ह्रीं हूँ औं

ॐ अस्य श्री अग्नि मंत्रस्य वसिष्ठ ज ऋषिः गायत्री छन्दः अग्नि देवता ह्रीं बीज हूं शक्ति चतुर्वर्ग सिद्धअर्थे रूद्राक्ष धारणर्थे जपे विनयोगः

After performing Adi Nyas, Karnyas and Hirdeye Nyas, wear rudraksh as per above directions. The sadhaka should recite the mantra during the day or in the morning. It is ruled by Mars and pacifies the evils of Mars viz land litigation, widowhood, blood poisoning and accidents.

Four Faced Rudraksha: This rudraksh is of Brahma. It is auspicious for general popularity, leadership and for rulers and good for eye disease. It bestows sweetness in speech, helps one to perform religious deeds. It is also good for Vashi karan and attracting others .

Main Mantra:

ॐ व्रां क्रां तां ही ई ॥

ॐ अस्य श्रीब्रह्मामन्त्रस्य भार्गव ऋर्षिः अनुष्ट्य छन्दः ब्रह्मा देवता वां ब्रीजं क्रां शक्तिः अभीष्ट सिद्धयर्थे रूद्राक्षधारणार्थे जपे विनियोगः ॥

rudraksha as per above directions. The sadhaka should recite during the day or in the morning. This rudraksha is ruled by the planet Mercury. It can be used for intelligence, printing, publishing, Astrology, Mathematics and other such activities. It is a Must for students, researchers and scholars.

Five Faced Rudraksha: It is penta faced. It is also known by the name Kal Ani. It bestows on the sadhaka popularity comforts, peace of mind and fame. It wipes away the sins of adultery and gluttony. It is good against Jupiter afflictions. It gives vital power, wealth, knowledge, fortune and happiness.

Mantra

ॐ ह्रां क्रां वां हांक्

ॐ अस्य श्री ब्रह्मा मंत्रक्य श्रीब्रह्मा ऋषिः गायन्त्री छन्दः ब्रह्मा देवता ह्रां क्रां वां हां अभीष्ट सिद्धतर्थे रूद्राक्षधारणार्थे जपे विनियोगः ॥

After that perform Adi Nayas, Kar Nayasa and Hirdeye Nayas and wear the Rudraksha as per above directions. The sadhaka should recite the mantra during the day or in the morning.

Six Faced Rudraksha : This is also called kartake. It bestows on the wearer the fulfilment of desires. It enables a person to perform good deeds, and become contented and virtuous. The main mantra for this rudraksha is given below. It is worn on the Left arm and is good for propitiation of venues.

ॐ ह्रीं श्रीं क्लीं सौं ऐं।

ॐ अस्य श्री मन्त्रस्य दक्षिणामूर्ति ऋर्षि पतिछंदः कार्तिकेय देवता ऐं बीजं सौं शक्तिः क्वीं कीलकं अभीष्ट सिद्धयर्थ रूद्राक्ष धारणार्थ मपविनियोगः॥

After that perform Adi Nayasa, Kar Nayasa and Hirdeye Niyasa. Wear Rudraksha as per above direction. The sadhaka should recite the mantra during the day or in the morning. It cures gynaecological troubles, love, frustration and loss of semen.

Seven Faced Rudraksha : This blesses the Sadhaka with secret wealth. Ladies Vashi Karan, destruction of enemies etc. This is treated as most auspicious, the Evils of Saturn are checked.

Mantra

ॐ ह्रीं त्रीं ह्रीं सौ

ॐ अस्य श्री अनन्तमन्त्रस्य भगवान ऋषि गायत्री छन्दः अनंतो देवता क्रीं बीज ह्रीं शक्तिः अभीष्ट सिद्धयर्थे रूद्राक्ष धारणार्थे जपे विनियोगः

After that perform Adi Nyas, Kar Nayas and Hirdeye Niyasa. Wear Rudraksha as per above direction. The sadhaka should recite the mantra during day or in the morning. It is used effectively during misfortune, danger and threatened death also against accidents.

Eight Faced Rudraksha : This rudraksha is assigned to Lord Vishnu. It is beneficial particularly for longevity; popularity, education and good health. The Beeja or main mantra is as below. It is ruled by Rahu.

Main Mantra

ॐ ह्रीं ग्रीं लं आं श्रीं

ॐ अस्य गणेश मंत्रस्य भार्गवाऋः अनुष्ट्प छन्दः विनायको देवता ग्री बीचं आं शक्तिः चतुवर्ग सिद्धियर्थे रूद्राक्ष धारणार्थे जपे विनियोगः

After that perform Adi, Kar and Hirdeye Nayasas. Wear the rudrakshas as per the above directions. The sadhaka should recite the mantra during day or night. ॐ हुं नमः

Nine Faced Rudraksha : This is assigned to Lord Bhairon. It is auspicious for spiritual attainments, wealth, property and other worldly affairs. The main mantra for this is given below. It is ascribed to ketu.

Main Mantra

ॐ ह्रीं वॅ यॅ रॅ लॅ

ॐ अस्य श्री भैरव मंत्रस्य नारद ऋषिः गायत्री छन्द भैरवी देवता व बीजं ह्रीं शक्ति अभीष्ट सिद्धार्थ रूद्रक्ष धारणार्थ जपे विनियोगः

After that perform Adi, Kar and Hirdeye Nayasas. Wear the rudrakshas as per the above directions. The sadhaka should recite during the day or in the morning. It is useful in checking abortions and to get moksha.

Ten Faced Rudrakshas : This is assigned to Lord VISHNU. It is worn to cut off the evil effects of all planets the fear from snakes and against litigation and imprisonment. The main mantra for this is:-

Main Mantra

ॐ श्रीं ह्रीं कलींव्रीं ओम

ॐ अस्य श्री जनर्दन मत्रस्य नारद ऋषि अनुष्टुय छन्दः जनादनी देवता श्री बीजं ह्री शक्तिः अभीष्ट सिद्धयर्थ रूद्राक्ष धारणार्थे जपे विनियोगः

After that perform Adi, Kar, Hirdeye Nayasa. Wear rudraksha as per above directions. The sadhaka should recite during the day or night. Evil spirits and ghosts are pacified through its use. All the nine planets are propitiated through its use and the wearer gets happiness all round.

Eleven Faced Rudraksha : This has been assigned to Lord Rudra and is worn for the attainment of popularity, strength and worldly comforts. The main mantra for this is as below.

ॐ रूं मूं औं ॥

ॐ अस्य श्री रूद्रमंत्रस्य काश्यप ऋर्षि अनुष्टुप छन्दः रूद्रोदेवता रूं बीजं क्षुं शक्तिः अभीष्ट सिद्धियर्थे रूद्राक्ष धारनार्थे जपे विनियोगः ॥

After that perform Adi, Kar and Hiredeye Nayasa. Wear Rudraksha as per above directions. The sadhaka should recite during the day or morning. The mind is controlled. One has wealth and finally becomes a Param Yogi.

Twelve Faced Rudraksha : This rudraksha has been assigned to the SUN god otherwise called Suriya. It bestows progeny and removes the difficulties of life, protects one against theft, and fulfills the hopes of the sadhaka who wears it. The main Mantra for this is:-

Main Mantra

ॐ ह्रीं क्षौं घृणिः श्रीं

ॐ अस्य श्री सूर्य मंत्रस्य भार्गव ऋषिः गायत्री छन्दः विश्वेश्वरी देवता ह्रीं बीजं, श्री शक्तिः धृणि कीलकं रूद्राक्षधारणार्थे जपे विनियोगः

After that perform Adi, Kar, Hiredeye Nayas and wear it as per above directions. The Sadhaka should recite the mantra during the day or morning attributed to Twelve Adityas. It makes the wearer, give protection against accidents, Rulers and Kings who want to rule over the world should use it constantly.

Thirteen Faced Rudraksha : This is assigned to Lord INDER. This sadhaka is blessed with power of Sidhi, Vashi Karan etc. Also one attains Comforts etc.The main mantra for this is as:-

Main Mantra

ॐ ई यां आप औं

ॐ अस्य श्री इन्द्रमंत्रस्य ब्रह्मा ऋषि पंक्ति छन्द इन्द्रो देवता ई बीजं मू आप इति शक्तिः रूद्राक्ष धारणार्थे जपे :

After that perform Adi Kar and Hiredeye Nayasa and wear this rudraksha as per above directions. The sadhaka should recite the mantra. (ॐ ह्रीं नमः विनियोगः) during the day or morning. Best for divine powers and for attainment of desires.

Fourteen Faced Rudraksha : This is assigned to Lord Hanuman JI. It gives courage, protects one at the time of adversity, removes all difficulties. The main mantra of this rudraksha is :-

Main Mantra

ॐ औं हस्फें खब्फें हस्त्रौ हसख्फें ॐ अस्य श्री हनुमन्त्रंस्य रामचन्द्र ऋषिः, छन्दः श्रीं हनुमदेवता औं बीजं हस्फ्रै शक्तिः अभीष्य सिद्धयर्थे जपे विनियोगः ॥

After that perform Adi, Kar and Hiredeye Nayasa and the rudraksha be worn according to above instructions. The Sadhaka should recite this mantra ("ॐ नमः") during day or in the morning. It is rarely available but has infinite virtues, enabling the user to reach the highest heaven.

Rudrakshas have been discussed in detail. We will further add that at the time of wearing rudraksha, one must donate alms, perform pooja and Homa. The bead destroys the accumulated poision from body, mind and soul. So everybody can derive benefit out of rudrakshas. It is very effective in high blood pressure, epilepsy, madness, cough, gynaecological troubles and mental disorder.

The rudraksha if used properly with recitation of proper mantras as detailed above will give tremendous results.

Used for Planetary Affliction

Rudrakshas have four colours. White, red, yellow and blue. It is so said in the old srutis that the white coloured one can be used when the Moon, Jupiter and Venus are afflicted in a birth chart so as to remove their malefic effects. Red coloured are beneficial for Sun, Mars and Ketu. The yellow coloured rudrakshas are the safest for propitiating Mercury and Jupiter. Blue coloured ones are used for Saturn and Rahu. Rudrakshas upto Nine faced are akin to the properties of Nine planets. But from Ten faced to Twentyone faced rudrakshas are representative of higher heavenly powers which transcends the planetary kingdom. These rudrakshas control the heavens and the basic instincts of man. It is hot by nature and controls the thermo dynamics and electromagnetic vibration around the human body. It is best used for Tantras for checking evils, cleansing the soul and realising divinity.

Other Uses of Rudrakshas:

1. By the use of Rudraksha rosary, diseases of the blood, Heart and heart attacks are controlled. Rishis have held that one gets peace of mind as it takes out extra heat from the body.
2. If the ash obtained by burning rudraksha is mixed with the ash of gold in equal proportion and taken, one ratti as a dose in the morning and evening, high blood pressure is controlled if it be taken with milk, Curd or Malai of milk.
3. In case of small pox, take rudraksha ash with black pepper in equal proportion with water, kept at night for three months. One will be cured positively.
4. If a big rudraksha is rubbed and paste is applied on a poisonous wound it will heat immediately without effecting the patient adversely.
5. Taking rudraksha with Muraka and Bhang (Hashish) increases Sadhana and prayer power. One has sound sleep. In India Baidya Nath Pharmacy has used Rudraksha in medicines. One of their medicines is Madhur Munaaka, which is used as tonic.
6. The wearer of rudraksha remains free from fear of Yamraj Ghosts & souls.
7. One gets long life and Aakal Mritya is averted.
8. A barren lady using rudraksha is blessed with a child.
9. It helps in awakening the kundalina.
10. It protects the wearer from bodily diseases.

How to Recognise Rudraksha

The following are points to check the genuiness of rudrakshas.

The English name for this tree is UTRASUM BEAD TREE and its latin is called ELAEOCARPUS GANITRUS ROXB.

1. When a rudraksha bead is put in a glass full of water it will dip and will not float. In case it is made of wood or is infested with insects it will float on the water.
2. If a ripe rudraksha is closed in a fist and taken near the ear and moved it will emit a pleasant slow sound.
3. If a rudraksha is placed between two copper Coins, it will move when pressed.
4. The rudraksha is found raised at places, hard and of rough surface. Each piece has naturally carved lines, which are called FACES of the rudraksha.
5. In a natural rudraksha, you will find a shine and a greasiness which appears after its continuous use by wearing and using it as rosary.
6. A few rudrakshas have eyes like that of a coconut near the carved lines. The three eyed rudraksha is attributed to Lord SHIVA, which helps in early attainment of Siddhi.
7. Rudraksha always has a rough surface but is not thorny. Thorny surfaced rudraksha is artificial.
8. Rudraksha of smaller size is always held in high esteem than bigger size ones as the smaller the size the more effective it is supposed to be.
9. The natural rudraksha has no hole in it. These are made later on. The piece, which has a natural hole is most auspicious.
10. In natural rudraksha the lines are not equidistant, but in an artificial one, these are found carved at equidistant.
11. In natural rudraksha the lines are not equidistant, but in an artificial one, these are found carved at equidistant.

Auspicious Mantras

Gayatri Mantra

ॐ भू र्भव स्वः। तत्सवितुर्वरेण्यं भर्गो देवस्य धीमहि धियो नः प्रयोदयात्

"Om Bhoorbhava Sva Tatsaviturvareniyam Bhargo
Devasya Dhimahi Dhiyo Yo Nah Prachodyat"

Mahamaritanje Mantra

ॐ त्र्यम्बकं यजामहे सृगन्धि पृष्टिवर्धनम उर्वा।

रूकमिव बन्धनान्मृत्यों मृक्षीय माम्रतात ॥

"Om Tryambakam Yajamahe Sugandhinam Pushtivardhanam Urva, Rukmiv Bandhanan mrityormukshiya Mamratat".

Method to Purify one Face Rudraksha

Mantra

ॐ श्री गणेश जी को नमः ॐ ह्रीं श्रीं कलीं एक मुखा भगवतेनुरुपाय सर्वयुगेश्वराय त्रेलोक्य नातेऽय सर्व काम फलप्रदाय नमः ।

SHRI Ganesh Ji Ko Namah. Om Hareeng Shareeng Kaleeng Aikmukha Bhagwate Anuroopaye Survayugeshveraya Trilokyanathay Sarvakampahalpraday Namah".

In chaitra month and Ashtami of Shukal Paksha Pooja of rudraksha bead be performed with coloured flowers. Hoop Kesar, chandan and deip can be used in purifying. Tilak of chandan, camphor be used. Each flower should be purified with the above mantra. After that the bead should be kept in the cash safe or around the neck.

Hath Jori Kalp

As already explained, it is a rare Tantric article. It is used very effectively after making sidhi of it. The uses of Hath Jori are:

1. At the time of talking to a person, keep it on your body the opposite party will agree with you.
2. The person to whom you want to put under your control (Vashi Karan), Perform Japa after reciting his or her name. One will become under your control. Do not use for nefarious means.
3. It is also worn in talisman of three metals (Gold, silver and copper) to give victory over enemies and fulfil all desires.
4. After use, it should be kept in a silver box with sandoor (vermillion) in it.

METHOD: On Sunday in Pushy Nakshatra, Hathjori be given bath in Panch-Amrit and Pooja be performed according to following method. The mantra be recited for 12500 times and its siddhi be made. Sitting towards East on red Asana with red colour rosary, the Japa be performed. Also keep an idol of Bhairon and its pooja be performed with oil, Sandoor and red flowers.

Mantra

ॐ नमो नमिउणा विसहर विस प्रणाशव रोग शोक, दोष

ग्रह कप्पदुमच्चाजा यइ सुहनाम गहण सक्ल सुह देॐ नम स्वाहाः

After performing above sadhana, put vermillion in a silver box on first day morning of Krishna Pakash and place Hath Jori in reverse position. Then again it should be reversed on first day of Shukla Paksha. Repeat this process for three Krishan and Shukal Pakash, it will be in reverse position which be kept for ever. Keep the box in cash safe. This is very good sadhana for finances.

Yantras, Mantras and Tantras have been explained in this valuable book. The sadhakas are requested to use them with earnestness, following all rituals and directions for good purposes and the welfare of mankind.

OM TAT SAT

OTHER TITLES ON OCCULT SCIENCES

SECRETS OF ASTROLOGY

Based on Hindu Astrology

Dr. L.R. Chawdhri

Secrets of Astrology is a ready reckoner for the lay reader to find solutions to his problems. It tells him how to know his own personality and that of his spouse, friends, and others. It gives tips on how to choose one's ideal life-partner. Love marriages, delayed marriages and divorce are also dealt with, as are lucky numbers and colours according to one's personality.

Love, character and sex have been discussed with the help of a Lover's Guide and sex-life barometers, linking the signs and showing how opposite signs attract each other.

Guidance is provided about predicting lucky times to acquire money, property and conveyance, win lotteries and make gains from horse-racing. Travel, employment, business, children, politics and spirituality are other subjects on which clear directions are given.

To overcome difficulties remedial measures, including use of tested Yantra, Mantra and Tantra, are prescribed.

Dr. L.R. Chawdhri has an experience of 39 years in the fields of Astrology, Palmistry and Numerology. He has specialised in remedial measures through these sciences. He is author of 17 widely acclaimed books on occult subjects.

ISBN 81 207 1065 7, Rs. 75

SECRETS OF OCCULT SCIENCES

How to read Omens, Moles, Dreams and Handwriting

Dr. L.R. Chawdhri

Occult sciences like Astrology, Palmistry, Yantra, Mantra and Tantra are the sciences of the secrets of nature—physical and psychic, mental and spiritual. These secrets are also revealed by nature through moles on one's body, dreams, twitching of body parts, omens and other means.

This book in 11 chapters unveils the hidden meanings of the existence of the small dark spots found on the human skin, the dreams one dreams, nervous movements of the body parts and objects and happenings that foretell the coming of fortune or misfortune. To know their meanings is to be forewarned. Only one has to interpret them correctly. This book provides the guidance to do so.

The reader will find the book a most profitable tool for use in daily life to attain health, wealth and happiness.

Various aspects of the 'Occult Sciences' have been grouped in this book for easy consultation by the laymen, astrologers, palmists, readers and the public at large.

Dr. L.R. Chawdhri has an experience of 39 years in the fields of Astrology, Palmistry and Numerology. He has specialised in remedial measures through these sciences. He is author of 17 widely acclaimed books on occult subjects.

ISBN 81 207 1067 3, Rs. 65

SECRETS OF NUMEROLOGY

A complete guide for the layman to know the past, present and future

Ravindra Kumar

Secrets of Numerology, written in a language the ordinary reader can understand, unfolds the Indian system of this occult science, which has been found more accurate than its western counterpart. Based on true life-cases, it shows that given the name and date of birth of a person, the pattern of his whole life can be foretold.

The book presents methods by which the reader can make his own numerical chart and analyse his character, know his own past, present and future. Knowing the physical, mental and emotional forces at work in his life he can mould his future. The book shows how to know one's right vocation, lucky numbers, colours. It also suggests which stones to wear for success in love, marriage or business, as well as a technique of changing one's name to influence one's circumstances—sometimes even within six months. Often a mere change in the spelling of one's name is enough to bring about good results. The book is the outcome of the author's study and experimentation for over 15 years.

Ravindra Kumar is at present Professor of Mathematics at Addis Ababa University, Ethiopia. He has set up an Institute of Numerology in Delhi for research in the subject.

ISBN 81 207 1363 x, Rs. 125

EVERYBODY'S GUIDE TO PALMISTRY

S.K. Das

This book unfolds the secrets of the science of palmistry discovered over centuries of human endeavour. It presents, in simple language, traditional as well as modern methods of hand-reading, blending them to arrive at sound predictions.

Among the highlights of the book are: scientific analysis of the hand; judgement of character and personality; choice of profession; selection of spouse; diagnosis of diseases; advance warnings of adverse life situations.

Sri Krishna Das has devoted 35 years of his life to the study of palmistry. He has written three other books. He figures in the Directory of Indian Writers, *1983, and in the 1985 editions of* Learned India *and* Reference Asia.

ISBN 81 207 0564 6, Rs. 125

HEALING THROUGH GEMS

A Simple Treatise on Gem Therapy

N.N. Saha

Gems have for long been considered to possess wonderful healing powers. Gem therapy is known to have worked where medicines had failed: in paralysis, spondylitis, heart attacks, acute fever. Gems can bring good luck, wealth and longevity, power and popularity.

This book is a simple treatise on healing through gems. The emphasis is on prevention and cure of physical problems.

N.N. Saha is an astrologer, gem therapist and occultist. He believes that gem therapy and astrology practised in conjunction can even cure chronic diseases. He has written several books on the occult sciences.

ISBN 81 207 0054 6, Rs. 70